When the Hills Ask for Your Blood

www.transworldbooks.co.uk

When the Hills Ask for Your Blood

A Personal Story of Genocide and Rwanda

David Belton

Doubleday

LONDON · TORONTO · SYDNEY · AUCKLAND · JOHANNESBURG

TRANSWORLD PUBLISHERS
61–63 Uxbridge Road, London W5 5SA
A Random House Group Company
www.transworldbooks.co.uk

First published in Great Britain
in 2014 by Doubleday
an imprint of Transworld Publishers

This book is a work of non-fiction based on the experiences and recollections
of the author. In some limited cases, names, dates and sequences or the detail of events
have been changed or conflated according to the author's recollection, to protect the
privacy of others, and for narrative reasons. The author has stated to the publishers
that, except in such minor respects, the contents of this book are true.

A CIP catalogue record for this book
is available from the British Library.

ISBNs 9780385615648 (hb)
9780385615655 (tpb)

Addresses for Random House Group Ltd companies outside the UK
can be found at: www.randomhouse.co.uk
The Random House Group Ltd Reg. No. 954009

The Random House Group Limited supports the Forest Stewardship Council® (FSC®),
the leading international forest-certification organisation. Our books carrying the
FSC label are printed on FSC®-certified paper. FSC is the only forest-certification scheme
supported by the leading environmental organisations, including Greenpeace.
Our paper procurement policy can be found at www.randomhouse.co.uk/environment

Typeset in 11/15pt Sabon by
Kestrel Data, Exeter, Devon.
Printed and bound by
CPI Group (UK) Ltd, Croydon, CR0 4YY

2 4 6 8 10 9 7 5 3 1

For Jules

CONTENTS

AUTHOR'S NOTE

On 6 April 1994 Rwanda's president, Juvénal Habyarimana, was assassinated. Within hours violence had erupted in the capital, Kigali. Soldiers of the Hutu government sought out and executed political opponents of the regime: hundreds of liberal voices from inside Rwanda were targeted and killed – from both the majority Hutu and minority Tutsi ethnic groups.

In response, the Tutsi-dominated rebel army, the Rwandan Patriotic Front (RPF), invaded the country from its bases in Uganda. As the RPF headed south, the Hutu government ordered its army, police and civilian militias to begin a sustained and pre-planned campaign to murder all Rwandan Tutsis. The killings were heavily propagandized. Urged on by their government, thousands of ordinary Hutus participated in the mass slaughter.

Within days, tens of thousands of Tutsis had been killed. On 19 April, Human Rights Watch contacted the United Nations to advise them that the killings amounted to genocide of the Tutsi people. But on 21 April, the UN Security Council voted to withdraw more than two thousand of its troops from Rwanda, leaving a staff of just 270. By late April, the

International Committee of the Red Cross estimated that 250,000 Tutsis had been murdered.

On 2 May 1994 I was sent to Rwanda by the BBC's *Newsnight* programme, to cover the crisis. By then I knew a little of the recent political history of the country.

♦ Rwanda is comprised of three ethnic groups – the majority Hutu (around 85 per cent of the population), and the minority Tutsi (14 per cent) and Twa (1 per cent).

♦ Rwandans share the same language and religions but, historically, many Tutsis were pastoralists, cattle-herders, whereas many Hutus settled on the land, growing crops.

♦ In the pre-colonial era Rwanda was ruled by a Tutsi monarchy and Tutsis were the elite. But ethnicity was a fluid concept. Hutus loyal to the Tutsi court could be rewarded with cattle, and if the herd were large enough, would become Tutsi. Intermarriage between the two largest ethnic groups was common.

♦ In 1919 Rwanda became a Belgian colony. The new colonialists favoured the Tutsis and further entrenched their position in Rwanda with greater economic and political privilege. This was reinforced fourteen years later with the introduction of identity cards, which labelled each Rwandan's ethnicity – Hutu, Tutsi or Twa.

♦ In 1959 a popular revolution by the majority Hutus against the Tutsi rulers provoked Belgium to abandon their colony three years later. Thousands of Tutsis fled the country and more followed when, in 1962, a Hutu government was elected.

♦ Throughout the 1960s and 1970s there were periodic massacres of Tutsis by forces of the Hutu-led government of, first, Grégoire Kayibanda and, following a coup in 1973, Major Juvénal Habyarimana.

♦ In 1990 a military force of exiled Tutsis, the Rwandan Patriotic Front (RPF), launched a series of attacks into northern Rwanda from its bases in Uganda. The RPF largely consisted of Tutsi exiles from the pogroms of the late 1950s and 1960s.

♦ Between 1990 and 1993 the war escalated. The RPF encountered fierce resistance from the Rwandan army, which received military support from France. Inside the country, violence against Tutsis increased, as did the level of state-sponsored anti-Tutsi propaganda by Hutu extremists, many of whom held senior positions in government.

♦ In 1993, international pressure to end the conflict forced both sides into peace talks. Over the vociferous objections of Hutu extremist politicians, President Habyarimana signed the Arusha Accords, which set out a power-sharing agreement that would usher in a new transitional government that incorporated the RPF.

♦ In October 1993, a UN peace-monitoring force, UNAMIR, comprising of two and a half thousand soldiers, was sent to Rwanda to help prepare the country for its political transition.

♦ On the night of 6 April 1994, President Habyarimana was returning from negotiations in Tanzania when his plane was shot down.

It was during the first of two assignments into Rwanda to report on the genocide that I met Vjeko Curic and stayed at his friary in Kivumu. It was not until 2003, however, when I returned to Rwanda in preparation for a feature film that I was producing, that I met with Jean-Pierre and Odette Sagahutu. Over the next ten years, I returned to Rwanda on several occasions and began to write the story of Jean-Pierre, Odette and Vjeko.

INTRODUCTION

I am staying at the Christus Centre, which sits enclosed behind a tall brick wall and a curl of razor wire, close to the heart of the city. The rooms have single metal beds and small windows, like cells. The heat in the afternoon is draining. The small courtyard looks bleached as if the sun has sucked the colour out of the pale brickwork. The sky is white – white-hot – and there is no join between earth and sky. The rooms are a good place to hide.

The Centre was home to Jesuit priests but now they are all dead. They were herded into the room next to where I sleep and gunned down. That was two months ago and there are still brown smears of blood on the walls. From the small window at the back of my room I can see the garden which is wild and overgrown. A rose, puce with colour, has wound its way up an avocado tree. The bush grows fast here. Especially in April when dense, grey curtains of rain sweep across the city and the streets and gardens are full of the sounds of metal pangas hacking away – *swish swish swish* – at the undergrowth. Another journalist who is staying here said he stumbled across a dead body when he walked through the garden late one evening. I don't believe him. You would smell the body long before you came across it. But it is true that you can find bodies anywhere. At the nearby hospital I watched quicklime being thrown over a pit of tangled corpses that had been discovered under a patch of shrubbery behind the canteen, weeks after they had been murdered. Anyway, the bush grows fast and you need to cut it back – a little every day – just to keep it under control.

The last remnants of the defeated army left the city a few days ago. The soldiers had bayed like dogs, punching the air and screaming that they would be back. The city teeters, as if it is catching its breath – not yet daring to believe that the criminals have left and that the people who remain are safe to emerge from under their rusted corrugated roofs. We Westerners hare around like anarchists, oblivious to traffic signals, looking for people. There are only a few. They stand awkwardly by their doorways and seem uncomfortable talking about what has just happened. 'We are alive,' they say.

The market at Nyabugogo opens but there is little food. A few women walk through the afternoon haze, in their broken plastic shoes, along concrete pavements that rot and collapse into steaming open gutters. They shake their heads at slowing taxis whose exhausts burp gouts of diesel at the lorries that have started to return to the city and which are sprawled at the side of the road, cabins cranked forward, broken-necked, their engines' entrails picked over by yawning drivers. Building begins. Small boys with bright, quick eyes and manly hands heave buckets of concrete porridge up through precarious wooden scaffolding, shield their eyes and gaze down at the convoys of white jeeps full of *awuzungu* – the white men – in pressed cotton shirts who browse through sheaves of paper and rehearse their opening remarks to the new Minister. Repugnance at the crime, condolence to the victims, hope for the survivors.

Ten years pass.

When I return there is nothing, outwardly, that I can see that points to what had taken place a decade earlier. Apart from the Parliament, that is, with its mustard walls still peppered with gaping, man-sized shell holes. I'm told that the President has no current plans to repair the building, preferring to keep it as a symbol of the war his rebel army fought to defeat the government and rescue the country. He likes to drive visiting politicians past the building too – an unspoken dig into the flabby ribcage of Western guilt. Now, that I do believe.

Otherwise, it is hard to imagine that in 1994 blood soaked the streets of this curvaceous, luminescent city. Even the city's genocide memorial seems to have actively divorced itself from the past; its spick-and-span white paint and smart grey roof tiles make it more Virginia Water golf club than place of remembrance. But what I begin to understand is that to imagine that Kigali, or anywhere in Rwanda, or any Rwandan, for that matter, carries the familiar, well-thumbed signs of genocide – that indelible visual shorthand that proclaims 'crimes against humanity' – is to misunderstand what happened here. There were no ghettoes, no tattooed numbers on wrists, no propaganda showing trains shuttling the victims off to a 'new' homeland – a cold death in a concrete and steel tank in a dark Polish wood. There were no epic forced marches from cities and towns to the privacy of a rice paddy. No grinning monster surrounded by his flunkeys. No satellite images of mass graves exist – no satellite bothered to swing by. Isolated, unimportant, African. The West cared not one jot for this impoverished thumbnail of land, except as somewhere to escape from as quickly as possible. Aid workers, diplomats, peacekeepers, doctors, missionaries – the ubiquitous mob of transient helpers that descends on a sub-Saharan, aid-dependent, autocratic, dysfunctional state – were hauled on to waiting aircraft by burly European soldiers the moment trouble broke out. Within two weeks, all but a couple of hundred from the force of two and a half thousand mechanized and heavily armed UN soldiers who had been in the country since the previous summer had left, too.

Rwandans were killed quickly, Tutsis mostly; but Hutus too – those the state mistrusted. A sophisticated, expertly communicated, highly propagandized campaign to racially and politically purify the country. Eight hundred thousand murdered – not in the one hundred days speechmakers favour, but more like fifty. Eight hundred thousand dead, in less than half a school semester. Maybe closer to a million (people argue over the number but it's an exhausting, airless argument). There was no need for death camps – the killers lived next door to their victims. The extremists called themselves the interim government and told people that what they were doing wasn't murder but communal work. Or sometimes, more grandly, they called it *national duty*. But it was murder and it happened everywhere and involved everyone. Across Rwanda, one Monday in early April, a farmer compared his bean harvest with his neighbour's, schoolteachers moaned together over cuts in funding, midwives organized their monthly rotas. Then a few days later ordinary Rwandans, civilians, rose up, in a murderous spasm, against people they worked with, drank with, had married. Occasionally they got their hands on guns or grenades but usually the killing was conducted with machetes, knives, hammers, clubs and, if they were desperate or maybe just imaginative, wrenched-off bicycle handlebars. In hospitals, nurses were hacked to death on the wards where they worked, new mothers slaughtered in their beds, their babies smashed against the walls. In schools, children were murdered and stuffed down latrines; in villages, storekeepers rounded up and thrown alive down wells. In churches, gangs with machetes and clubs tore into the thousands that had sought sanctuary there. Across the valleys and fields and marshes of Rwanda, no Tutsi was safe. The contamination of unhinged violence – and of ungraspable guilt – runs through every city street, every district, every hillside village.

The scars of this genocide are not found in slaughter-houses – though there are plenty of those – but embedded, like a migraine, in the crenulated bone of the inside of the minds of all those who survived, who took part, or just gawped as blunt metal edges rained down on brittle, bowed, heads. In the minds of those who endured and who, now, have no choice but to live alongside each other. In the mind of the woman who walks, unblinking, to the market every day, past the butcher's stall where a man stands with bloodied apron and watches her; the same man who ended her husband's life on a wet April afternoon in 1994; a man who was the envy of the village because his blade was never blunt, he never broke sweat, and when the day ended he still had the energy to lift a bottle of beer to his lips.

In his peach-coloured office, I sit and talk to President Kagame. He has presided over Rwanda's slow recovery since the forces he commanded defeated the Hutu extremists in the summer of 1994. In a cabinet behind him are several books on business management and a biography of Lee Kuan Yew. Kagame's long, elegant hands drape themselves over his crossed knee, his tapered fingers clasped delicately together. He talks about his plans for the future. Rwanda will be the nexus between east and west Africa. Kigali will become a hi-tech business centre built and run by an educated, urbanized population. Its smallness, Kagame says, helps with his analogy that Rwanda will become the African equivalent of Singapore. His thin frame seems to wallow about in his blue suit as he talks. His shirt collar is too big for his thin neck. I want to reach over and cinch the knot of his tie more tightly.

This talk of IT and invisible exports is tiring. I ask him how his vision can be reconciled with life, as it is currently lived, on the streets of Kigali, where the surviving victims of the genocide live next to the killers. Kagame shifts in his oversprung, gilded chair. There is a faint air of exasperation in his thin, fluttery voice. Not this again, he seems to be thinking.

'You are wrong. We are all victims here. Not just the survivors. The killers, too.'

He tells me that Rwanda was the victim of an appalling crime perpetrated by extremists and racists. But it is time to move on. 'Not to forget, of course. But we are one nation now. No more Tutsis or Hutus. Just Rwandans.' The President pauses. I think about Jean-Pierre. We have been working together for a few months now, on a film that is being made in Kigali. We have become friends. He dropped me off at the President's compound earlier but he will be home by now. Sitting on his steps, talking into his phone.

Smart grey steps – polished and perpendicular – he poured the cement himself when he built the new house on the foundations of where his old house had stood. Not many Tutsis survived the slaughter in his district of the city. The houses were so densely packed some said the killers stood at night with their ears pressed against the walls, waiting for the *inyenzi* – the 'cockroaches' – to give themselves away. Jean-Pierre survived. For two months and sixteen days, he hid and they never found him. When the killers left, he went home and there was nothing left of his house. Not a brick, a door lintel, a window frame, an electrical wire, a scrap of carpet, a flake of paint. Jean-Pierre likes to tell me that they didn't just want him dead; they wanted to wipe out any evidence that he had ever existed.

'Is it possible,' I ask the President, 'for Rwanda to outpace its ethnic past?' Kagame looks away, out on to the compound – a neatly trimmed lawn bisected by a meandering crazy-paved path of blood-red bricks. Soldiers stand guard at the small doorway at the edge of the compound. They are huge men, bedecked with oiled weaponry. I'd been told that they come from Tanzania, specially trained, unequivocally loyal. Kagame sits back in his chair. 'We have to,' he says. There is a long pause. The two presidential aides sit motionless, watching him, like cats staring up at a tree where a bird flutters in the branches. When he next speaks, his voice is whispery quiet.

'We have to,' he says. 'We have no choice.'

PART I

1994

'I cannot but remember such things were,
That were most precious to me. Did Heaven look on,
And would not take their part?'

Macbeth, Act IV, Scene iii

CHAPTER ONE

Jean-Pierre

The hole was fifteen foot deep. Deeper, Jean-Pierre reckoned, than most septic tanks in Nyamirambo. Deep and dark enough for anyone who could be bothered to heave off the metal cover checking for Tutsis to think him dead and surely not worth the effort of finding a rope and going down to check. They could always fire a few shots into his prone body but how many people in this part of town had weapons or enough ammunition to waste on a shapeless, grey shadow. There had been few bursts of gunfire accompanying the screams that Jean-Pierre had heard from down here in his hole. Machetes or clubs, he suspected, had done the job. Anyway, there was nothing he could do about the guns. All he knew was that cesspits in this part of Kigali were often only eight or ten foot deep. So he was lucky.

The district of Nyamirambo lay at the southern edge of Kigali and had been home to Jean-Pierre for the past month. Densely packed, undistinguished, it sat mostly on the flattish ridge of a hill staring at a dull, blunt peak called Mount Kigali, attracting only the poor or the cultural outcasts – Muslims, musicians, cross-dressers, drug addicts. There were few here who could afford the extra work to dig a cesspit into the soft red soil deep enough to keep the stench away. And little point if the houses either side were less civic-minded.

The deep holes were dug in Kacyiru or Kiyovu, for the ministers and their lackeys who roosted like cockerels in their oversized villas, oblivious to their privileged views of the valleys that unfolded for miles and, under a full moon, glowed like alabaster; their families lounged on imported tan leather sofas, wilting under the weight of their ennui, sucking on orange Fantas, ignoring the grunts of the man of the house as he screwed the new Tutsi maid against the bathroom door upstairs.

The walls of the hole were reddish-brown and had been dug with care and attention – smooth to Jean-Pierre's touch. His fingers travelled across their surface. Gentle undulations, patches of roughened soil that bumped his fingers as they ran along the sides; some wetness too – though he was sure that the foot of water at the bottom of the hole was from rainfall rather than from any pipe. He liked to touch these walls. In the darkness his hand could span an area that was quite different in texture and feel to any other part, as if each had its own story. Intricate personal crevices that earthed him to the world beyond his hole. The echoed shouts of life outside spiralled downwards to where he sat, staring in the darkness at his walls, rubbing grains of dirt between his thumb and forefinger, kneading the earth into his skin. Each circumference the tip of his thumb drew around the print of his forefinger triggered a mild trembling down the left side of his body, proof – as if he needed it – that he could still respond to the delicacies of touch. Each circumference felt like his personal mini planetary orbit. A rotation in time. And (and this was important to him) another second off the time left in his hole.

Jean-Pierre had chosen well to climb into that particular cesspit on the morning of 11 April. In fact, for the whole of the previous two months, his decision-making had, he reckoned, been nigh on impeccable. By February his home in Gatenga, like many other districts in Kigali, had become tense. The peace process had stumbled, lurching between moments of optimism when liberal politicians proclaimed that a power-sharing deal between the Hutu government of Juvénal Habyarimana and the Tutsi-led Rwandan Patriotic Front was close at hand, to despairing darkness as the same politicians were set upon, beaten up or murdered by Hutu extremists. News of each latest wave of violence swept into the squeezed mass of small brick houses in Gatenga, which stewed with gossip. Jean-Pierre's home was wedged between two larger houses and only when he retreated to the cramped bathroom where, under a trickle of water from the ancient showerhead, he washed each morning could he escape the flow of chatter from his Hutu neighbours as they argued over the latest Tutsi 'plot' to destabilize the government. Really, it was Odette who suffered most; it was she who had to walk past the gangs of young Hutu boys, not yet confident enough to shout at her but old enough to curl their lips and scratch their testicles, snorting at her as she made her way to the bus stop and her job at the state electricity company. With no regular hours, Jean-Pierre could stay at home instead to look after Sandra, now two, and their nine-month-old, Vanessa.

By early March, Jean-Pierre decided that Gatenga was too

enflamed by the political turmoil for Tutsi families. Odette and the girls should leave Kigali and, for the time being, live with her parents, Bernard and Joséphine, in Gitarama – little more than thirty miles south-west of the capital. He told them not to worry. He would remain in Kigali but move to another district, Nyamirambo, where most of his clients had their businesses. He promised he would come and stay with them the following weekend.

Unlike Gatenga, Nyamirambo was a cacophonous mix of Tutsi and Hutu, Muslim and Christian, sweat shops and street stalls, the city's poor and downtrodden who, after years of exclusion, were now largely unbothered by the racist blasts from the government radio station. It was also home to Jean-Pierre's best friend from his student days in Zaire. Ernest lived in a small side street in the heart of Nyamirambo with his new wife and baby daughter. Jean-Pierre felt safer here, closer to the city limits if he needed to get away to Gitarama, and better placed to assess the mood of the capital.

For a month Jean-Pierre continued his daily routine. Several businesses in the district needed an accountant to manage their books. The money was not much but after the government department had got rid of him, the work kept his accounting skills up to scratch and it left him time to manage the two music stalls he had opened on a street close to Avenue de la Justice. Twice a week he handed boxes of tapes he had had shipped from Zaire to two boys who ran the stalls. A good day would see his mix of funk, reggae and Zairean Afrobeat earn him five thousand francs – thirty dollars – and sometimes double that. The weekends with his family in Gitarama were short and leaving Odette and the children again was difficult. But he felt sure that the uncertainties of the previous few weeks would come to an end soon; the President was close to signing a peace deal and that, enforced by a UN presence in Kigali, would surely put an end to the recent violence.

Jean-Pierre listened to the announcement on the state radio station, Radio Rwanda, on the morning of 7 April. The President had been assassinated. A long time later, people would relish telling Jean-Pierre how they had heard the President's plane crash: the scream of engines as the Falcon F-1 struggled to stay airborne after the surface to air missile slammed into its port engine, the magnificent, swollen boom that thundered around the hills as it ploughed – with its own rather unique homing instinct – deep into the President's own vegetable patch in his back garden. But Jean-Pierre heard none of this and suspected people who claimed that they had simply liked to pretend they had witnessed Habyarimana's demise in this way. The radio that morning told people to remain calm. A transitional government was already in place. But the crackles of gunfire that Jean-Pierre could make out from other districts suggested reprisals had already begun. It prompted both he and Ernest to keep inside the house and out of sight from any neighbours or passers-by. Ernest's wife, Anny, and their baby were told to stay in the bedroom at the back of the house. Initially, the shooting sounded distant, and they whispered to themselves that it must be from the wealthier districts of Kigali where all those deemed by the ruling Hutu elite to be untrustworthy or subversive were likely to have been put on extermination lists, just as they had been in earlier massacres in the 1970s and 1980s.

Nyamirambo, they thought, held little value for the Hutu

government. The poor and the marginalized had never been a priority for the military or the politicians. Yet, by late morning, there was a knock at the gate of Ernest's house. A gendarme stood there. A few locals loitered behind him, some peering over his shoulder, craning to see past Ernest into the small rectangular compound. Who was he, the gendarme demanded. Ernest Balola. From the Republic of Zaire. The gendarme asked if he was harbouring any Tutsis. No, Ernest said, he wasn't. The small crowd shifted, a few murmurs, but the gendarme was satisfied and walked off. The civilians followed obediently but some heads were still turned, watching as Ernest, his shoulder bent into the gate, slid across the metal latch.

Crouched at the back of the house Jean-Pierre could hear the shouts of the crowd on the street. There was excitement in their voices but also a kind of frenzy. He spent the day moving from room to room – somewhat embarrassed by his boyish commando crawling – below window height, trying to assess how close the killers were. The house had an inner courtyard and from the privy situated in the corner of it, Jean-Pierre could look out on to the main street. There were gangs of men being directed by the shouts of a local *conseiller*, who led them through the warren of small streets as they conducted house-to-house searches. Towards evening there was a deafening crash – a gunshot, not far away. Ernest poked his head out on to the street. A man called Jean-Marie – quite old, a resident of the district for many years – had been shot at the top of the lane, someone said, by the wall that bordered the Republican Guard barracks. Inside, Jean-Pierre listened. He had known Jean-Marie. The old man was surely nothing to them – nobody important.

The shooting intensified, echoing around the hills that dissected the city. Ernest whispered to his friend and together they crept across the courtyard to their spyhole in the privy. From the little window Jean-Pierre could see a small truck. Machetes, clubs – a few rifles – were being unloaded from the back and the *conseiller* was handing them out. They heard more shouts. There didn't seem to be any method to where the men went or whose houses were searched, merely a response to a series of urgent barks by a gang leader acting on snippets of information that he received. The murder of the old man whirred around Jean-Pierre's head. It was pointless – there was no sense to it. And now all these weapons being handed out. Jean-Pierre began to suspect that what was taking place was not an isolated massacre like those when he was a small boy or even targeted killings but something more malevolent.

At dusk they ate. Bowls of beans and, over the brazier, they cooked maize. Jean-Pierre watched the rich plume of smoke spiral up from the compound and disappear into the darkening sky. Perhaps the uneasy hush that had fallen over Nyamirambo had unnerved him but the smoke felt like a signal to the killers outside, roaming the streets. He thought about Odette and the children. It was possible that the waves of anger and paranoia that echoed around the walls of the small compound in which he sat would dissipate and not produce the same intensity of violence elsewhere in the country. Then again, Jean-Pierre reasoned, he could be entirely wrong. Perhaps this frenzy that he detected meant all of Rwanda was now in flames and every Tutsi had become a target. He wondered if Odette had had any choice in what course of action to take. If she had, he felt sure that she would have chosen well.

Years earlier he had watched her as she walked past his office on the lakeshore road in Kibuye each morning and evening. Hardly a road – more a series of ruts in the hard red earth that children used as tram lines to run their wooden carts along. When he was small he'd had a similar cart. A cart that became a sailboat when the rains in April turned the road to soup. The ruts brimmed with rainwater then. He and his brothers used to watch the contorted faces of drivers staring wide-eyed through their windscreen wipers, ship captains suddenly ploughing into deep, gloopy brown seas. The dry season brought dust – thick, smutty clouds that lined the inside of Jean-Pierre's mouth and stained his old T-shirt with red smears of snot. Government cars rarely ventured on to the roads that Jean-Pierre played on so there was little chance of having their surface metalled. The Chinese road crews that criss-crossed their way through Rwanda in the seventies and eighties – dropping like flies with malaria and tuberculosis and later, as they whored, AIDS – paved only the roads used by President Habyarimana and his cronies.

Somehow, on her journey to work, Odette never tripped or stumbled as she walked past Jean-Pierre's office. Her step was light and never rushed. Her head sat precisely on her slender neck, like a pea perched on a plastic straw. When her body moved and swayed as she negotiated the next obstacle, her head stayed perfectly still, balancing an invisible pot. He liked her calmness and the way she ignored men's leering stares. He loved her courage and he wanted to protect her. When she walked behind the *umurehe* tree outside his office, with its grey trunk and long leaves, he had to crane his neck through the window to catch sight of her.

Images slid into his mind: her hand carrying her briefcase, low-heeled shoes picking their way carefully through the ruts, her shapely bottom in a dark skirt, her dead-ahead look – before she was gone, up the hill to her office and Jean-Pierre was left wondering how he would ever find a way to talk to her.

On the morning of 8 April 1994, Ernest left his house and walked to the crossroads twenty-five yards down the road. At the junction was a yellow-painted office. Pinned to the door was a list of names. When Ernest came back to the house he reported that Jean-Pierre's name was on the list. They spent the day discussing his options. Ernest and his wife were Zairean so they and their baby were in no danger. But Jean-Pierre worried that they were risking their lives by having him in their home. Ernest disagreed. Nobody had spotted Jean-Pierre recently at the house and if anyone asked he would say that his friend had gone with his family to Gitarama.

At five o'clock that afternoon it began to rain. A steady rain, powerful enough to send the gangs back to their homes. The neighbourhood grew quiet. Crouched, his back against a wall, sitting below the window, Jean-Pierre listened to the battering on the corrugated roof. It lasted nearly an hour – about right for April – beating out its pattern above him. Then, like the last swish of gravel being swept off a concrete path, the rain moved on. He did not dare look out but he knew what he would see if he did – that mesmerizing clarity of the sky, a cold, hard blue, washed clean of its mugginess, the soaked streets shining angrily, smouldering with the last moments of evening light. He could hear drips landing in the water buckets outside – innocent plops that he sometimes used to imitate in front of Sandra to make her laugh as she scribbled nonsense on the dirt by the back door. The rain had lasted just long enough. Judging by last night, the gangs of killers would not begin their hunt again until the following morning.

Curic

Thirty miles south-west of Kigali, up a narrow bumpy track off the main Gitarama road, lies the parish church of Kivumu. Adjoining the church is a series of small, single-storey buildings, joined together and set, on three sides, around a patch of neatly mown grass. On 7 April 1994, the pastor of Kivumu, Vjeko Curic, was on the telephone, talking to his old friend, Father Sebastijan Markovic; they were discussing the assassination. Markovic had been unable to get back to his friary in Kigali after giving a Mass out of town the previous day. But at least that meant he was able to speak with Curic now. The telephone lines had been cut in the capital but here, out in the country, the lines still worked. Curic explained that he had seen little out of the ordinary in and around Kivumu, but he admitted that he had not ventured far that day so it was difficult to make a proper assessment. Despite the poor quality of the line, he could hear Markovic's heavy breathing. His friend was stressed. He was cut off from the other Salesian Fathers, holed up in a relatively unknown backwater and unsure how the events of the last twenty-four hours would unfold. Curic advised Markovic to leave early for Kigali the following morning and to be ready to bribe the soldiers at any military roadblocks he might run into. It was impossible to say for sure what would happen next but certainly he, like Markovic, feared for the country and worried that his Tutsi parishioners could become targets for Hutus bent on violent revenge.

Later that evening Curic took prayers in the small chapel just off the sitting room. The ancient generator surged like an old man clearing his throat, causing the chapel lights to flicker.

'O Lord, I cried to you for help and you have healed me.
I will thank you for ever.'

Curic, his brown habit worn with age, tried to concentrate on the prayers but all he could think about was the vow he had made to his old friend before he put down the telephone: 'You know this, Sebastijan. You know I will be staying – whatever happens.'

There was nothing surprising about what Curic told him – the moment of decision for the two priests had been building for some time. But the words that crackled down the line seemed to press against the side of Markovic's temples – thick, like a pulse inside his head.

Before the assassination of President Habyarimana, Sebastijan Markovic coaxed his old Toyota saloon up the bumpy track to Kivumu most weeks to visit Curic, his closest friend. Markovic enjoyed the respite from Kigali; it was quieter here, there was none of the political intrigue that dominated the nightly conversations that he endured in the capital with two of his fellow priests. Both Belgian, and much older than Sebastijan, Father Pierre and Father Matthieu irritated the hell out of him. Matthieu, in particular, was an infuriating gossip, sniffing out information with the suppressed eagerness of a teenage radio ham twiddling his dials long after bedtime, falling upon snippets of news with unreserved delight, concocting half-baked theories about which he would pontificate over dinner.

Markovic and Curic were both Bosnian, both in their late thirties and both had worked in Rwanda for many years. As men who had grown up in Yugoslavia, surrounded by Orthodox Serbs, Muslim Bosnians and Catholic Croatians, they were attuned to the often unspoken but deeply felt grievances of ethnic division. Spending time with Curic was always a relief for Markovic after days in the company of his Salesian brothers who, he felt, spent too much of the day gossiping and politicking and not enough ministering to their parishioners. But recently, he had been coming to Kivumu for reassurance. Kigali had begun to frighten him. It wasn't just politicians who were being attacked. His own parishioners had started to turn up at the parish house fearing for their lives and asking for protection. Tutsis harassed and intimidated by their Hutu neighbours. In February another member of the order, Father Jean-Paul, a French Canadian, had had a service interrupted by the arrival of a gang of young men dressed in the uniform of the militia, known as the *interahamwe* and notorious for being the blunt end of state-sponsored violence. Jean-Paul had protested, calling them 'hypocrites' for wearing rosaries when they were known to be killers. He was lucky, Markovic reckoned, not to have been attacked on the spot. Kigali was simmering with a mixture of fear and anger from the overwhelmingly Hutu population: anger that the internationally brokered power-sharing deal between the Hutu government and the Tutsi rebels risked a return to the colonial days of Tutsi rule; fear that thirty years of Hutu oppression of the minority Tutsis would lead to horrific reprisals should they lose power. The city felt like a clenched fist, itching to lash out. On Markovic's last visit to his friend, he had sat hunched forward in his chair, hands clasped together, and poured out his worries. His contemplative, slightly preachy manner was gone. His thinning hair was plastered with sweat, his short-sleeved shirt clung damply to his body. The calm authority that Curic so admired and which typified the intellectualism of the Salesians had drained from his friend's voice. Curic loved Sebastijan, but whilst he enjoyed his visits to the École Technique Officielle in Kigali, the Fathers' secondary school where Markovic lived and worked, he had never had much time for his Belgian colleagues – pudgy, complacent, old-school Europeans, who basked in their former role as know-it-all colonialists. He was sure, too, that some of the Belgian Fathers were politically suspect. They were Flemish men – part of the Dutch-speaking majority in Belgium who had, historically, been ignored by the minority Walloons who resolutely had kept the country Francophone – and who, in his analysis, naturally sided with the Hutus, another oppressed majority whom independence had ushered into power. Curic suspected it ran even deeper. The Belgians, he knew, felt inferior to – even intimidated by – the Tutsis who they knew they couldn't manipulate. 'I can tell a Hutu that it's a nice day and whatever the weather he will nod in agreement,' one priest had told Curic when he first arrived in Rwanda. 'But don't ask a Tutsi,' the man continued. 'He'll look at the sky and if he disagrees he'll tell you.'

'What do *you* want to do?' Curic had asked Markovic that evening.

It was a question that had whirred around Sebastijan Markovic's head for several weeks. But now, at last, he knew the answer and saying it to Curic felt like a release. 'I want to leave. I mean, if something bad happens, I will leave. In all probability, I think anyone who stays is in very grave danger.'

The room in which they sat had grown quiet. Curic could hear another colleague talking to the Hutu cook, Oswald, in the kitchen. Dusk was approaching and the grey light had softened the bright sheen of the polished-cement floor and dropped both men into contemplative shadow. Out here in the country Curic had witnessed little of the intimidation and violence that Markovic had experienced in the capital. He suspected that Kivumu's wide valleys and the remoteness of its hillside villages helped dilute the intrigue and tension. But he didn't doubt his friend's analysis. Recently he had watched groups of young Hutu men gather in villages – private conclaves to which he was not invited nor welcome. Curic had become deeply immersed in Rwandan life. He spoke Kinyarwanda like a local – not the arcane, eye-watering textbook version but the sweat-stained language found in the fields and markets. Here, from the silences between words, the hesitations and pauses, the syllables dying on lips and the downcast eyes, Curic learned to interpret true feelings. The prejudice that Tutsis endured but which they were careful to leave unspoken; the boredom of the jobless young Hutus who hung around the market stalls; the numbing frustration of the farmers who squatted by their huts most afternoons, drawing deep on their straws dipped into bottles of fetid banana beer. The gatherings had left him uneasy.

It was a while before Curic spoke. Then he said, 'Sis, there comes a time when you have to make a choice – either to stay or go. You cannot escape reality all the time.'

Markovic was unsurprised by Curic's barbed reply. He was aware of his friend's irritation with the easy life embraced by the priestly enclaves that had prospered ever since Rwanda had been first colonized. The country offered missionaries an existence of unchallengeable isolation, tucked away comfortably in the folds of Rwanda's hills, careful to keep the poor to whom they ministered at arm's length. For decades they had pootled along the potholed roads in their old Peugeots and Toyotas to hold Masses, tend to the sick and dying, visit schools. In the evenings they returned to their friary houses where Rwandans mutely struggled in the kitchens to produce a passable version of European cuisine. There was usually electricity and, if not, Rome would find funds for a powerful generator, to offer the Fathers light for their evening prayers and bedtime reading. It was a quiet life – uncomplicated by the startling modernity they saw on their occasional visits to Europe, which sent them scuttling back to the stolid communal rhythms they beat out daily in their Rwandan parishes.

From the moment Curic arrived, barely twenty-six, a single suitcase in his hand, to embark on the rest of his life, he had shown little tolerance of the smug religious torpor that had settled over Rwanda's hills. At times, even to Markovic, the zeal with which Curic immersed himself in Rwandan life seemed like an affront to some of the more delicate

Catholic sensibilities. But Curic was a Franciscan. He had chosen to follow in the footsteps of St Francis. Christian fellowship for him came not through the pulpit but from walking and living among the poor. Curic had been ruthless in his interpretation of his vows. In his first few years at Kivumu, he had declined the use of a car, preferring to walk for several hours into the valleys, some of which dropped hundreds, even thousands of feet below the narrow dirt roads, or climb escarpments that stretched back past the nearest ridge of hills, peppered with dwellings, high into the deep creases of the mountainsides, so he could reach the remote farmsteads where he took off his trainers and, in bare feet, tilled the soil alongside the farmers. At night he ate the food they cooked and settled down to sleep next to them in their huts. He learned their language faster and better, his tutors said, than any European they had ever taught. He recruited a core group of young Rwandan novices and together they travelled to the north of the country to build a novitiate on a remote hillside that was owned by the Franciscans. The Rwandans were astonished to watch a white man – an *umuzungu* – haul water, for seven days, from the valley floor to the hilltop to make the mud bricks needed for the house. Back in Kivumu, he managed the local youth football team and could taunt the opposition in Kinyarwanda as well as any of his players. By the late eighties, Curic had squeezed money out of Germany, Italy and Canada and had begun what he believed would be a lifelong programme to bring improvements to the parish at Kivumu – to create a sustainable community consisting of a health centre, schools, a new church, agricultural stores, a residence for the Christ the King Sisters, a house for

Franciscan novices – all aimed at offering Rwandans access to education, employment, health care and spirituality.

Curic had fought with the local builders from Gitarama. He doubted they were skilful enough to undertake the construction work needed for these developments, and he suspected they were corrupt. Don't cheat me, this is God's house, he had yelled at them. He went in search of a builder in whom he could trust. He was recommended Aimable Gatete, who lived and worked in Kigali. In the past Curic had railed against workers who failed to turn up on time and hid behind shoddy work. But he liked the way Gatete looked him in the eye and told him upfront what things would cost. He was a Tutsi, too, which carried weight with the Bosnian. To those he trusted, Curic admitted that he favoured Tutsis over Hutus when he had the chance; he was disgusted by the discrimination they suffered, particularly in terms of their schooling: Tutsis were eligible for only 10 per cent of secondary-school places. Gatete was an able draughtsman and builder and, in 1987, designed with Curic a new church for the parish. It was heptagonal, made of brick, with a smooth cement floor and long polished-wood benches that could seat several hundred. A new primary school was next; then living quarters for the Christ the King Sisters, a health centre and, finally, barns and a silo for the new farm cooperative Curic had formed. The silo would hold the farmers' surplus beans which Curic bought and then sold back to them the following season at cost price, undercutting the inflated prices the infuriated merchants were charging. '*Umuzungu, umuzungu,*' the children used to shout as he walked through their villages. He despised the word – the cry from an African that heralded the arrival of the European interloper. 'Your mother is an *umuzungu*,' he used to yell back in Kinyarwanda – half snarl, half smile, leaving the children open-mouthed and their mothers, sitting outside their huts, hooting with laughter. No one shouted '*umuzungu*' at him any more. He was 'Vjeko' or, if they were yet to be formally introduced, '*padiri*'. Be with the people, endure with them, and you will understand Christ's love, his old professor had told the class back at theological college in Sarajevo. Eleven years after arriving in Rwanda, Curic had trodden every path in his parish and woven himself into the community. It was not in him to leave now, whatever Markovic's decision.

For the two days following the assassination and the phone call from a worried Markovic, Curic received several more calls, mostly from Nairobi but some, too, from Sarajevo. Priests had not been specifically targeted but some had already witnessed traumatic scenes of violence. In Rusengo, Italian soldiers had rescued two Polish priests who had spent more than thirty hours holed up in their sacristy – chairs and tables thrown up against the church door to keep the killers out – listening to the screams of their parishioners being killed outside. There were eyewitness accounts on the BBC of a round-up of any Rwandans who had prompted suspicion amongst the increasingly paranoid and extremist members of President Habyarimana's inner Cabinet. By 9 April, more than two thousand prominent Tutsis and Hutus who belonged to one of Rwanda's new opposition parties had been killed. Journalists had been shot in their front gardens, opposition politicians blown to pieces by grenades thrown under their beds where they hid with their children. Rwanda's Prime Minister had been dragged out of her house, baited and kicked, before an officer from the Presidential Guard drew his pistol and blew her head off. 'Madness' was the word that Curic heard most often in these conversations – a madness had visited the people – and what, when faced with such horror, was one supposed to do about it? How could a priest stay and fight such deep-rooted evil?

Curic learned that Sebastijan Markovic's Salesians were now being protected by Belgian paratroopers from UNAMIR at the École Technique Officielle in Kigali, along with dozens of other Europeans who had fled there at the onset of the violence. The priests were trying to feed, water and guide spiritually the two and a half thousand Rwandans who had taken refuge in the school. But few believed that the UN force would remain there much longer, and if they evacuated the European civilians, most priests were reconciled to leaving as well: to remain meant almost certain death and their duty was to stay alive, they told each other – to minister to those who were also alive. Curic bristled with irritation. 'I took a vow to be with these people,' he said to his Provincial Master on the telephone to Sarajevo, 'to endure with them.'

By Sunday 10 April, almost every European priest was preparing to leave the country. In the southern university town of Butare, several were preparing to travel over the border into Burundi, and in Kivumu Curic discussed with a colleague, Father Darius, the possibility of the latter joining them. Markovic borrowed a satellite phone and reached Curic, telling him of the rumours that the Belgian paratroopers would be leaving his school early the next morning. Apparently, trucks had been arranged to take all the Europeans to the airport, from where they would be flown to Nairobi. The Rwandans who had sought refuge at the school would not be coming with them. Things had got very bad. 'Not here,' Curic replied, 'here there is nothing.' It seemed impossible to Markovic that only thirty miles away life could still be calm. For several days he had watched as Hutu militias began to gather around the gates of the École, taunting the Belgian troops and threatening the Tutsi refugees. Earlier that week a dozen Belgian soldiers had been captured in another part of the city and butchered. He knew that the small contingent at the school offered little protection against any sizeable Hutu attack. 'Just you wait,' he told Curic. 'It's coming your way.'

Odette

Just a few miles from Kivumu parish, in Gitarama, Odette reacted to the radio bulletins with calmness and practicality – just as Jean-Pierre suspected she would. In the hours following the assassination she and her parents assessed the situation and decided to remain at their house and wait. It was true that people were agitated by the news but the town was quiet. The house was large enough for them all, with a spacious compound where Sandra and Vanessa could play, and they felt safe. There were large metal double-gates and a lattice of elegant steel curlicues protected the windows. Even as the radio broadcasts became more extreme Odette's father, Bernard, felt confident enough to walk his elder granddaughter down the small path behind the house to the two-acre plot he owned to help him dig for sweet potatoes and pick beans. Through his grove of banana plants Bernard could look out across the small valley to the next village. Nothing had changed. A woman washing her child in a pail of water outside the door of her mud hut, a man swiping his panga, back and forth, at the weeds that festooned the countryside in the rainy season. A wisp of smoke. Sandra stumbled over the earth furrows, grabbing on to beanstalks, squeaking with pleasure as her grandfather gave her a sweet potato to carry back to the house.

Two days after the assassination they received a visit from Jacqueline. She was a friend – a woman whose family Bernard and Joséphine had helped in the past. She was worried: the killings in Kigali were spreading. She knew this because her daughter was about to marry an important local Gitarama politician – a vice-mayor. The woman was upset. 'They are going to kill all of you,' she said. 'All Tutsis.' She had quizzed her future son-in-law. He had told her the country was at war now. And in a war 'people die'. But he was powerful and could protect them. He had bodyguards. People were afraid of him. She was going to ask him for help.

Help came to Bernard's family in the form of a letter – a laissez-passer that the vice-mayor had signed. As the violence spread beyond the city limits of Kigali and into the surrounding villages and towns, they felt protected. But when Sandra fell ill with malaria, Odette felt she had no choice but to take the two girls to the local hospital at Kabgayi, just three miles away. She carried the vice-mayor's letter with her. Hundreds of people were on the main road. No bad thing, she reckoned, since the three of them merged into the seamless mass of people passing through Gitarama. Some were Tutsis although most were Hutu refugees who had fled their homes ahead of the advance of the Rwandan Patriotic Front, which, on learning of the death of the President, had immediately invaded Rwanda from the north. As she passed her local church, St André, Odette saw dozens of families slumped on the steps, surrounded by bundles of clothing, carts, old bicycles. She had brought practically nothing with her and wore a pair of work shoes, her suit trousers and a T-shirt, with an *igikwembe* – a traditional shawl – wrapped around her waist into which Vanessa was tightly strapped, pinned to her back. Sandra, she carried in her arms.

The Kabgayi hospital heaved with people, mostly Tutsis who had fled their homes, although some rooms were strewn with wounded government soldiers. The corridors stank of putrefaction. Groups of people sat outside on the brick steps that surrounded the hospital. A low murmur seemed to hover, like the pall of smoke from the fires that had been lit, just above the crowd. At dusk, passing vehicle headlights panned across them and people yelped in panic. No one seemed to be in charge and Odette wanted to put her hands over Sandra's ears to stop her listening to the whispered rumours that wormed their way around the huddled groups:

'The army are coming to kill us.'

'My brother's sister-in-law is from Ntarama. She saw young men with machetes killing children.'

'They swung the children by their feet on to concrete walls, smashing their heads in.'

Odette found a nurse who took her and the girls into a room at the back of the hospital. Children lay quietly on mattresses spread across the floor, their mothers beside them. The nurses were kind. Sandra was quickly diagnosed. Malaria, as suspected. Odette found a corner of the room and settled her daughters down. There were moments when she thought of Jean-Pierre. The stream of people she had walked with that day gave her some encouragement that her husband would be on the road too, probably heading south from the capital to find them. Or west, to Kibuye, where his father and mother had recently moved.

The following morning, a government man in a brown suit arrived to address the huddled mass of people that had spent the night outside the hospital. He told them that they could not stay there any longer. It was a large crowd since throughout the night even more people had arrived. He spoke with the self-satisfied pomp of the petty bureaucrat, confident only in the orders he had been told to issue. When people asked where they were supposed to go he grew defensive. How was he to know? This was not his problem, he shouted, as he marched about, close to defeat. People looked away – ignoring his orders – and he grew angry. He seemed to shrink inside his baggy suit, blinking vacantly, swamped by his own pettifogging. More people arrived. Wearily they dropped their belongings on to the ground. The stuffed bags and bulging foam mattresses spoke of their last frantic moments of leaving – shrill arguments, a lurch back into the house for an arbitrary possession that meant something, sometime, a long time ago.

By mid-afternoon Sisters from the local convent had arrived, distributing food and water to the old and sick and the children. A fierce debate took place between Brown Suit and a Sister. The bureaucrat spent much of the time turning away from the argument, shrugging with exasperation at the misfortune that had befallen him. Then, just before dusk, an announcement. Walking through the mass of people, the Sister and a solitary priest told them to pick up their belongings. It would be a short walk to the cathedral. Nothing too strenuous.

Like a large, decrepit animal rising reluctantly to its feet, the crowd lifted itself and began to walk slowly out of the hospital grounds towards the cathedral a few hundred yards away. Some attempted to climb the steps into the building, but Brown Suit had re-emerged from his sulk and positioned himself by the doors, from where he angrily barked commands and pointed people towards a stony path that ran down a small hill, past the Bishop's residence. At the bottom was a large enclosed field. At one end were several cowsheds; at the other, the Bishop's garden. A fence – part wooden, part wire – ran around the perimeter. And in the nearest corner there was a rickety wire gate, through which the refugees began to walk into the field.

Odette had not heard Brown Suit's shrieked reprimands. She hadn't left the hospital room and would not do so for a further week. Caring for Sandra rooted Odette to her corner of the room in any case, but she had already made up her mind that she would remain here for as long as possible. Leaving the room – even to walk the hospital corridors – would, she was sure, risk attracting unwelcome attention. The room baked with the collective sweated heat of half a dozen families. No one felt safe with the windows open, except at night, but then each shout from outside or roar of a truck produced a collective moan of fear from the room's inhabitants. There was little food but the nurse who had provided anti-malarial drugs for Sandra's fever brought pails of water to the room each morning. After two days the fever broke. With Sandra out of her delirium Odette could focus on rehydrating her. It was a relief to be able to nurse her elder daughter – to occupy her time and force the deepening anxiety she felt about her family back in Gitarama to the back of her mind. For those two days, as Sandra lay prone on the floor, Odette's mind had swung from her life here in this room, as the mother of two small children, to her life as a daughter, just a few miles away. As much as she tried to reassure herself that the vice-mayor's influence had proven effective, the whispered reports of the country falling into murderous chaos made her fearful that this assurance of protection was paper-thin.

Curic

Long before dawn on 11 April, Vjeko Curic woke to the sound of insistent knocking at the metal gate. Outside was a young couple with a small child. They were trembling. He knew them – they were called Barabaganda. Another family emerged from behind a copse of eucalyptus trees. He ushered them all inside and took them into the sitting room. Most stood awkwardly, staring at the calendar on the wall and the figure of Christ that hung above the fireplace. Barabaganda sat on the old sofa with his arms wrapped around his knees. He was trembling badly. He and the others had left their houses the previous evening. During the day he had heard his neighbours talking about 'the Tutsis next door' and had watched the arrival of the local *bourgmestre* who had spent a few minutes talking with the neighbours before leaving. Their village was transfixed by the news of Habyarimana's death, but until now it had been calm, as if unsure what to do. The local politician's appearance had energized people. Now Barabaganda and the other Tutsis felt that every whimper and cry from their children drew attention to them.

At nightfall, the family had slipped quietly out of the back of their house and walked, cross-country, to Kivumu. He told his story quickly and, judging by his trembling, Curic suspected that there was much the Tutsi had not spoken of.

He knew too how difficult their journey must have been. Years before he had walked the same paths to the same village with some of his young acolytes. Dressed in old jeans, a short-sleeved shirt and a pair of leather sandals, Curic had balanced a twenty-litre water container on his head as he followed the goat trails from Kivumu. It had taken them several hours – the village had seemed deceptively close but three ridges lay between them and their destination. It had been late afternoon when they climbed out of the last valley, the green mess of fields slowly blackening as dusk settled. They had sung hymns as they walked, the *padiri* teasing the teenagers that he, an old man of twenty-six, was a better walker and singer than any of them. Curic remembered the greetings from people perched next to the houses he passed. Women sat back on their thick haunches, feet together, knees splayed, pounding cassava or shelling beans. The men, barefoot, trousers cinched at the waist with old string, work shirts stained and sour. He remembered he felt scrawny and loose-limbed compared to the muscled compactness of these men. Habyarimana's forgotten underclass, he had thought. Stuck up on a hill, out of sight, pre-modern. The same men who would now be hunting Tutsis, clambering through thickets of maize with machete or panga, club or knife – it really didn't matter – crossing streams, wading through rice paddies, urging each other on. He remembered he had passed dozens of houses that day. God alone knew how these people had managed to evade capture.

Curic took his set of keys and told the families to follow. They walked out of the courtyard, past the cowsheds to the novices' house. It was empty. Curic told the families they would be safe here. The house was tucked below Kivumu's ridge, visible to few people and then only from the other side of the valley. He told them he was going to lock them in – for their safety. He would send Oswald over later with food. The priest walked back to his quarters through the dark and stood in the doorway looking into the living room. On the chair next to where Barabaganda had sat he noticed the small cushion still bore the imprint of his friend Sebastijan, from his last fraught visit a short while before. It struck him that the past few days had characterized the differences between the two men. Their physical disparities they had always laughed at – Curic whippet-thin and fidgety, Sebastijan fleshy and immovable. Emotionally, Curic was fiery and passionate; he would proclaim, denounce, uphold an opinion and critique on any subject or person. Sebastijan took longer to decide what he thought and then, once certain, anchored himself permanently. When Curic enthused about his latest ideas – a new health centre, literacy classes for adults – Sebastijan sat quietly in the small living room, blinking slowly behind his lenses, his hands perched on the promontory of his large midriff, listening as Curic's ambitions grew and the plans began to slip gently away from the realms of practicality. His mouth would slowly form a fleshy circle, ready to intervene delicately and guide the idea – and his friend – back into the world of the possible.

Curic looked back out at the path down which he had led the small band of frightened Rwandans a few minutes before. He guessed that by now Sebastijan was on his way out of the country. It was hard not to smile at the empty chair, at the inevitability of his friend's decision and at the implausibility of what he had decided to do himself. He picked up his car keys, spent a few brief moments in his room and then walked to the battered old Passat that sat parked by the cowshed. He would not judge Sebastijan, that much he knew. He hoped that however things turned out now, Sebastijan would not judge him either.

For forty minutes Curic drove in silence along dark roads. Musambira, Gihembe, Buhoro, Gatizo, roadside villages, dark now, deserted, uncluttered by barefoot children running for school, ancient minibuses stopping for pick-ups on their morning ride to the city, loiterers by the beer stalls, eyes following the *umuzungu* drivers. As he drew closer to Kigali he passed clumps of people walking away from the city. In the flash of headlights that swept over them he could see the piles of belongings perched on their bicycles. At the Ruyenzi bridge which marked the city limits, Curic encountered a military roadblock. He slowed to a halt and switched off his engine. Two soldiers approached. They were heavily armed and their uniforms identified them as members of the Presidential Guard. Curic leaned out of the window and explained that he needed to get into the city. One soldier asked why. He replied that he needed to pick up an employee. The soldiers looked down at him and then quietly spoke to each other. The sky had lightened and Curic saw there were more troops than he first realized; both ends of the bridge were fortified with sandbags. He was reminded of the day three years earlier, in the north of the country, when he had crossed from Tutsi-rebel territory back into government-controlled Rwanda. As he left the rebel checkpoint, soldiers had asked him for any books or newspapers they could read. On the other side of no-man's-land he encountered soldiers from Rwanda's national army. They asked for money and whisky. It was a sign, he was sure, that the Tutsi rebel army, the RPF – well disciplined, ideological, incorruptible – would one day defeat the Habyarimana regime. Now the soldier who had asked the question turned back to him and explained that it was impossible for him to go any further. The *inkotanyi* – the rebels – were close to the district he was headed for. He'd have to go back. Below him, Curic could hear the greasy, chestnut-coloured Nyabarongo river make its way under them. He looked at the soldier who stood above him. The man had already told him to leave. Curic brought out a wad of dollars. He would pay, he said. Five hundred dollars – eighty thousand francs – if he was given an escort.

It was still before dawn when Curic drove into Kigali with the two soldiers. The city seemed deserted – the call for a curfew from the interim government seemed to have worked. There were several military roadblocks. Curic noticed that grouped close to the troops were gangs of men. They carried homemade weapons – machetes and clubs with nails hammered into their ends. One or two carried rifles or had grenades hooked into their belts. At each roadblock Curic halted while the soldier in the front passenger seat leaned across him and talked to the soldier peering through the driver's window. Sometimes they shared gossip – mainly about the proximity of the *inkotanyi* – but they were rarely held up for long. They made their way past the bus station at Nyabugogo, up into the quiet residential district of Kiyovu before turning right, past the military barracks towards Nyakabanda. It was light now and Curic began to see bodies. They lay close to houses that looked to have been looted, in the street gutters, as though they had been pulled off the broken-down pavements to allow people to pass by unimpeded. Many of the dead had arms across their faces as though they had been attempting to protect themselves as they were attacked. Curic noticed, too, that a jacket or shawl concealed their faces, as if someone had deliberately covered them after they had been killed. The limbs of some of the bodies had become swollen, so he guessed that they must have been killed some time ago, almost immediately after the President's death was announced.

'What does your worker do?' the soldier next to him asked.

It was a loaded question, Curic knew. A white priest on the road at dawn retrieving an employee was almost unheard of and served only to provoke suspicion.

'He is my cook. He has been with me for years.'

Nyakabanda district was a nest of alleyways and side roads. At the junctions Curic saw makeshift roadblocks. Groups of men stood by them. They stared deeply into the darkness of the car as the priest was made to stop. Many of the men sucked on straws plunged into old plastic containers. They stank of cheap alcohol and woodsmoke. At one barrier, behind flames that crackled out of a blackened and rusted metal barrel, the priest could see several bodies piled just off to the side of the road, within spitting distance of the militia at the roadblock. He presumed that these were people who had been killed more recently.

It had taken more than an hour to drive the few miles from the Ruyenzi bridge to Aimable Gatete's house. Curic knocked as loudly as he dared on the metal gate. After a few minutes he heard Gatete approach. Speaking quietly, his mouth close to the wire grille, Curic told him that he was here to get him out but that they didn't have much time. When Gatete slid back the lock and opened the gate he saw the two soldiers climbing out of the car. The priest told him that the men were there to protect him, but in truth he could not be sure how much protection they would provide. Once inside, they discussed Gatete's family. It would hardly be possible to bring them all out. And it was prominent Tutsis who were being targeted, they reasoned, not women and children. Gatete was a well-known Tutsi businessman.

The soldiers walked up to the two men and told them to hurry. They were nervous. Gatete ran back to the house and a few seconds later re-emerged with his wife, who closed the gate behind them. Their escort told them that it was impossible to drive back the same way through the roadblocks – the *interahamwe*, the militia, could not be trusted. They would have to find a different route to the bridge. For Curic, the soldiers' admission that the Hutu militia was a more potent force than the army was an important lesson in the hierarchy of power that now ruled Rwanda. Soldiers in uniforms, carrying the latest weaponry, deferred to gangs of raggedly dressed civilians armed with little more than clubs and knives. It started to make sense. Soldiers were professionals, paid to protect the President and the country. But the gangs carried a greater authority in that their murderous work was voluntary and an expression of patriotism – a direct response to the country's leaders' exhortations for Hutus to leave their homes and work all hours of the day and night to carry out their national duty.

Curic dropped the two soldiers off at the Ruyenzi bridge roadblock. As he began to drive away one of them leaned in and looked past Curic directly at Gatete who still sat in the back of the car. 'I know he is not your cook,' the soldier said. 'No one pays that kind of money for a cook.' He stepped back from the car and waved them on.

Jean-Pierre

If he twisted his body, moving carefully on his metal drum, Jean-Pierre could look up and see the small crack of light between the walls of his hole and the manhole cover. With each shift of his head the light swept over him, fragmented crystals of colour shimmered and skated as his eyelids hovered, half shut. He saw blues and greens. They reminded him of the shafts of colour that he'd seen through the cracked windscreen of the bus he had taken the weekend before last to see Odette in Gitarama. Bright green hills. He was not especially fond of the countryside south of Kigali. The hills were stolid and uniform, the land overly farmed, the people slow-witted. The weekend had been short and leaving Odette and the children had been difficult. But he had been right to send them to Gitarama. Just as he had been right to come to Ernest's. His head knocked gently against the earth wall – as if to reinforce each of his decisions. Given what had taken place here in Nyamirambo, he knew that if he had stayed at home in Gatenga, he would be dead by now.

The events that led him to this hiding place were still hazy. Jean-Pierre remembered the hammering on the metal gate of Ernest's house and the conversation as Ernest stood at the gate, the men outside peering in. Like the visit the previous day, a gendarme was with them. He had a rifle. He demanded to enter the house. Ernest had no choice. Jean-Pierre had thought about hiding under the bed but it was pointless and risked the life of Anny and her baby. He came to the door and the policeman grabbed him. Someone shouted, 'I know him. He is a Tutsi.' The policeman shoved him back into the compound, close to the corner with the privy, from where, the day before, Jean-Pierre had watched the *conseiller* handing out weapons. He heard the shot from the rifle and felt his head hit the ground. Then nothing. When he came to he heard Ernest's voice but he couldn't make out what he was saying. He thought, I am dying. Then he felt Ernest lift him up and he found himself struggling back into the house. The bullet had seared his skull. The rest of that day he lay on the floor. Ernest came back from checking the list at the yellow house. Jean-Pierre's name had been scratched off it. 'That means they think you are dead,' he said. But Jean-Pierre didn't believe anything. 'They will come back,' he insisted, 'and if they find me here they will kill me and they will kill you.'

That night Nyamirambo was drink-sodden and lawless. Several houses near to Ernest's were set on fire. Through the privy window Jean-Pierre glimpsed people walking past, heaving furniture, telephones, beds, blackened kitchen pots and pans. Gangs of young men ran hooting with excitement, others walked more slowly with radios pressed to their ears. Radio Mille Collines was a new, privately owned station that had been started by businessmen loyal to the regime. It had become wildly popular with Hutu extremists for its invective and its frenzied exhortations for Hutus to kill Tutsis. Now, the tinny, metallic voices urgently gave out information and news of what they were describing as a Tutsi plot to kill

Rwanda's beloved President. Jean-Pierre knew that he could not last another day in this house. He had to move. If he was to stay alive then he had to get out of there.

He woke Ernest at four that morning. They unbolted the gate and Jean-Pierre slipped out. Twenty-five yards from the gate, to his left, was the crossroads. It was dark but he could see the militia roadblock quite clearly. Several men lay asleep, close to a brazier which still glowed. It would be impossible to step around the roadblock without the risk of waking one of them. Theirs was not a deep sleep – they lay prone but uncomfortable, curled up under old jackets, their heads bent on the crook of an elbow. Jean-Pierre looked up the road. Fifty yards up the hill the road came to a T-junction. Left would take him back towards the centre of Kigali; right, deeper still into Nyamirambo. There was an hour of darkness left. If he was caught on any road he would be killed. He walked a few steps up the slope towards the T-junction. On the right, close to Ernest's house, was a small alley with an open drain. He stepped into the alley and edged slowly along it – feeling his way in the dark between the two walls of the adjoining houses. The alley turned abruptly right and then left before it stopped and opened into a small courtyard. The house seemed deserted. There was a metal manhole cover in the courtyard. It was heavy. Jean-Pierre struggled to slide the cover half off. It smelt earthy, not putrid, as if it were newly dug. The cover was certainly new. He sat looking around the compound. It was enclosed on three sides, only visible from the alley. He could hear people beginning to stir, throats being cleared, doors being opened, the sound of a tap being run into a plastic pail. He lowered himself into the hole, his hands gripping the edge. His legs dangled in the air. As he released his grip he felt his feet plunge into tepid water and then hit the bottom of the hole. Looking up, he could see his head was between six and eight feet from the opening. The hole was perhaps four feet wide – he could easily touch both sides with his arms outstretched.

Jean-Pierre had been standing like this for more than an hour – long enough for the sky to have lightened and for him to have started shivering in the water – when a face peered down into the hole. It was Ernest. He said he had seen Jean-Pierre disappear down the alley. 'How did you get down there?' he whispered. 'I jumped,' Jean-Pierre told him. 'Wait, I am getting a torch.' Ernest's head disappeared. A few minutes later, Jean-Pierre heard the noise of a metal chain being dragged nearby. Torchlight beamed into the hole, flashing across Jean-Pierre's face. It hurt his eyes. He cried out for Ernest to stop. The torch blinked off. Then a chain was lowered in. At the end of the chain was a bucket with a few inches of water. Jean-Pierre plunged his hand in and found an old plastic cup. He drank. Two, three cupfuls. He'd had no idea he was so thirsty. As he dipped the cup in again the bucket was yanked from his grasp and began its journey up out of the hole. Jean-Pierre tried to say something to his friend but Ernest had begun to slide the cover over the opening. The light drained from the hole, leaving Jean-Pierre in darkness.

Curic

That night, after Mass, Vjeko Curic sat at the small wooden table with a glass of rakija. As bad as the scenes had been that morning on his journey into Kigali to find Gatete, he still wondered if the violence would not burn itself out. Since independence, extremist Hutu politicians had carefully manipulated their history to stir up nationalist sentiment against the minority Tutsis. Children were taught that the Belgian colonists had favoured the Tutsis, retaining the monarchical dynasty that had oppressed the poor rural Hutus for generations. It was effective propaganda – twisting a shared culture and political heritage between the two ethnicities into a racist message that in moments of dire poverty helped avert the gaze of the vast majority from the feeble-minded failings of their government. Curic remembered an old Hutu man pulling up his shirt and showing him the scars on his back from a beating he said he had received when the Tutsis were last in power. He had no way of knowing if what the man said was true, nor if it had been a Belgian or a Tutsi hand that had held the lash. In the dank hut in which he crouched, examining the man's back, the brooding silence spoke of a bitter memory – one that the Hutu government could rework, creating a potent brew of ethnic hatred which wove together the threads of ancient Tutsi supremacy and colonial oppression.

When they flared up, as they had done every few years since independence, the massacres were savage and ritualistic, but they burnt only briefly. The dead would be buried, the perpetrators would soon return to their barracks or neighbouring villages, and the survivors would suffer in silence. There was a Rwandan saying that Curic knew and that seemed to sum up the self-containment of the people he had chosen to live with: '*Amarira y'umugabo atemba ajya mu nda*' – 'the tears of a Rwandan man fall inside into his belly'. It seemed to Curic that all Rwandans – not just the Tutsis who had suffered thirty years of intermittent state-sanctioned violence and murder – were accustomed by now to a level of brutality that was unlikely to divert them from their daily trudge to the fields or the market. Three years earlier – in response to a state of emergency declared by the government after the first invasion by the Tutsi rebel forces of the RPF in northern Rwanda – soldiers had walked into Kivumu and ordered Curic not to leave the parish. But within weeks life was back to normal.

Yet the bodies that Curic had seen that morning on the streets of an unremarkable district of Kigali – pulled out of their houses and killed, quite possibly by their own neighbours, only hours before he had driven by – conjured up an unpleasant memory. It had been two years before. He and his Novice Master, a fellow Bosnian, Father Pero, had sat in this very room with a Rwandan priest they had trained – a man they liked and in whom they had invested years of teaching and spiritual encouragement. They were ruminating on the RPF invasion and wondering if the war would force both sides to the negotiating table. For most of the conversation the two Europeans had done most of the talking. Until the Rwandan blurted out that, in his opinion, peace talks were a waste of time. 'It would be better,' he said, 'that we kill all of the Tutsis before they kill all of us.'

Curic made his way into the kitchen and stared up at the shelves, counting the bags of rice and beans. With Aimable Gatete safely installed, the novices' house was full. If others came, he would have to think of new places to hide them. He understood why they had come. They had nowhere else to go.

Terrified, mumbling stories of their families being attacked, their houses burnt or destroyed. Curic had responded the only way he could. But he had committed himself to a dangerous course of action. Remaining in Rwanda for his parishioners, bickering with local functionaries over food supplies, monitoring the movement of people in and around Kivumu, these all fell within the boundaries of permissible behaviour for a priest known in the higher echelons of the Rwandan church to be an independent spirit. But secreting Tutsis inside his own home was probably a treasonable offence. His status as a European would mean nothing to the extremists.

It would only be a matter of time before someone informed on him. Then, the faith his new houseguests had shown, that he could stand between the people and the killers, would be revealed as hopelessly naive. He would be cut down just as they would be. He thought back to his professor, Milan Babic, who had taught him at theological college in Sarajevo. 'You are Franciscans,' he would say, blasting the words out from the front of the class with all the enthusiasm his small frame could muster. 'Invest in people, not power. The people come first. Then Jesus.'

Curic looked again at the imprint from Sebastijan's large frame on the cushion. He wondered where his friend was now. Earlier that morning he had got through to the École Technique Officielle and learned that they were in the process of being ferried to the airport. Markovic, he was told, had gone – loaded on to an earlier truck by French troops. And probably now on a plane to Nairobi. Curic had replaced the phone slowly. There had always been an air of unflappable permanence about Sebastijan. As well as a friend he had been a counsellor to Curic – an audience for his opinions, his plans, his occasional rants. Now there was no one to argue with or give Curic advice. No Rwandan would provide a counterpoint to Curic. He was, he realized, entirely alone. If he shouted, the words would echo as if they were spoken to an empty room.

There had been times in the past, when he had travelled north to Byumba and stayed with farmers high up in the hills, when he had felt this kind of isolation. He had spent evenings listening to the grumbles of old farmers who moaned about the days under the Tutsi monarchy. The men drank their *urwagwa*, murmuring their discontent, a morose drunkenness settling over the hut like dense afternoon rain. The beer – made from banana plants – was fetid and sour but alcoholic. He looked through the murk at the men – worn faces that seemed like a throwback to a proletariat that had hacked and toiled under the watchful eyes of the Tutsi rulers – the *bami* – for centuries, then submitted to a colonial government that sent scientists to measure brow and nose widths, length of calf muscle, degree of intelligence, and drew maps tracing ancient journeys from the Horn of Africa that the Tutsi cattlemen had made long ago. All this science produced identity cards, labelling the ethnicities. It was laughable, Curic knew that. There were no unknown souls in Rwanda. Pio was a Hutu and the cattle that trod and shat on his fields were Tutsi cattle – owned by Vénuste and his father, Ignace, before him. Évariste brewed the best *urwagwa* and his father had taught him. Hutu, both. Francine the midwife was a Tutsi, but she pulled babies from between the legs of women who were Hutu, Tutsi and even Twa. The storekeeper, Jean-Baptiste, was a Hutu, and said he was a Hutu even though his grandfather married a Tutsi who was known to have been tall and beautiful, with slim hips when she was young, but ended up just like all the other women once she had bent herself to the harvest for a few seasons. In a land that no one left and few ever visited, there were no strangers.

Existence was a ritual, a pre-determined life cycle of un-questioning labour where squat, powerfully built men gripped sacks of coffee beans, threw them over their shoulders and began a slow walk down sheer steps carved out of the hillside – the muscled arches of their feet strained to screeching point – to markets several miles from their small plots. When they were young they carried bundles of sticks gathered from the bush for their mothers to fuel their fires. Jerrycans next – twenty-litre, dirty-yellow, plastic monsters that bent their necks sideways as they hauled water from the stream at the bottom of the valley back home to their huts perched halfway up the hill, arms craned upwards, hooked over the barrels, muscles burning. School intervened, but only just enough for them to learn to read a little. The kleptocrats in Kigali expected little of Rwanda's rural poor – that is, most of the country – other than to leave their classrooms soon enough and piss off back to their hills, cut away the brush, fornicate, spill out more children, brew their banana beer, die uncomplainingly and bury each other under their acacia trees. Do as they were bidden.

When the men had fallen asleep Curic had crept from the hut to look out across the dark, soundless valleys. The huts sprinkled across the landscape, the links that bound this country together, had disappeared under a moonless night, inked out by thick black brushstrokes. No electricity up here – houses had settled into darkness hours ago. No sweep of headlights that slowly wound along the contours of the hills – no roads existed. He could reach into the darkness, eyes straining, and see nothing, hear nothing. He was entombed and entirely alone. Away from the mental funk of the farmers, he was exhilarated. He could whisper a prayer and the furthest point would catch every word. He could hurtle down hills and across valleys, at impossible speeds, with no fear of falling, the thick night air cushioning him. A brightly lit stick-man on a canvas of black. Untouchable.

From the edge of the compound Curic saw the tall, dark outline of his cook, Oswald, making his way slowly back from the novices' house. It was cold tonight. Wind gusted through the eucalyptus trees. Oswald walked slowly, head bowed, a man wading through water. Behind him, the building was a shadow – a ship marooned in a sea of maize that quivered in the wind. Barefoot, Curic walked back across the patch of grass, the dampness chilling the soles of his feet, to his living quarters. With just the glow of the oil lamp throwing a small crescent of light across the long oval table he wrote a short note to Sebastijan.

Sis, my darling,

We're still holding out. I've managed to get Aimable out of hell, well not me, but God did it. Judging by the ones who escaped from Kigali, some of the long ones [Tutsis] managed to get away. J.B. with his wife and child came to me on foot. They are all somewhat disorientated. There are lines upon lines of refugees here. The situation is complex. I remain here until someone kills me! And someone definitely will; I just hope it isn't a long one, because it will be a grave sin for him, and he won't be able to get over it afterwards.

Maybe you come to visit Vjeko through Burundi. Who knows!!

*Love and greetings from your
f. Vjeko*

PS: I know that it's worse for you than for us, but hold on. Forget as much as you can. All connections are broken. Till when? Fuck it!

CHAPTER TWO

Jean-Pierre

In the blackness of the soil Jean-Pierre sometimes thought he could see his reflection. His fingers brushed the dirt away and traced the lines. An ancient mask, unearthed. It showed a man who was not quite handsome – his head was too squat and his ears too rounded – but he was certainly attractive. His mouth curled slightly up at each end, giving him a look of gentle, half-suppressed amusement. But when he brought his fingers up to trace his jawline and cheekbones the reflection disappeared. Jean-Pierre had been in the hole for more than a week and already he could feel the effects of his incarceration.

Next to him where he sat in his hole was the bone of the chicken leg that Ernest had lowered down to him the day before. He had been asleep, cross-legged, on his oil drum. The cold metal of the bucket clanged against the drum and woke him. There was no bowl inside, just a damp chicken leg. He smelt it. The bucket travelled back up the hole. Ernest scraped the cover back into place.

The two men had developed an unspoken system that they

hoped would keep him alive and avoid Ernest attracting any undue attention by making too many visits down the alleyway. Ernest had dropped a five-litre jerrycan of water to Jean-Pierre. Every two or three days, the bucket would swing down into the hole with a small bowl of food inside. A few beans. Perhaps some maize or an onion or a carrot. Whatever Ernest found in the depleted marketplaces of Nyamirambo. He had lowered the oil drum to Jean-Pierre the night after his friend had first jumped into the cesspit. And a small cushion to sit on. The water at the bottom of the hole was receding, but for the time being the drum kept Jean-Pierre's feet from getting wet again.

Jean-Pierre stared at the chicken leg. Meat was a rarity. Perhaps it was his training as an accountant, but it prompted a ritual that required absolute discipline, following a strict algebraic formula where every molecule of this piece of dead animal could hop over the equals sign and be reinvested back into Jean-Pierre, who was still alive. First, the shreds of skin were removed and eaten. The grease from the skin was sucked off each finger. Then he gnawed off the few morsels of flesh that remained before ripping the tendon off the bone and letting it sit on his tongue and slowly dissolve into gooey mulch. This would take some hours as it dripped down the back of his throat. Later, he would lick the bone clean. Then, he planned to snap the bone in two or three pieces and suck the marrow out. If he was careful, he reckoned the bone would last until Ernest came again.

He had a recurring thought that circled around him, about what it meant to be frightened. On the one hand, he reasoned, the hole he sat in was the end of his life so there was nothing to be frightened about. But it was also true that the hole gave him hope that it might be possible to survive. After all, no one had found him yet. He was not sure he wanted this kind of hope. If he thought he might get out alive, then it made him fear even more the prospect of not surviving – of being dragged out and killed.

He did not think he slept but he must have because sometimes he dreamed things. Then, later, when he was awake, he saw them again – sparks in the darkness.

'Eat your food and be quiet!' Jolie shouts.

Ten children are sitting around the table. Jean-Pierre is at one end because he is the oldest boy. His older sisters are next to him – Jeanne Nors, Donathila Uwamahoro and Aimée Nyiramatama. Then all the boys crowd around the other side – Joseph Mukassa, Jean Mugabo, Job Munguhanacoyo, Jacques Muhire and Joseph Binego. Didier Nors – just a baby – is at the other end staring at his brothers and sisters, his hand clutching a piece of papaya. Everyone is talking and talking.

Jolie is fierce at supper. Too many kids. But she smiles when you say, 'Jolie, I want some more.' Her real name is Taciana. But her nickname is Jolie because when she was young she was very pretty. Joseph first saw her when he was a student doctor and she was sick and in the hospital and Joseph said, 'She is pretty, I am going to ask her out when she is better.' Joseph was tall and handsome and funny, and when they married they moved to Ruhengeri where Joseph worked in the hospital as a doctor and a surgeon. Then they moved to Rutongo, not far from Kigali, and now they have ten kids. Joseph is not at the table. He is still at the hospital with his patients. Everybody at the hospital calls him *muganga* Joseph. *Doctor* Joseph. The main corridor is long and at either end you can see the trees and the red dust of the hills because there are no doors, and the breeze ripples through the corridor, which is green and shiny and you can see your shadow as you walk, and it feels like you are staring into a bottle. When Muganga Joseph walks past the nurses and greets them by name they giggle. Rutongo is a good hospital with good doctors but outside his office there are always people because he is the favourite doctor. Muganga Joseph listens to his patients. They tell him about their lives – not just why they are feeling sick – and he tilts his head, and outside the queue grows and the corridor starts to hum like bees. When he gets home Jolie is still shouting because one of the children is not home yet and she has told them that if they are not at the table by eight they will get no food. 'Jolie, come on,' Joseph says. 'Leave them some food out and they can eat when they get home.' Joseph likes it to be peaceful. At home he is never Joseph. He is always called *Papa Joe*. Jolie shouts at the children but she never shouts at Papa Joe. He has pens that poke out of the pocket of his shirt, like a schoolmaster. Parker pens. He loves the Parker ink pens. If he has had a beer you can ask him for things. You can ask him for a Parker pen – but make sure you get it from him then and there. He will give it to you, no problem. But if you wait until the next morning he will smile at you and you'll know it's too late. You see, you have to time it right.

Curic

In the early morning during the rainy season, Vjeko Curic liked to sit after Mass and look out across the valley, still coated in moisture from the previous night's rain, as if blanketed by a layer of fine grey muslin. Even though the country reminded him of Bosnia, he had always been careful to avoid making too many comparisons between it and his new, adopted home. People, on learning where he came from, would frequently come out with trite, facile observations, which they delivered with the authority and excitement of a scientist uncovering a new molecular linkage: the undulating landscape of Bosnia and the hills of Rwanda; the historic ethnic divisions in the two countries; the mirror-like presence of a powerful, oppressive all-seeing state in both.

But between the violence that had erupted in Rwanda and the war in former Yugoslavia, soon to enter its fourth year, it was difficult not to draw parallels. The year before, Curic had been on his way to visit his family when he was stopped at Mostar by the vicious fighting between Bosnian Muslims and Croats. His parents, he was told, were trapped – part of a Croatian enclave in Zepce, surrounded by the Bosnian Muslim army. And now he had discovered there were people in his own parish who were in a similar, if not more precarious position.

It was his cook, Oswald, who on his daily commute by bicycle from his home to the friary had told the priest that people – Tutsis – were leaving their homes and walking towards Kabgayi and its cathedral to seek protection from the Bishop. This was on 12 April. The President had been dead for almost a week. Curic drove the seven miles to the cathedral. People were sitting on its steps, just off the country's main north–south highway. Others were making their way down a stony path that ran alongside the Bishop's residence.

Curic followed them. He heard a hum of noise and then a strong smell of human shit hit him. The path fell away sharply. He could look back and see the Bishop's gardens – neatly manicured lawns edged with dense thickets of low hedge – perched loftily above a small field in which perhaps a thousand Tutsis now camped. Most stood around in groups, though the old sat, heads bowed. Some lay in the dirt, sleeping on their few belongings. There was little room for people to move through the camp. He noticed several younger men hacking at the branches of trees. At one end of the field there were sheds and some of the corrugated iron from the eaves had been stripped off and propped against the walls, offering those too weak or too old to move a measure of shelter from the rain that came most afternoons, turning the land into a quagmire. Barbed wire had been hastily erected above the old six-foot wooden paling. Curic noticed that it was still being put up, not by the soldiers who were staring at the arrival of this *umuzungu*, but by the people inside the camp. They were fencing themselves in; hardly the actions, Curic reflected, of people who think they are in a safe haven. But it did suggest that the Tutsis had, in a minor way, some degree of control over their predicament.

On his return to Kivumu his car edged past a steady trickle of people on the road, carrying their belongings with them, heading to their parish church. Curic told Oswald to prepare what food he could – particularly for those who came with none of their own or with young children. He made sure that Oswald separated off a portion of the supplies for the people in the novices' house and told him that he should let the families know that they must not cook their own food; Oswald knew to feed them only after dark.

Looking into the kitchen, Curic could see his cook working at the table, his tall frame leaning over, his brow creased in concentration. He had met Oswald seven years before – when he had been one of the many young Hutu men who had helped build the new church. It had been an eye-opening experience. Employing locals on an ambitious building project with regular wages would, he expected, be welcomed or, at the very least, produce in the community an energizing jolt. But it had not played out that way. The men seemed indifferent to the work they were doing. They gathered each morning under the eucalyptus tree where they sat, quietly, and waited. Curic watched them. There was a kind of bovine subservience to their patience. Each day they would wait for Gatete or one of his foremen to show up. And, Curic guessed, if no one came, they would have sat and waited there all day. In Kigali he met white expatriates who raised exasperated eyes heavenwards as they told tales of their work-shy employees.

'"It's my time to eat," that's how they are. Doesn't matter if you are a peasant or a President,' they said.

'The problem is that Rwandans never look beyond tomorrow.'

But what was beyond tomorrow for the mass of Rwandans who lived outside the gaze of spoilt, myopic Westerners, Curic wondered. The horizon for the dirt-poor was a twenty-yard strip of maize and beans, an airless dark hut, a brood of uneducated, undernourished children, a small hole nearby to shit in, and a government that sat in distant, undisturbed, corrupted silence, dragging its people downward. Tomorrow would be the same weary plod to a small patch of earth as today, as yesterday had been, and the day before that.

Curic remembered his young postulant, Aphrodis, explaining that Rwandans seemed content because they were all poor. No one was rich so they didn't know anything else. The problem was that they were content not working. Like the others who gathered each morning, Oswald had been shy and careful to avoid too much eye contact with the *umuzungu* priest. But Curic had noticed how hard he worked, how carefully he listened to Gatete's instructions. He was the first to raise himself off his haunches each morning and the last to leave his work at the end of the day. By the time the friary had been built, Curic realized he needed a cook and, in Oswald, he believed he had found a worthy apprentice. He taught him European-style dishes, for the stream of *awuzungu* who visited. When it was just him, Curic preferred Oswald to produce food as he would at home. *Amashu* – cabbage, fried and mixed with roasted *intoryi*, miniature aubergines that looked like Christmas tree decorations, swamped by ladles of soupy *ibishshyimbo* – brown beans, rich and earthy as the soil in which they grew – that growled and chuntered through your bowels and spattered the toilet-bowl enamel. And sweet potatoes in garlic and chilli, Curic's favourite. Oswald's frown of concentration, as he brought the dish through from the kitchen, would break into a look of wide, high-cheeked, squirming embarrassment at the roar of approval from the priest.

When Curic left the camp at Kabgayi he walked back up the hill and sought an appointment at the cathedral office with Bishop Thaddée Nsengiyumva. It was not an easy decision for Curic. The Bishop was high up in the ruling party's hierarchy and would doubtless be torn between his ecclesiastical duties and his political loyalties. But if the Tutsis who were moving into the camp below his quarters were to be protected, they needed the Bishop's explicit authority. The Bosnian was told that the Bishop was busy – too too busy, his unctuous secretary said – and was not to be disturbed. Things would be better tomorrow. Curic should be sure to visit then.

As he climbed back into his car he could hear the hum of the camp just out of sight. Earlier, at the entrance, the crush of people had been so great he had had to turn sideways and squeeze his way through the gate. He had walked slowly past a group of heavily armed gendarmerie. Two stood on the low wall that overlooked the camp. Their eyes gleamed as they watched the people that gathered behind the wire fence. If they had been cats their tails would have been twitching.

The next day Curic drove to Burundi. It was a journey of seventy miles to the border and a further fifty to Burundi's capital, Bujumbura. There he met with an aid agency, Catholic Relief Services, and explained that he wanted to begin a weekly food convoy from Bujumbura into Rwanda. He had drivers he trusted but he needed a truck. The agency lent him a Mercedes jeep to replace his battered Volkswagen and began a search for a suitable lorry. And they gave him money – dollars – which he explained he would need for bribes. He spent one night in Bujumbura and by the time he turned round and drove back into Rwanda, he learned that the violence now extended well beyond Kigali. There were daily reports of fresh massacres across much of the country. People, he was told, were flocking to their churches for refuge and, in some instances, were being encouraged to do so by the local government officials. Once there, the Tutsis were surrounded and set upon by gangs of *interahamwe* who encouraged villagers and onlookers – people who had previously been friends and neighbours – to turn on them. At the École Technique Officielle in Kigali, the two thousand Tutsis and dozens of Hutus who opposed the violence and had sheltered alongside Sebastijan Markovic and the other Salesians under the protection of the UN force, had been marched two miles from the school and murdered.

Odette

Sandra was better. The fever had gone. She toddled between the blankets and belongings of the people who lay quietly in the room. A squawking two-year-old whom her mother struggled to control. It was partly her daughter's high spirits in such a small room that encouraged Odette to leave the hospital. Mostly, however, it was the whispered news from a neighbour of her parents, Mukaruziga, who had come to Kabgayi to find them. She did not know what had happened to Odette's family in Gitarama. Frightened by the violence, Mukaruziga had not been home for more than a week. But she knew Odette had gone with her daughters to the hospital. That was why she came. She would help them get back to Odette and Jean-Pierre's home in Kigali. The rumour was that large pockets of the capital were now in rebel hands. Such was the success of the *inkotanyi*, the Tutsi rebels, that the government had fled Kigali and was now in Gitarama, where Odette had been staying with her children. But its presence nearby didn't mean that life here was about to become any safer. Odette looked at Mukaruziga. She had known her for much of her life – a Hutu woman only a few years younger than her own parents, whom she had worked for, helping rear Odette and her brothers and sisters. She had lived close to their house for many years and her small plot of land adjoined the two acres Odette's father owned. It was impossible to imagine this woman betraying her. And her ethnicity might provide them with the 'cover' they needed to travel.

They left just before dawn. The room was quiet. Most were asleep although some, lying sideways on their blankets, watched them leave. They told no one where they were going. Vanessa was wrapped in Odette's *igikwembe*, Sandra clung to her mother's front like a crab. She needed them with her, Odette told Mukaruziga when the woman offered to carry Sandra. They joined the main road and moved into the middle of a large group of refugees, inconspicuous, half obscured by the barrows and carts and detritus. She felt the eyes of people walking past, in the opposite direction. Some stopped and watched, as if looking for someone they might know. She kept her head down, following Mukaruziga's feet as she paced out the road, just in front. They passed the camp behind the Bishop's residence. Some in the group veered off towards its gate. Odette said, 'If we go there we will be killed. They will put us on a list and we will be killed.' Mukaruziga agreed. They kept walking. Since leaving the hospital Sandra had not uttered a sound. She lodged her chin on Odette's shoulder and rocked slowly with the rhythm of her mother's steps. Odette could feel Sandra's breath on her face. If she turned her head her mouth would brush against Sandra's ear. 'Everything is fine,' she whispered. Odette felt her daughter's small hand tighten around the hem of her T-shirt and her throat thickened and ached and she thought she would suffocate. When they stopped in the shade of a eucalyptus tree and Mukaruziga gave them water, Sandra sat next to her, wordless – staring at the refugees as they pushed past. Odette pulled Sandra into her. She wanted to weep for them. Her cubs. She felt the energy of their warm bodies pouring itself back into her as their hands searched for and then fastened on to hers.

They reached the village of Musambira on the road to Kigali in the late afternoon. They found the local primary school. Other families were already there. Some had settled in the classrooms but there was not enough space inside for everyone. Odette staked out a small piece of territory away from the road. It was close to the edge of the school, next to fields where she could watch farm labourers come and go from their work. There was no fence around the school but she felt more anonymous here – away from those gawping from the road. Once a man came and asked her name. Otherwise, they were left alone.

That night they were woken by a gun battle. Booming crashes in the fields nearby and bursts of gunfire that made a wild slashing noise through the air like cloth being ripped close to your ear. They ran inside a classroom, clambering across people. Someone said that the RPF were close and that they should try to get across to the *inkotanyi*. 'That's impossible,' a voice replied. 'We'll be caught in the crossfire.' The noise had become deafening. People began to get up and run from the school, in the opposite direction from the battle. Odette gathered up Vanessa, gave Sandra to Mukaruziga and followed. They crossed the main road. She heard screaming and people crying out but she was too busy following the path through the field to open her mouth. She could hear

Mukaruziga behind her as they stumbled through the dark. At first, they followed small, less well-known routes north – a lattice of spidery paths spread across the countryside – and then they rejoined the main road. Not to Kigali. The fighting had dissuaded them from trying to reach the capital. But twenty miles west, to Kayenzi. Odette had an aunt who lived there, she told Mukaruziga. She was married to a Hutu who was high up in the village. He knew the mayor.

Curic

Curic swung his Mercedes jeep on to the road out of Kabgayi. His latest trip to the camp had not been a success. The men, women and children behind the wire were starving. Their numbers were growing. They were pressed against the fence. His protests had been met with hand-wringing by people from the local government. War, they said, the country was at war. There was little enough food for ordinary people – let alone those that had decided to barricade themselves behind barbed wire. Curic could hear the sneer in their voices. It was pointless to argue – they knew what was really going on. And in their sour shrugs he recognized too the deadening hand of Rwanda's shambolic local bureaucracy. A whole class of functionaries that sat, in every town across the country, midway up the ranks of the ruling party. They worked – if sitting at an old desk in a worn suit jacket doing nothing all day could be described as work – in grubby back offices, where filthy ledgers lay around unopened. The walls were tired yellow, stained dirt-brown, the bookshelves empty, the telephone seemingly poised to ring but disconnected. They cowered in front of their superiors who despised them for their ignorance, their small-mindedness, their mumbling social inadequacy. But with the limited amount of power they were given they could exact a vicious, barked retaliation on those beneath them for the ritual humiliation they were forced to endure.

Farmers were beginning to leave the fields and make their way back to their homes. Curic drove more slowly than usual. They walked in single file, in tattered, grimy shirts and old sandals, their faces flitting past his windscreen. The priest noticed that, as usual, there was none of the hooting and banter and argument that he'd seen on the roads in Uganda. Nor the screaming schoolchildren – chasing and waving as he passed – a ragtag army of smiling, vociferous belligerents. Rwandans seldom talked as they walked. Automatons, back from their daily grind, an impassive trudge from fields to dwellings. When they turned to watch Curic – which they invariably did – they would stop and stare at him, their eyes would meet, and then, long after he had passed, Curic could see them in his rear-view mirror, motionless, rooted, still staring blankly after him. On this particular stretch of road he sometimes recognized one of them and waved. Usually he was met with a quizzical frown, although the man or woman might half-heartedly, as if in embarrassment, lift an arm in acknowledgement. But, even though his mirror was dusty and cracked, Curic could see that people never seemed to talk to each other about the white man who had just waved at them as he drove by. They would watch the back of his disappearing car as if they were memorizing his number plate. If there was any interest, it was kept to themselves.

Curic was reminded of Bishop Nsengiyumva's pastoral

letter, written and published three years earlier in the Kabgayi diocese. They had walked slowly through his gardens behind the cathedral. The palms of the Bishop's hands were pressed together like the hands on the chipped figure of Jesus that hung above the doors of the cathedral, nailed uncomfortably to the wall by his thighs, the blue paint on his cloak flaky and dry. The arms of the Bishop's thick, black-rimmed glasses clung to his neatly cropped hair. He was excited by its publication but, Curic supposed, he must have been nervous too. '*Convertissons-nous pour vivre ensemble dans la paix*' was as close to pamphleteering as Rwanda got. From a senior cleric who was a senior member of the regime's ruling party, this kind of self-criticism was controversial and risky. Carefully phrased, the article had, nevertheless, demanded an end to the relationship between the Catholic Church and the ruling elite; it urged the government to address the terrible poverty that afflicted the peasantry.

Curic slowed to a stop. A large sow was being dragged screaming across the road to a butcher's stall. Several men stood by their wooden shacks, watching the animal's executioners struggle to control her as she screeched her protest – her eyes blazed furiously at this late-afternoon indignity and her tongue lolled in foamy exhaustion out of the corner of her mouth. Curic looked at the men who were laughing at the sow, he saw the butcher sharpening his knife and the small boys who, encouraged by their elders, were aiming pointless, sadistic kicks at the animal's snout and drooping teats. A sense of menace pressed on his temples and then swept past him, like the hot eddies of wind that kicked up suddenly and blew dust into the dark corners of his church.

He sat quietly in his car watching the scene and thought

again about the Bishop's publication and their garden talk. What had intrigued him at the time was the blunt acknowledgement by the Bishop of the Catholic Church's failure to spiritualize the country. Every Sunday millions of Rwandans took to the roads, pacing out their journey not to the fields but to their *padiris*: to sing, pray and take the Sacrament. But, as Nsengiyumva noted, whilst the ritual may have been followed, there appeared to be no palpable sense that the experience was understood. People knelt to receive the blood of Christ not because they wanted to but because they were told to. The Bishop had fretted over his countrymen's unthinking acquiescence in matters of the spirit.

As they walked, Curic had pointed out that governing Rwanda was predicated on unquestioning obedience. The Hutu peasantry sat, ill-educated, in their valleys, bullied into sullen silence by their political masters who, on detecting the faintest whiff of disgruntlement at the lack of food or jobs or, bluntly, hope, would quickly play the nationalist card, accusing Tutsis of plotting to undermine the Hutus' natural, rightful hegemony, demanding unswerving loyalty from the rank-and-file Hutu, encouraging vicious attacks on Tutsis. The invasion in 1990 by the rebel Tutsi army had only fuelled the sense of paranoia in the country and assisted the government of President Habyarimana in suppressing any protest at the desperate lives people were forced to live. The Bishop had listened quietly to Curic and nodded. Curic knew that it was nothing Nsengiyumva didn't already know.

They had reached the end of the Bishop's garden. Two men cutting weeds with their pangas moved discreetly backwards out of their way, bowing gently to the Bishop, murmuring quietly, as if, Curic thought, we are two great panjandrums, arriving here for the first time, at the head of a hundred-mile camel train from far-off Eastern lands. He watched the Bishop smile beneficently at the two men before he turned to face Curic. He spoke quietly to the Bosnian. He had news that he knew would disappoint him. Curic's application to enrol in Butare University's medical school had been rejected. Rwanda needed more *Rwandan* doctors and, besides, his primary mission was to fulfil the country's spiritual needs.

Curic looked at the Bishop. Six years earlier his request to study medicine had been turned down by the Provincial Master back in Sarajevo. The young priest had been told to focus on his spiritual role in the parish. Later he learned that senior Franciscans in Bosnia had worried that splitting his time between church and hospital would have tempted him to leave the order. As irritated as he had been at the time, he could see how those who did not know him could think that might happen. The decision to reject his application now, however, was preposterous. For nearly a decade Curic had demonstrated an unswerving commitment to his spiritual mission. For the last three years, the Bishop had watched the young Franciscan energize his parish with a series of practical flourishes that had transformed the community. New schools, new farming cooperatives, a properly functioning health centre and jobs, real jobs. The *padiri* was loved and respected.

Between the swipes of the gardeners' blades cutting the Bishop's grass Curic could feel the stifling throb of prejudice, an echo from his own past as a Catholic growing up in an atheistic Yugoslavia. It was ludicrous, he knew, to imagine that Butare's medical school was burdened by the weight of Rwandan applications. Most of the country was overwhelmed by poverty, and those who were not preferred – Curic believed – a more politically advantageous and less effortful life shuttling paper files between various government departments to working in hospitals. And hardly any Tutsis were offered a chance to study at university. The Bishop mumbled his apologies and pressed the pinkish pads of his fingertips delicately together as if his hands held an airless bubble in which he – and perhaps Curic too – were enclosed. Curic looked out across the garden to the fields below. Rwanda – landlocked and wedged between savannahs to the east, impenetrable jungle to the west, and enemies north and south – a cultural desert, a brutal throwback to medieval times; its government able to raise the drawbridge on the world outside, content that its citizenry will never realize its isolation. For the first time since he had arrived in the country, Curic suddenly felt trapped.

The sow had been dragged into the dark insides of the butcher's badly lit store. The entertainment was over. The men wandered off. The boys turned their attention to a small woven basket of twigs and began to kick it down the road. Dusk was grey and quiet as Curic drove slowly away. A mile further down the road Curic was forced to slow once again. This time it was for a roadblock. There were civilian militia on the barrier which Curic had not seen before. Several men seemed to be involved. They were squat and powerfully built – years spent trudging up and down steep-sided hills. They carried machetes and wooden clubs. Some people had been stopped by the side of the road. They queued like shoppers, their tired pink identity papers clutched in their hands. They shuffled forward, their faces now as mutely blank as they were in the small black and white photographs that were stapled inside the cards.

Back at Kivumu, Curic parked by the church. He had heard the reports on the radio since the assassination that spoke of roadblocks being hurriedly built across the country. And he had known for months of the whispered gossip that extremist members of the government had constructed a secret plan for a mass killing, had stored weapons and trained a civilian militia. Yet, looking out over the fields of sorghum and maize, he saw nothing that suggested a heinous, countrywide mass crime was about to take place. The bodies on the road when he had driven to Gatete's might have been a typically violent but isolated reaction to the death of the President. Yet something was nagging at him, and had been ever since the roadblock.

He watched the last of the small figures working in the fields. This was a busy time for any farmer: the heavy rains were behind them and, left untended, the ground would soon be overwhelmed. A few goats herded by a small boy trotted past. The sky was darkening and from behind the cloud came soft thuds. *Boof, boof, boof.* No crescendo, no crackled boom, not thunder, then. Artillery. The battle for Kigali, between government soldiers and the rebel Tutsi army, was now several days old. As he watched the goats skitter through the narrow courtyard, he understood what it was that had been gnawing away at him. Earlier, as he had driven away from the roadblock and looked back at it in his dusty mirror, he had seen the gang leader and his men march up to the group of people who were patiently waiting for their identity cards to be checked. None of the roadblock gang had hung around to watch him – the *umuzungu* – drive away. Too interested in their quarry, they hadn't given the white man a second glance.

Jean-Pierre

For more than a week Jean-Pierre had sat in darkness. When he heard the cries from outside or the crackle of gunfire he felt protected. It was as if he had been enveloped by a thick amniotic fluid. Sometimes he felt that it was slowly absorbing him. If a killer slid off the cover, Jean-Pierre was sure he would look down and see nothing but a warm, soupy darkness. When Nyamirambo was quiet, however, the blackness made him panic. The pulse in his ear throbbed like a metronomic downdraught of wind. He banged the heel of his hand against his ear and scraped at his head. It could last for hours and made him sob with frustration.

He had developed a hunger for news. Unlike the physical ravages which he could control by rationing the food Ernest gave him, the ache he felt for the outside world gnawed at his conscience. He knew that it would be impossible to find out about Odette and the girls – Ernest had already told him that even he, a Zairean, could not contemplate a journey to Gitarama. But news of any kind was, in Jean-Pierre's mind, intimately linked to his decision to send his family away. So when the cover slid open and Jean-Pierre saw the shadow of Ernest's head, news was always his main concern.

'I heard gunshots earlier, what happened?' he asked.

'It was Alphonse. There was a massacre at the mosque.

And Rugarama was killed today in Nyabugogo. I think you knew him.'

Jean-Pierre was surprised to discover that, as shocking as it was to hear Ernest's abbreviated reports of the senseless deaths of those he knew, the news offered some comfort. It allowed him to put a pin in the mental map he had formed of Kigali. With each pin, with each senseless death, he was reassured that the decision to move his family out of the capital had been the right one. He replayed his conversation with Odette over and over again. They had first discussed leaving back in February. They were united in thinking the violence was political, targeting specific Tutsis and Hutus who had publicly backed the peace negotiations that had led, just a few months before, to an agreement for new, democratic elections. But people had been assassinated; there had been riots in some districts of the capital. Why risk the children getting caught up in it?

In the dark as he marked out his map, there were moments of doubt. The reckless, feral noise that he had listened to over the first few days had dissipated and he guessed that roadblocks – such as the one he had seen on his brief journey from Ernest's house to the cesspit – had established some calm in Nyamirambo. Perhaps, after all, the violence was isolated in certain parts of the city. Then he heard the sound of distant shelling and he made a mental calculation as to its location – Rebero or Kimihurura. Kiyovu or Kacyiru. He had always had a good sense of direction. He used to tell Odette the best way home through the traffic or guide her down streets in the dark. Perhaps it was because he was well travelled, as a child following his father around the country to new hospitals, being schooled in Zaire, working in different towns. He soaked up new places quickly – the streets and shortcuts, the areas to avoid. Odette rarely disagreed with him. When they drove, she sat staring straight ahead. Sometimes she would make a murmur of assent, but mostly Jean-Pierre sensed that she was not too bothered by such things, her mind was elsewhere. It was the same when they got married. He had been very nervous, but she had seemed so calm throughout the day that it was hard sometimes to know what she was thinking. When they started to live together he had learned not to let the flutters of panic he felt deter him. He realized he must trust his instincts. In a room in Kibuye – far from the suffocating atmosphere of the capital – surrounded by people dancing and the noise of his music, he had done just that, falling in love with Odette because she was different. She did not rush about. She moved slowly, talking to people, never distracted by the noise of the music. With Odette it was always better to watch and to wait.

Curic

When Curic made the short walk from his friary on 14 April to conduct morning Mass, he discovered the church was packed. Normally he might find fifty or sixty parishioners there. This morning there were four hundred gathered inside. People sat slumped against the outer walls or on the polished wooden seats. Some were praying by the altar. A group was attempting a hymn, but it was hard to sing the way they usually did at Mass now that no one felt like clapping their hands. They were terrified. Each had a story. Some had travelled for two days, across valleys, hiding in the fields during the day, moving at night. In the stumbling darkness families had become separated. Pierre-Célestin Ncogoza was a farmer who made the weekly journey to Sunday Mass with his wife, Béatrice, from their smallholding two miles to the south. He looked starving. He had lost Béatrice and their two children. A gang of Hutu militia – the *interahamwe* – had attacked their home two days ago. They ran out of the back of the house into the fields. They lay in a banana grove all night and all the next day, their old clothes merging into the frayed yellowed leaves and brown stalks, their children lying in the ditches amongst the piles of maize husks. They lay for hours like that, not moving. Like dogs, motionless in the afternoon heat. The second night they began to walk towards Kivumu. People heard them and they fled their pursuers in panic. Pierre-Célestin hid in a drainage pipe for several hours. His wife and two small children were dead, he was sure. They had been following him as they ran but then he heard only his own footsteps, his breathing. At Kivumu church he had wandered through groups of people looking for his family. He saw people he recognized, but there seemed to be little energy for talking. Pierre-Célestin asked if anyone had seen his wife and children. No one had. People were restless and frightened. After Mass they told Curic they would not leave the church.

At the primary school, Curic found groups of men standing around the front of the building holding clubs and machetes. Inside, more than a hundred people were hiding in the classrooms. Béatrice was there – with her children. She was badly injured and her elder son lay by her side, breathing heavily. She explained how they had managed to walk to the school. But that morning the men outside had started to beat them. Her son Olivier had been hit on the side of the head by a club. He had run screaming from his attacker. Béatrice wept as she described how Olivier had run round in circles, the palm of one hand pressed into the side of his head, as if he were trying to shake water out of his ear. Then a man came up to her with a machete. She said, 'Please forgive me,' and he hit her across the back of her head.

Curic left the school and approached the men outside. They paid him little attention. Initially, Curic was restrained – quietly explaining that he was the priest at Kivumu and that this was his school and the people were his parishioners. Through the door he could see frightened faces peering out and his voice sharpened and grew louder. The people they had attacked were his parishioners. *His* parishioners. Curic was working himself up into a fury, spitting Kinyarwanda at the men. They were to leave, immediately, or he would report what had happened to the chief of police who, he told them, was a man he knew well. The men shuffled their feet, watching each other, waiting to see who would wilt first under the verbal barrage. Initially no one made a move, but then they all collectively swung away down the road, clubs lolling jauntily. Curic watched them leave. He wanted to keep shouting but he knew the risks of humiliating them further.

An hour later he sat with Bishop Nsengiyumva in the quiet of his study that adjoined Kabgayi cathedral. Curic explained that the diocese faced a moral and physical crisis. Right now, there were several hundred people camped at his church and school in Kivumu. It was likely that they would be murdered if he did not get permission to move them. The Bishop blinked slowly behind his glasses. Curic understood the tortuous balancing act the man sitting across the wide expanse of desk faced. Thaddée Nsengiyumva was the second most powerful Catholic in Rwanda. To be seen to condone the massacres would be professionally ruinous. Yet his elevated political position left him little room to manoeuvre. Curic liked him, too. Unlike other senior bishops Curic had met – in Africa and Europe – this man showed none of the pretensions of high office. The room was sparsely furnished. A calendar on a wall. Two small chairs under each of the windows. A single bookcase. Behind the Bishop hung a simple dark-wood crucifix that was partly obscured when Nsengiyumva leaned back in his chair.

'It is very difficult. The war we now have. What to do with all these poor people.'

The Bishop pressed his palms together as if in prayer and touched them to his lips. He murmured, half to himself, 'What to do, what to do.' Curic watched him and thought, this man is caught in a web. Even if he takes responsibility for these people he can't be seen to accept culpability for why they are here. An ill-considered suggestion would, Curic grasped, prompt a retreat from the Bishop – like pulling the wrong thread and seeing the knot tighten.

Curic presented his idea to the Bishop in careful, modulated language. He couldn't be seen to press his case too hard, but his journey that morning to the Bishop's office in Kabgayi had convinced him of the sense of his plan. Curic had learned that the intensity of the fighting for Kigali between the two sides had forced the government to flee the capital and requisition a college in Gitarama, just a few miles from Kabgayi. Only an hour ago, Curic had chanced upon a column of refugees who had followed their government out of the capital, trudging in driving rain and under darkening skies towards Gitarama. The column was at least a mile long, perhaps twenty thousand people. Fearful of straying too far from the men who had confidently proclaimed on state radio that the country was safe in their hands, this mass of people, mostly Hutu but surely some Tutsi as well, were a walking humanitarian crisis.

Kivumu lay just north of Gitarama and Kabgayi. The crush and chaos of people on the road, Curic reasoned, offered him the chance to move his Tutsi parishioners the seven miles from Kivumu to the makeshift camp below the Bishop's residence at Kabgayi. Positioning them here, under the direct gaze of Bishop Nsengiyumva, would offer them the best chance of survival.

From national radio announcements Curic had learned that Tutsis throughout the country were being ordered by local politicians and the gendarmerie to gather at churches, schools or hospitals, ostensibly for their own security. Tutsis would most probably have run to their place of worship at a time of crisis, anyway, but the BBC's World Service was now reporting that the large number of Tutsis collecting in churches allowed the extremists to murder people quickly and efficiently. In Musha, a small community east of Kigali, the army had kicked down the doors of the church one morning and murdered nearly twelve hundred people who had gathered there. First with guns and grenades and then, to finish people off, they had waded in with wooden bats and machetes. More than six hundred of the dead were children. Curic's church at Kivumu, hidden up in the hills and now full of Tutsis, would surely be targeted too.

But if he could move them to the camp at Kabgayi, they might stand a chance. Kabgayi was not some mud-brick church in the middle of the bush, surrounded by hills and impenetrable roads, where Hutu killers could murder Tutsis with impunity. The Church might be able to get away with expressing its sorrow at such massacres and regret that owing to the situation – 'a most desperate civil war' – it was impossible to visit these parishes and calm the local population down. But Kabgayi was a vast slab of red-brick cathedral situated on the main road that ran north–south through the country, home to a powerful member of the ruling elite and spiritual home to hundreds of thousands of Rwandans. A massacre there could not so easily be dismissed.

Curic explained that he wanted to move his parishioners to where they could receive proper pastoral care. He needed a letter from the Bishop that proved he was working for him on behalf of the diocese. A laissez-passer – written in simple language – which he could show to any 'authorities' he met on the road. He chose his words carefully, offering explanations that he hoped Nsengiyumva could use himself to anyone who might question his decision. Bringing the people to Kabgayi would, he said, bring order to the diocese. It would help cauterize the wound that had opened up in Rwanda.

When Curic returned to Kivumu he drove to the primary school where he told people to walk to the church. He would meet them there later. He loaded Béatrice and three other injured women into his jeep and took them to the hospital in Kabgayi. Her children were left with a woman Curic knew would look after them. By midday there were several hundred people gathered at the church. Curic was brisk. Standing in the footwell of the jeep, he told them that staying at Kivumu was not safe. They would travel in groups, with him, to Kabgayi. A hundred at a time. He showed the letter from the Bishop, a guarantee, he said, that they would be safe.

Curic led the swathe of people in his jeep, the engine idling in its lowest gear. At the top of the first hill he saw a roadblock. It was an old tin drum with some recently cut branches of what looked to be eucalyptus strewn across the road. The roadblock had appeared since he'd returned from speaking to the Bishop that morning. Curic guessed that news of the evacuation had leaked out, and he realized that there were likely to be many more of these impromptu roadblocks between his parish in Kivumu and Kabgayi. In that moment, as the car slowed, he resolved to avoid, wherever possible, bringing it to a complete stop. The drive became a series of small, carefully measured pas de deux between the will of the Bosnian, trying to get through the barricades quickly and efficiently, and that of each successive roadblock leader, attempting to retain an air of command in front of his gang. If Curic stopped the jeep, then the power shifted irreversibly to the gang leader. The man could amble slowly across, slouch over the car, lean inside and initiate a ritualized interrogation of the priest – where was he going, where had he come from – which was as much about asserting himself as it was about eliciting information. The trick was to keep the car moving – at a brisk walking pace – while he leaned out of the window, showing the Bishop's letter to the man, telling him, before he could ask, the answers to his questions, as he kept up alongside. Thus, an imperceptible and unspoken bargain was struck between the two men: the gang leader had been gently deferred to, and Curic – a priest busy with parish duties – was quickly past the roadblock.

Safely through, Curic parked his jeep twenty-five yards beyond the barrier – close enough to watch the refugees pass the men, but far enough away that he did not risk any further conversation, any potential haggling. Less than half a mile later, on a bend in the road, another roadblock had materialized. This time the militia gang lashed out at some of the people as they passed by. The column slowed and a murmur of panic spread through it. Curic reversed his jeep back towards the barricade. The whine of his car distracted the men. Curic called the leader over and began to talk quietly to him. After a few moments, the man leaned in through the window. Curic had dropped his hands on to his lap where he was counting out several ten-dollar bills. He was careful not to show the man how much money he had, but sufficiently clumsy to demonstrate that he had more. Curic folded the money in two and thrust it into the leader's hand. He sat back in his seat. Through the crush of people walking past the jeep he could see the gang glancing at his car. The file of people moved faster through the roadblock and Curic shifted his jeep into gear and crawled back slowly to the head of the column.

A few hundred yards later, another barrier. Then, at an even shorter interval, one more. By the time Curic's convoy had made the seven-mile journey to Kabgayi he had counted eleven roadblocks that had been erected that very morning. The journey had taken an hour longer than it should have done. At that rate, Curic calculated, it would be well past midnight by the time everyone had reached the camp. He needed to double the number of the next group, but that risked him losing control of it since it would be hard for him to see what was happening at the back whilst he was leading at the front. Curic had little choice. He knew that moving the Tutsis at night would be extremely dangerous. The column palpated with fear anyway. By dusk the gangs would be drunk. The road would be pitch black. It would all add up to too much opportunity to lash out at his parishioners, however much the bribe.

Curic was unsure of the precise number of people that he escorted that day to Kabgayi. But by evening all those who had run to his church and school were inside the wire of the camp. He guessed seven or eight hundred had been added to the camp's growing population. As he left he felt torn by his decision to bring people there. The bursts of rain meant that the ground underfoot had been churned into mud. People lay exhausted by the heat of bodies pressed next to them. There was little food. But they were collecting rainwater in sheets of corrugated plastic they had ripped off the shed roofs and distributing it around. There were a significant number of people – several thousand – situated within earshot of Bishop Nsengiyumva's living quarters. As bad as conditions there were, Kabgayi represented the best possible chance of survival for his parishioners and for the thousands more who had fled their homes in search of sanctuary. It would be here that he would focus his efforts. In this stench-ridden hole, he would embark on his task of keeping people alive. Back in Kivumu, Curic ate ravenously – his first meal of the day. He laughed when he told Oswald that he had felt like Moses, leading the Israelites out of Egypt.

Jean-Pierre

Jean-Pierre had not been present at the birth of either of his daughters. He had been warned that Sandra's birth would be difficult and that had decided it for him. He preferred to wait outside. It had been a cool night and he had paced up and down the corridors of the maternity ward. It was true they were by no means dirty, but they were not up to his father's standards. Papa Joe was meticulous and demanding about cleanliness. When the children heard his car come down the track they used to rush to their rooms and tidy up. He was never angry, but Jean-Pierre could sense the disappointment in his father if he felt the house had not been cleaned or his children had not bothered to bathe.

Jean-Pierre rubbed his index finger up the crease of flesh from the base of his neck to behind one ear and shuddered to think how he would look to his father after ten days in this hole. Short, greasy sausages of dirt, which he flicked off into the tepid water, at the bottom of the hole. He flexed his legs and rubbed the backs of his knees. The sweat that gathered there as he sat cross-legged on his drum had started to chafe the skin. He had developed a routine. Every few hours he alternated between standing on his drum or sitting and letting his legs hang loose over the edge which, now the water had subsided, meant his feet remained above the waterline. He hoped his father would understand why he had not washed. Papa Joe and Jolie had moved to a village just outside Kibuye only three months before. The *muganga* was supposedly retiring, but he had let Kibuye hospital know that he was available to help out. The town was the prettiest in Rwanda, wedged between tall green valleys and Lake Kivu that shone, silently, like a sea on an airless day. Jean-Pierre knew it well. He had lived there for three years when he had worked at the Chamber of Commerce. It was where he had met Odette.

Odette. Just mouthing her name was enough to return him to that time.

There is a party organized by Jean-Pierre. He is the president of the Association des Célibataires. In Rwanda, everything is an *Association*. Nothing exists unless it involves your name being taken, categorized and labelled. Even men meeting women. The usual routine was that someone suggested a date, Jean-Pierre booked a room in town, sorted out the beers and a music system. People came and danced to reggae and funk and disco. Jean-Pierre brought his tapes of Fela and Papa Wemba from his days at college in Zaire. Steaming nights of Afrobeat. No *Associations* there. In college you finished your studies late at night and friends would drag you out to eat sugar cane and parcels of *cassava* on the street, and plunge you through dark wet corridors into clubs where Zairean girls danced and did not stop. Jean-Pierre used to watch those girls. Their arms pumped the air. Their eyes grew wide and he thought they were so intense that they looked like men. They looked like boxers.

At this *Association* party, Jean-Pierre recognizes Odette. The girl who walks past his office window. She is very beautiful, and when she moves to talk with someone her body stays still, only her head moves towards the person. She does not flit around the room but, as far as Jean-Pierre can see, prefers to spend time with one person. He thinks, she is not one of those silly girls, who are always laughing and flying around like birds. He cannot imagine her at a club in Zaire, sweat pouring into her dress. He sees her at several parties after that, but he does not talk to her until they find themselves on a trip to a tea plantation. There are six of them on the bus, and since he isn't driving he makes sure he sits next to her. He asks the usual things. Where is she from? Gitarama. What work does she do? Accountant at Electrogaz. They talk about funny things. About their families. Jean-Pierre tells her a story about Papa Joe and she laughs and looks away as if she is shy. And he thinks to himself, I want to make this girl laugh again.

After that trip Jean-Pierre starts to ring her office and ask if he can walk her home. Sometimes she has left already, and later that evening he walks past her house and sees her through the windows and watches her lock the doors and he thinks, that's OK, she's safe now. One day the *Association* has a swimming party, and on the way back in the bus she sits at Jean-Pierre's feet and her back presses just a little into his legs and he puts his arms around her. She doesn't move away. The road is bumpy and the bus driver grinds his gears, but all Jean-Pierre can hear is his pulse beating in his ears. With each bump his hand shifts a little and he feels her body follow his hand – a gentle press as she moves too – and he knows that it is happening and he is closer to her now, and he knows that she can feel him breathing in the soft tang of her skin.

When he gets home he writes a letter to Odette. It is long – five pages – and he tells her what he feels about her and asks her if she will agree to be his wife. When she sees him next she comes up to him and says, 'Yes.' They marry in Gitarama because that is where her parents live. But they have a party in Kibuye because that is where they fell in love. Some of the guests complain that Kibuye is like a village compared to the capital, Kigali. 'People are not civilized here,' they tell him, 'look how they dress, how they talk. They never escape from this town, let alone take a bus to Kigali.' Jean-Pierre smiles and nods and thinks, I have lived in Zaire, under the rule of Mobutu Sese Seko, who dines at the White House. Zaireans fly to Brussels to shop, and Europeans come to Kinshasa to do business with their copper-dollars, and gaze out at the mighty Congo river as it makes its way to the foamy Atlantic shore. Jean-Pierre knows that it is Rwanda that is the village.

CHAPTER THREE

Curic

After two weeks of the camp's existence, Curic was not sure what would kill the Kabgayi internees first – the ravenous soldiers beyond the wire or the camp itself. A pall of smoke hung just a few feet above the refugees. At first this grey shroud seeped into people's clothes. Then, into their bodies. Within a few days there was an endless cacophony of racked, cavernous coughing from the thousands who sat, blankets draped over their heads in an effort to protect themselves from the cold of the dark valley, like a vast herd of abandoned cattle, sodden with thick rain, lowing bleakly against the elements and their fate.

The soldiers who stood outside the wire were heavily muscled men with neatly pressed camouflage uniforms and red berets wedged expertly on to their cropped heads. Their skin glowed with health and vigour. They prowled around the fence, prompting people to shrink towards the centre of the camp – like a sea anemone that has been poked with a stick – leaving only the bodies of those who had died in the night, wrapped in old blankets, lying by the fence. The soldiers sometimes shouted at the internees, telling them to bury their dead, not leave them rotting by the fence. But bury them where? The camp was packed, seething, bulging with a mass of bodies that swayed like vast, industrial fields of corn, rooted to the earth. When the soldiers shouted, people cried out. A mewling wail spread infectiously through the camp. Curic hated this sound. This keening. But he understood it. The people inside the wire were being terrorized. Ostensibly they were under the protection of Bishop Nsengiyumva, but when Curic returned every two or three days he was told how soldiers had walked through the camp, sometimes on their own, sometimes with the *interahamwe*, who would comb through the crowd, looking for those they knew. 'That is Isaac,' they would say, 'he is a businessman in Cyogwe, take him'; or, 'This is Beata – she is married to a doctor, get her.' The refugees pointed to the forest at the far side of the camp. People were taken there and shot. 'A few days ago a bus came,' they told the priest, 'and the teachers from St Joseph's were found and put on the bus. They have not come back.'

Curic heard all this at dawn – his preferred time to deliver the sacks of rice and beans. He knew he was within his rights to come when he wanted – the increasingly grubby-looking Bishop's letter was his surety – but he was less likely to be hassled in the early morning when the guards were often reluctant to throw off their covers, under which they had finally got warm after the restless chill of the spring night. By now, he was making two food runs a week from Burundi up to Kabgayi in the truck loaned by the aid agency. He had a satellite phone, the jeep and a constant supply of dollars to help him through the roadblocks. He travelled in the jeep while Paul, his Rwandan driver, drove the truck just a few feet behind. They never went faster than forty miles an hour, so that the roadblocks both heard and saw them long before they arrived. The seventy-mile journey to or from the border could take up to seven hours, depending on the number of roadblocks they met. Some were permanent and manned by men whom Curic came to recognize. Others cropped up on the bend of a road one day, but had disappeared by the time he made the return journey. The truck and the jeep were well known, as was the priest's simple, conditional offer: dollars for passing through unhindered. The food was distributed by Curic to feeding centres throughout the diocese – which was now home to thousands of homeless Hutus who had fled the fighting in the north – and to the Tutsi camp in the Bishop's garden. Curic was doing what he always told the Bishop was his aim as a priest – helping the people, whoever they were. But, with eight thousand at the camp, it was at Kabgayi that the food was most needed.

Through the wire Curic heard the chatter from the soldiers' radios. Radio Mille Collines. The words were spat out – foamy, shrill demands for people to avenge the death of their President. It had been a difficult language for Curic to fall in love with – all those orchestrated conjugations, nouns stuffed with consonants – and, when the speaker was angry, it could become high-pitched, neurotic, like the yelp of a saw on wood. Several times over the radio Curic caught the word *inyenzi* – 'cockroaches', the racial slur aimed at the Tutsis. Looking at the camp, he could see that it was as if the propaganda was working on the inmates. The mud and smoke had drained all colour from their clothes. The grey mass of people no longer seemed to walk as individuals. They shuffled, blankets draped over them like an insect carapace. There were times, in the past, when he and Sebastijan had privately joked about the Long Ones – the Tutsis – and the Short Ones – the Hutus. Curic had sometimes made Rwandans laugh when he squashed his nose and said he was Hutu, or stood on his tiptoes and looked down his nose. 'I am Tutsi,' he said. Now such jokes no longer seemed funny. As he watched the food sacks disappear into the grey stew of the camp, he imagined that the hum of humanity, which rose over the wire to greet the guards each morning, must indeed seem, to their propagandized ears, like the buzz of trapped insects.

Odette

Even though her aunt's house in Kayenzi was set back from the main road and land surrounded it on all sides, Odette took no chances. She refused to let the children outside and, for the first few days after they had arrived in late April, she insisted that they all stay in their one room at the rear of the house. Her aunt rarely ventured into the room and her aunt's husband remained a distant figure. Odette sensed that they were tolerated but little more which, given the risk that her relatives were taking in hiding a Tutsi family, was understandable.

Outside Odette could hear the thrum of the town and the sounds that had once been the innocuous background patter of daily life now formed whole narratives in Odette's mind. The chatter of a portable radio was, she imagined, the latest broadcast from Radio Mille Collines warning people that the enemy was amongst them; the whine of a motorbike meant local militia had despatched a message to the town gendarmes asking for reinforcements; the tramp of feet on the dirt road was a new gang of killers beginning a house-to-house search.

Odette and Mukaruziga struggled to keep the children occupied. In the afternoon, the heat from the sun crept round to their side of the house, leaving them irritable and lethargic, sodden with their own sweat. The children yowled like bored cats. There was enough water for them to take a shower every three days, but it was difficult to wash their clothes. They found lice on their bodies. Each morning Odette and Mukaruziga inspected the seams of the children's clothes, crushing the insects between their fingers. As she watched the older woman sitting in the corner of the room with Vanessa balanced on her knees, Odette realized how much she had come to depend on Mukaruziga. When she left to walk through town in search of food it was not just her calm, down-to-earth attitude or her help with the children that Odette missed. It was as if the empty space in the corner of the room where Mukaruziga had her few small possessions grew, her absence pressing outwards into the rest of the room, squeezing Odette against the walls, suffocating her. Odette could feel her heart hammering, her breathing growing faster. The noise from the town – shouts or car exhausts – pierced the room, needling her temples. It was difficult for her to hold the children when she felt like this. They twisted and writhed and complained. Their elbows and shins jagged her ribs, their hot hands scratched and pawed at her. She lay on her side on the single bed, staring at the blanket on which Mukaruziga slept and thought about

Jean-Pierre. Not practical questions – was he alive, where might he be – but bursts of memory. She saw his large, meaty hands as he bathed Vanessa. She heard the echo of his voice as he washed the steps outside and talked to Sandra. 'Bring me the cloth,' she heard him say. 'No, Sandra, *the cloth*. In the bucket. There. You see. I need the cloth from the bucket. Yes, to me.' She tightened her stomach and pressed her hand into her mouth to push back the sound that came roaring up from her gut.

Then Mukaruziga would return. Once she had shut the door quietly behind her, Odette could resume the process of shedding her past as if it were a familiar room that the closed door now held at bay. All that mattered now was their survival, and every decision she faced should be channelled through one all-consuming, basic question: would it help or hinder their chances of living through their nightmare? It seemed as if Mukaruziga understood this. They never spoke about the past. They talked only about what they needed that day or even that hour.

Mukaruziga was careful to ensure that she never bought too much food. She was frightened of arousing suspicion. When the government had relocated from Kigali to Gitarama, just over thirty miles away, hundreds of militia had travelled south with them. They had now come west, to Kayenzi, intent on pressing home the government message. The war, they said, was everyone's responsibility. People must help the armed forces to finish their work. The work, everyone knew, was to kill Tutsis, and any Hutus who were foolish enough to protect the *inyenzi*. The local *bourgmestre*, Odette's aunt reported, had run away after the militias accused him of failing in his duty to carry out the national directives. In her old shawl and frayed shirt, Mukaruziga was at little risk of being picked out since Kayenzi teemed with similarly tattered refugees. Each day the numbers rose as more and more Hutus from neighbouring districts fled the advancing Tutsi rebel army. Some were passing through but others decided to stay, often moving into the ransacked homes of Tutsis who had been killed in the first bloody week of the genocide. There was little at the market. Food supplies had dwindled, few trucks were on the road, fields remained unharvested. Mukaruziga scavenged and Odette's aunt obtained food from other towns. The children did not starve but they were hungry and when their stomachs hurt them they cried. Then Odette gathered them into her arms. Their bones showed, their little ribcages pressed against their skin.

Their safety depended on the man of the house. Odette trusted her aunt, but there was little way of knowing to what lengths her aunt's husband would go to protect his wife's niece and her children. Odette had heard countless stories on their journey from the hospital, until they had started to disgust her and she stopped listening. Hutu husbands forced to choose between dying with their Tutsi wives or handing them over to the militia and being made to watch as they were hacked to death. It was possible that her aunt's husband would help them, but nothing in her experience suggested that this was necessarily the case. Odette was a Tutsi woman living in Rwanda. For twenty-six years she had lived in a country that had ground her kind into a paranoid underclass, a group of people stooped under the weight of a constant psychological beating that suppressed them into angry silence or, even worse, made them start to imagine that the injustice they suffered was normal, just part of life.

She had heard bile pour out of the mouths of young men on to her dignified mother as she walked to the market each day. She had seen her husband lose his job, listened to his rage at a racist world that denied him the chance to put food on the table. She had been spat at, and she knew women who had been kicked. Every Sunday she had gone to church to listen to the *padiri* who stood in front of the packed, devoted congregation and requested they take the Sacrament, which she did. She sang hymns and prayed – as she was requested to do. Finally, the priest instructed her to ask God to forgive her sins. *Her* sins. The ones that she had visited on this world. She had done this, too. In her conduct and in her approach to life, she had done all that had been asked of her; she had worked hard, started a family, lived without complaint under the shadow of prejudice and violence and, without rancour, had placed her faith in others. Now, as she watched through closed curtains the outline of the man of the house returning home, she decided that she would not ask him for anything. Instead, she would keep her children close and trust only herself.

Gatete

For more than a week since Curic had brought him to Kivumu, Aimable Gatete lived in the novices' house with the other families. He had quickly grown tired of the cramped quarters and, despite Curic's strict instructions, he often let himself out of the house and walked through the fields that surrounded the parish buildings – many of which he had helped build. He was not popular with the others in the house. 'This house is small,' they hissed at him as he made to leave, 'and it is easy for anyone outside to see that there are people in here if you keep opening the door.' Sometimes Gatete picked up a hoe and started digging in one of the newly terraced strips of land. The work stopped him thinking too much about his family whom he had left days before in Kigali. Seen from across the valley, he would look no different to hundreds of other farmers out on their land.

The increase in killing and the surge of people into Kivumu in the second half of April put a stop to Gatete's wandering. On 20 April Curic came to the house and told Gatete to gather his things. They walked in silence to Curic's quarters. The priest sat Gatete in a chair and told him that he had just got back from Kabgayi where he had spoken to two Inter-national Red Cross workers who were now stationed near the camp. He already knew that the expatriate community had left the country – airlifted by French and Belgian commandos – but he had now learned that the aid agencies were in the process of being evacuated too. All of them – except the Red Cross. And even they were working in impossible conditions. *Interahamwe* at roadblocks regularly harassed their staff, hauling them out of their vehicles, threatening them. A few days earlier, six wounded Rwandans in the back of a Red Cross ambulance had been pulled out at a roadblock and shot by militia. Following that incident, the organization had suspended its activities until the Rwandan government had grudgingly agreed that its work should be unimpeded. In New York, the United Nations had voted to reduce the UNAMIR force from more than two thousand to just two hundred and seventy. Rwanda was being abandoned. They were entirely on their own. Curic poured Gatete a glass of rakija. 'All this,' the priest said, 'at precisely the moment that the world is waking up to the fact that genocide is taking place in Rwanda. The extremists want to wipe you out and they have to do it quickly, before they lose the war with the RPF.'

Curic told Gatete that he needed to move him to another part of the church complex. The militia would surely come soon, and they would be thorough, working systematically through each district, combing the area for Tutsis. There was intense pressure for people to inform on others; the radio had warned that any Hutu caught protecting a Tutsi would be killed. Curic needed to disperse people if he was to have any chance of keeping them alive. The Franciscan was calm but he spoke like a soldier, issuing commands, tolerating no interruptions. For now, Gatete would move to the small room behind the sacristy. If militia came to the church, they would not bother to search a room that had a mountain of old furniture and priestly possessions, under which Gatete could hide. But this was not the long-term plan – Curic brought a map to the low table where they sat. He seemed excited as he spread the map out and, with his finger, traced the road south from Kivumu, through Butare to the Burundian border. 'Somehow we have to get you out of the country,' the priest told him.

Jean-Pierre

Jean-Pierre Sagahutu. The name rolled around his mouth – each syllable enunciated with precision – working its way forwards from the back of his throat, out on to his lips where it sat, waiting to be pushed out like a smoke ring.

Sa-ga-hu-tu. It was funny. His name. For the last few days his mind had been occupied by trying to understand how he had ended up here, in this place, at the age of twenty-eight. Fate, happenstance, luck, a test from God, stupidity. But perhaps his ordeal was due to none of those things. Perhaps it was just his name. Or, at least, the way people interpreted it. Once, when he was nine, his teacher said to the class, 'Hands up if you are a Tutsi.' A few hands went up. The rest of the class shouted at the children with their arms raised. *Oooohhh*. Jean-Pierre was confused. Why did this man want to know who was a Tutsi? Then the teacher looked at Jean-Pierre. 'Why is your hand not up, you are a Tutsi.' He turned to the class and laughed. 'This boy is a Tutsi and he does not even know it!' Heads swivelled. The chairs creaked. Twenty heads. Even the boys with their hands in the air. The teacher shouted again, '"Sagahutu" means "not a Hutu".' Jean-Pierre looked at him, standing at the blackboard, and wondered if he should tell him that of course he knew he was a Tutsi but he had been given his name because of his size. The arms of the other boys had started to droop but the teacher told them to keep them up. Jean-Pierre saw the man's mouth moving, telling the class about the Tutsi kings that used to reign over Rwanda and punish the Hutus, but in his head he heard Papa Joe – laughing and laughing, drinking a beer and watching Jean-Pierre eat all the food on his plate. 'Hutus are small,' his father said. 'Even when you came you were a big baby. You are not a Hutu, that's for sure.'

Now the memory made Jean-Pierre tired. It was futile to look for reasons for his suffering. Staring into the dark earth that surrounded him, Jean-Pierre could see little point in any exploration. By crawling around inside his head for a rationale for his existence in this dark hole he reminded himself that there was a life outside – one that had existed before he entered the hole and one that might exist after he pulled himself out of it. But 'before' was irrelevant, and the idea of 'after' was beyond his comprehension. There was only this specific instant, and his world in this moment was confined to a hole, the dark, the chicken bone that sat by him. He snapped the grey shaft, placed one jagged end into his mouth and began to suck.

Curic

Some of the planks of wood lay down one side of the church at Kivumu but most had been carefully deposited round the back. They were pale – made from eucalyptus – eight foot long, two inches thick and perhaps a foot wide. Curic waved at the driver to start the truck and slowly he guided it back at right angles to the wall. Anyone who walked by on the dirt road past the church would think only that the truck had been parked there in preparation for the next food run to Burundi. Curic walked to the rear of the lorry and once between it and the church wall, dropped to his knees and squeezed under it. He lay there breathing heavily. Between him and the chassis were a series of metal spars. Two ran the length of the chassis and five ran across it. Solder had oozed over the joins where the spars had been fixed: frozen solid, it looked like ancient wax from an old altar candle.

Paul, the driver, slid a plank under the truck and Curic heaved it above his head and manoeuvred it on to the flat surface of the spars spanning the breadth of the truck. There was perhaps a gap of twelve inches between the wood and the bottom of the lorry. Another piece appeared from the side. Curic edged down a few feet, dragging the plank with him, and began the same process of positioning it above him, flat and across the chassis. After thirty minutes he had five planks lined up on the metal exoskeleton underneath the truck. He knelt down, pushed his arms forwards and, head first, wriggled on to the wooden platform. Swivelling his hips he lay flat across the planks, looking up. The darkness the layer of wood had created was perforated by occasional nodules of light from above – holes in the bottom of the truck's container – which made it look like a strange night sky. Cocooned, Curic had no sense of panic or claustrophobia. The smell of the eucalyptus wood made it feel homely, like a sanctuary. He lay there, his fingers rubbing against the coarse grain of the wood, his nose an inch or two from the container above, his mouth just a fraction away from one of the holes. He could feel the warm air from outside, feathering his face. He closed his eyes and consciously began to slow his breathing.

It was Paul who'd had the idea. One night, in the Burundi capital, he had confided to Curic that he needed to help a friend escape. He'd taken the priest to the hotel car park. Crouching down, he'd shone a torch up under the truck and shown Curic the spars that had been fixed on to the underside of the truck. Many drivers did it, Paul explained. They used it to smuggle goods illegally into the country. When Curic stood back up he noticed the heavy canvas apron that skirted the edge of the chassis. Its bottom edge was tethered and stretched by thick cord through brass eye-rings, making it difficult to lift up. Unless a border guard could be bothered to drop on to his knees and crawl under the truck it would be impossible for him to spot the metal frame.

Curic groaned and shifted his body slightly on the planks. Six years earlier he had injured himself carrying mud bricks up the side of a hill and had been forced to return to Europe to spend several weeks in hospital. His back still gave him trouble but he was content lying here, cut off from the outside world. The journeys with his small convoy to and from Kivumu were physically and mentally draining. Six times now he had brought food and medical supplies into the country. He was familiar to the roadblock gangs and he doubted they presented any difficulty. Curic had lost count of the number of times that they had been stopped and his papers had been pored over; a flickering torch or a brazier the only light for the men to peer at the documents, which were returned to him, thumbed and greasy, with a grunt and a muttered order for the barrier to be lifted. Only on two occasions had he been asked to open the truck's container. Curic was happy to oblige. The more he and his truck became known to the roadblocks the more likely, he reckoned, the delays and inspections would dwindle to nothing or as close to nothing as he could reasonably hope.

The guards at the border itself, however, were less predictable. They were idle, lethargic men who rarely left their half-broken office chairs and the festering heat of the small wooden guardhouse. But they were also mercurial and deeply unpleasant. Their afternoon torpor, oblivious to the flies buzzing over the bones of their half-eaten lunch, could disappear in a wave of vindictive, mercantilist fury if, for some reason – or none at all – they sensed guilt or weakness or commercial advantage. The genocide offered them a new sport, an opportunity – which they took in turns – to scrutinize with greater interest than before papers and identity cards, passports and *lettres d'assurance*. Their goal was no longer fines or bribes for petty illegal trafficking, but an officious handover to the militia for any Rwandan foolish enough to attempt to cross the border with suspect paperwork.

'*Padiri!*'

Curic leaned out of his cocoon to find Paul staring anxiously up at him. The priest heaved himself out. Three more lengths were placed on to the metal frame, filling the remaining space along the spars. They decided to tie the planks down with rope to ensure that they were securely fixed and didn't rattle. An hour later, Curic stood back and surveyed their work. Undetectable by anyone standing looking at the truck, hidden by the canvas apron, was a solid nine-foot-long wooden platform that spanned the width of the container. Curic felt a surge as he looked at their handiwork. Three people could lie on the improvised bed. Any more would be too risky. Noise from the escapees themselves or the creaking of the wooden platform could give them away. The priest clapped his hands. He had a plan to get Gatete out of the country. Stick it to those murdering bastards.

Odette

Now that they were back on the road, Odette rarely slept more than two or three hours a night. What sleep she had was dark and blank. When she woke it was from the ugly incessant ache that pressed into her abdomen. She could picture the inside of herself. Her stomach was bare, like the scraped-out skin of an old piece of fruit – a few remaining, intractable morsels of flesh had crusted themselves on to the skin and had become dry and abrasive and spiky. The ache pressed down through her guts on to her pelvic bone, leaving a hollow space above that made her feel quite sick. On bad nights it ground deep into her, a blunt bite. Then she allowed herself to reach for her children – something she forbade herself to do when they were awake. In the darkness she would curl them around her, press them into her body, warm her ache. Vanessa hardly moved or murmured but lay stretched out, arms thrown back. But Sandra whimpered in her sleep, burrowing into her mother, her small legs scraping like a puppy's into the ground for leverage to get closer.

In the early morning the mist from the fields mingled with the haze of smoke from the few smouldering fires of others who were on the road. Odette hated these fires – the way the smoke sat in pallid lumps above them – like signposts for the shadowy figures she could see making their way into the fields each morning. It seemed reckless to make a fire so near to people who might see value in informing on them or, worse, be killers themselves.

Dawn was the time she had always liked best. Though it had been the source of a longstanding debate with Jean-Pierre. He liked dusk – the moment when the city finally sat down and breathed long and deep. But she preferred the morning – then there was clarity and hopefulness and a cool freshness. This morning she watched the figures move slowly down muddy paths, their loping gaits, their hoes glinting in the early light like coins glimpsed in the soil.

They felt like touchstones, small and hopeful, to the calm world before the killing began. Then the sun burnt off the mist and the huddled shapes of her children, buried under a small blanket, jolted her back to the present – to a narrow dirt road somewhere west of Kigali, on the way to her final destination, Kibuye.

In the end, it had been fighting near Kayenzi in late April that had forced them to leave her aunt and the house they had stayed in for more than a week. But even before that, Odette was of a mind to try and escape anyway. From the house she could hear the gangs of young men gathering each morning. They were drunk, she could tell. They paused as they talked, sucking banana beer from bottles. The talk was always of where the *bourgmestre* would send them that day. Up into the hills to hunt for Tutsis, or to help out another district further afield.

The sound of shelling from the Tutsi rebel forces had halted those mornings of gossip and provoked a desperate, visceral panic throughout the town. Her aunt's husband reported that the militias had urged people to help finish off any *inyenzi* while they still had time. Kigali had yet to fall to the RPF but elsewhere large swathes of the country were now under rebel control. Everyone feared the reprisals from the Tutsi army and their response was to undertake fresh house-to-house searches in the hope of finding any last remaining Tutsis. Her aunt's husband had said he was sure that he could still protect them, but by the time Odette heard the sound of gunfire nearby she had already made up her mind.

She hoped that Kibuye, sixty miles away, protected by steep-sided and, in late spring, bitterly cold mountain passes, had avoided the massacres. She knew the lakeside town well from her time working there for Electrogaz, and she knew that her parents-in-law had been busy building a new home with a view of Lake Kivu and would welcome her and their grandchildren. She comforted herself, too, that the journey west to Kibuye, whilst full of unknowns, was at least one that many others were making as well. At points where the road steepened or narrowed, the grey surface disappeared under a shuffling walkway of people. Even when it flattened and straightened out and the mass of refugees became a thin straggle, Odette, Mukaruziga and the children were indistinguishable. Odette wore the same trousers and T-shirt in which she had left her parents' house – by now they were filthy and torn. If the trousers pointed to a woman unused to trudging along Rwanda's highways and lanes, the faded patterned *igikwembe* which she wrapped around her midriff and her eleven-month-old baby made her as unremarkable as any other mother forced on to the road during those days in early May 1994. Mukaruziga carried a basket on her back for her cooking pot; Sandra hung from her or, from time to time, walked on her own. Together, inching westwards, they were a shuffling archetype of an African failed state: homeless, female, half bent from carrying children, food and a little firewood, wary of strangers and fearful for the future.

During those first few days in May, they alternated between the main trunk road from Kigali to Kibuye and dirt roads. Sometimes they left the tarmac road in search of food and then, once off it, they stayed on the smaller paths that criss-crossed the countryside, grateful not to be scrabbling so much with other travellers for the few scraps of food that they could find. But they were never entirely on their own, and Odette calculated that this was just as well. They were strangers walking through these fields and even from afar she could see the flash of a face looking up, the movement of a man stopping his digging, leaning on his spade and watching. Their journey was being mentally tracked by those they passed and, on their own, they risked being approached and asked questions. But the countryside was awash with others like them, forgettable human spindrift that might momentarily catch the eye of a man digging in his field, but had disappeared by the time he looked up again from his work. She had torn up her identity card – the small piece of folded pink card, with her picture on the inside, her name and her ethnicity. *Tutsi.* To keep it would mean death. To not be able to produce it was risky, but she hoped that the vice-mayor's laissez-passer, which she still had in her pocket, might carry some weight if they were stopped. She noticed that her hand made small, involuntary brushing motions across the side of her trousers from the frequent checking to ensure it was still safe.

She rarely spoke to anyone, including fellow refugees. Some she thought might be Tutsi, though she guessed almost all had to be Hutu, struggling to escape the war and the advance of the RPF. There was no point sharing information with these people. They knew as little as she did and they were as hungry as she was. But they were not as desperate. Their identity cards – if they were Hutu – did not consign them to an instant death by the side of the road.

The children almost never cried. Odette guessed that their stomachs had shrunk so that the small amount of food that they scavenged was enough. They walked each day and they took care not to stop until late afternoon when the corner of the field they had chosen had fallen into shadow. When they were settled, Mukaruziga would head off through the adjoining fields to look for food. Bananas mostly, but she also took beans that still hung from the plant – green and raw. Together they dug for sweet potatoes, which they cut into slices and chewed slowly. Odette pulped the food as best she could for Vanessa. Sandra sucked on old sticks of maize. They drank from streams. At night Odette curled her daughters close. She drew her shawl over the three of them. She tried to pray, but she was often distracted by the sounds of people in their houses or camped nearby. She could smell the woodsmoke from their fires and tightened her grip on her children.

Rusumo, Rwanda–Tanzania border, 4 May

By the time the Akagera river passes under the bridge at Rusumo Falls the waters, which emerge from Lake Rweru in the south of the country, have travelled east along the border between Burundi and Rwanda before turning northwards and travelling two hundred and fifty miles, contiguous with Tanzania, on their way to the vast inland sea of Lake Victoria. At Rusumo the river narrows into a cavernous rocky gorge. On the metal bridge that spans the gorge, one morning in early May, a short, stout man, dressed in full military uniform, stood with one hand on the rail, peering over the edge of the bridge at the river below. Before the gorge the water meandered sedately, heavy and idle, the colour of milky tea. By the time it reached the bridge and dropped into the ravine, it churned with furious energy. Cross-currents tugged at it fiercely, creating swirling eddies and waves that hammered up against the walls of the gorge. One hundred yards below the bridge the river began to veer right until it slowly disappeared, still tumbling, under a crescent of vapour.

The man in uniform was a general. I knew this because he wore smart red flashes on his collar, there were stars on his epaulettes and he carried a swagger stick – which he used as a pointer when he talked to his fellow officers. He was impeccably turned out. His boots shone and the starched creases on his trousers were pencil-straight. He was barrel-chested and he walked with crisp, carefully articulated steps. His feet, I noticed, were small, and I suspected he would have made a natural ballroom dancer – his black patent shoes working with precision under his portly frame, surprising and flattering his partners.

The general told the few journalists that had gathered around him that he was angry. The war in Rwanda was a tragedy, he said, everyone was agreed on that, though neither he nor his government in Dar es Salaam was in any position to intervene in the internal politics of another country. 'But this,' he said, pointing his stick at the river below, '*this*,' he hissed, 'is disgusting.' Quite apart from the risk of the conflict spilling over into neighbouring countries, this was a public health calamity.

Below the general, I had noticed that waves crashed against a substantial rock that jutted out above the river, a few yards from the water's edge. The waves were thrown back on to another boulder that lay perhaps fifteen feet behind the first, larger one, creating an eddy that swirled, violently, in an anticlockwise direction. In the middle of the eddy was the body of a man. With each successive wave, the man was picked up and thrown against the larger rock before sliding off and being spun back around the eddy, feet at its centre, arms raised, before being swept again against the rock. While the general spoke I watched the dead man as, every few seconds, the waters span him around the eddy. His body had become bloated, his jacket so tight that his arms were forced back. His head was impossibly large, with puffed-out cheeks and eyes squeezed bulbously tight. His lips had been pushed out into a vivid swollen circle. During some of his circumnavigations the river tossed him over on to his front. The seat of his trousers had split apart, revealing his buttocks.

Most of the bodies that were being carried downstream, however, thundered straight under the bridge and were quickly swept along in the main current of the river. They hurried through the torrent, skirting rocks, slipping sideways down dark channels before disappearing from view, only to re-emerge a few yards later, limbs flailing, turning over and over until they sped around the corner and finally out of sight. Looking back up the river, I could see half a dozen bodies making their way towards the bridge. I calculated that three bodies were passing under us every minute, victims of government propaganda that had urged Rwanda's Hutu population to kill their Tutsi neighbours and dump them in the Akagera and send them back north – back to the Nile and the land they had come from. Mostly men and women that morning, but I saw children too – though in the swirl of water and choppy foam it was difficult to spot the smaller bodies.

The general brought the impromptu press conference to a close and walked briskly with his junior officers to the

Rwandan end of the bridge. Tom, my reporter, and I – the producer – along with Steve, our cameraman, and Monty, the sound recordist, shuffled after him, a few paces behind. Two soldiers waited for him. They carried Kalashnikovs and wore dark blue berets, plain green combat jackets and blue trousers, which were tucked into black wellington boots. The general disappeared inside a small border post where he was due, he told us, to meet with the local commander of the Tutsi rebel force, the Rwandan Patriotic Front.

Several of the rebel soldiers sat on the porch of the office. None of them spoke. Some cleaned their weapons, others stared back towards the bridge. From where they sat they could see the dead being carried down the river, at least until the river dropped into the gorge. I brought out my camera and asked if I could take pictures. They ignored me and I worked my way around the group. The porch was quiet after the rush and noise of the falls. I sat down and pulled out my cigarettes, offering them around. Small shakes of the head. A kite twirled above us – drifting in long, torpid circles towards some nearby trees. I asked them about the war (I knew they spoke some English. The RPF were Anglophile – decades as refugees in Uganda had made sure of that). They proffered a small smile, otherwise nothing. I felt clumsy – fumbling and twitching like a wind-up toy, whirring with pointless energy. The men were in their twenties, part of an army of just a few thousand that, in the past month, had driven the government forces – dug in, numerically superior, armed and advised by the French – from most of north and east Rwanda. What lay ahead of them was the battle for Kigali, the central stronghold of Gitarama and the southern one of Butare.

These men had been born and raised in the refugee

camps of southern Uganda, children of Rwandan Tutsis who fled their country thirty years earlier to escape a newly enfranchised Hutu majority determined to exact revenge on the men and women who had enjoyed favoured status under the Belgian colonists. The camps they built were well organized and disciplined; young people were formed into cadres, the brightest were sent to Europe for their education. In camp classrooms they learned that Rwanda was once a kingdom ruled by the Tutsi. In training exercises the soldiers were taught bush craft whilst their officers were sent abroad to Fort Leavenworth to learn infantry tactics from the Americans – funded by a rich and successful Tutsi diaspora that was dedicated to seeing their people return to their country.

The general emerged from the border post accompanied by the RPF commander. They shook hands at the bridge and the general walked back across to Tanzania with his entourage. We stayed in Rwanda. The RPF commander was dressed no differently to his soldiers – apart from the standard army boots he wore on his feet. The men, who moments before had slouched around the steps of the border post, lifted themselves from the ground and began to make their way towards two Toyotas. We followed the commander.

'What happened at the meeting? What will you do about all the bodies?' we asked. 'How difficult will it be to defeat the Rwandan government forces?'

The commander gazed over our heads to watch the Tanzanians take their last few steps off the bridge. We persisted with our questions. He watched the general. Then he turned, looked briefly at us and, for the first and last time, I heard his voice – a low murmur to his soldiers who climbed into the back of the two flatbed 4x4s. They sat on the edge of the trucks, legs trailing. Two soldiers slid their backsides on to the open tailgate of one of the Toyotas, rifles facing outwards. Above us the kites continued their aimless circling. The commander took one last look around, climbed into the passenger seat of the nearest vehicle, and the small mute convoy drove away.

Gatete

The truck that carried Aimable Gatete and two other Rwandans left Kivumu on 5 May. It was still dark, perhaps three in the morning. Gatete was unsure. For the last fortnight he had sat in the sacristy of the church going slowly out of his mind. The room was small and, cooped up, his thoughts had returned many times to the decision to leave his family in Kigali. He replayed the early morning when Curic came to fetch him over and over in his head. It had seemed clear-cut at the time: men were being targeted, not women and children. Evacuating his family would have been impossible – even if the soldiers in the car had gone along with it. The militia at the roadblocks would never have believed Curic's claim that he was picking up his employee.

But for over a week at the novices' house he had listened to stories about the indiscriminate nature of the killing that people had witnessed or heard about. Stories that were still whirring around his head when Curic moved him to the sacristy, where he had sat, on his own, dwelling on it all. Surrounded by Catholic paraphernalia, his world turned inwards. The furniture, the prayer books, the hymnals, the spare chasuble – all the arcane objects that he was forced to stare at seemed to expose the futility of his predicament. When, after more than two weeks, Curic had opened the door to the sacristy and told him that he would be leaving that night, the relief was as much about leaving a room in which he was powerless to do anything as it was about escaping the killers who, each night, he could hear patrolling the fields and pathways around Kivumu, searching for Tutsis.

Guided by torchlight, Gatete crawled under the truck. He was a large man and he struggled to squeeze himself on to the wooden platform that offered no more than twelve inches of vertical space. He pulled himself on to the planks, face down, and slowly twisted his body around until he lay flat on his back. Curic had been watching him and, now that he was settled, whispered to him to shunt his body sideways along. Gatete was unclear why he needed to heave himself closer to the front of the truck where it was darker and more enclosed until he saw another head appear and begin to wriggle into the space. The man, whom Gatete had never met, settled close to him. They both watched one more passenger slide on to the platform – this time a woman. They lay there breathing hard from the exertion, their breath settling on the underside of the metal container, which was just three inches from their faces.

The track from Kivumu down to the main road was bumpy and the three Rwandans groaned as their bodies jolted against the hard wooden surface. Gatete's arms lay alongside his body at first, but he found that if he drew them back as far as he could and turned the palms of his hands upwards, bracing them against the metal just above, he could stop his body and head hitting the container. His efforts to demonstrate this to the man next to him proved fruitless; the man was incapable of focusing on what Gatete was saying and gesturing. His eyelids had stretched back away from his eyes and he moaned with each bump that caused his body to be thrown upwards into the container. The woman was quiet. Gatete wondered how the man was going to cope, sandwiched between wooden planks and several tons of truck, for the distance of seventy miles to the Burundi border.

Once they reached the main road the journey became smoother. But Gatete's concern about his new neighbour only intensified when, a few minutes after joining the road, the truck stopped. He could hear Curic talking and, through the canvas apron that obscured them, he could see flickers of flame, which he imagined were from torches. Slowly he turned his head and behind him, looking down on to the road, he could see shadows of figures. It was difficult to tell how many men had surrounded the truck. He could hear them walking to the back. Curic, he thought, was still in his jeep. Gatete could hear the priest explaining that he had started earlier than usual because he wanted to try to get back to Rwanda the same day. He sounded casual, almost chatty. Clearly, he knew the men he was talking with. Gatete shifted his head to look at the man next to him. His breath came short and because he had pressed his lips together, it seemed to escape him in a high-pitched whistle.

When Curic got out of his car and walked to the back of the truck, Gatete's companion became more alarmed. Gatete heard the priest jump on to one of the rear bars and pull open the doors of the container for the militia to inspect. The man next to him began to shake. Before they left Kivumu, Curic had whispered that there would be many roadblocks but that he was well known at them now, so the militia merely talked to him and rarely checked the inside of the truck. Gatete closed his eyes and laid his hands flat on the planks. His fingers brushed against the rough grain. He tried to think about some of the work he had done recently, the jobs that he had submitted estimates for, the smell of wet cement, the scrape of sawn wood. At the rear of the lorry the inspection was over and Curic slammed the doors shut. Gatete could hear the militia making their way back up along the side of the container and he slid his hand over and rested it on the arm of the man beside him who turned his head in alarm. Gatete nodded encouragingly and then began to breathe slowly through his open mouth, hoping his example would encourage the man to slow down his own breathing. It didn't work. The flames from the nearby torches threw enough light under the truck for Gatete to see that the man was staring wildly at him, his breath still coming in short whistling bursts. On the man's far side, Gatete could see the outline of the woman, lying rigidly still. The truck gunned its engine, startling the man who now grasped Gatete's hand, and slowly the convoy made its way past the roadblock.

It was cold under the truck. The wooden shelf provided some protection but the wind nipped at them through the canvas apron. Gatete had little room to move so he simply had to endure the sharp chill of air funnelling into his body. A gnawing ache tore into his left shoulder and the tips of his fingers became numb. The noise of the truck grinding through its gears as it climbed the steep hills was deafening. As fast as the wind and noise suggested they were going, Gatete knew that their progress was painfully slow. Curic had warned them about this. When he was sure that the noise of the truck would drown out their voices, Gatete gripped the man's arm and reminded him what Curic had told them. There would be many roadblocks. The journey would be long. The man turned to look at the woman on his other side. Gatete could raise his head just enough to see that she had briefly looked at the man before twisting her head back so that she stared straight up. He was relieved. The woman was offering no support to the man, no pool of dark mutual fear they could both slip into. Shunned by the woman, the man turned back to Gatete. He looked bewildered rather than scared. 'Everything will be fine,' Gatete shouted. 'As long as you stay quiet at the roadblocks, everything will be fine.' Through the crack between the planks Gatete could see the tarmac racing underneath him. It was a grey river of concrete, he said to himself, and they were in the current – being pulled downstream to safety. He smiled at the man, wove his fingers through those of his left hand and squeezed gently.

CHAPTER FOUR

Jean-Pierre

By early May the frenzy of the initial days of the genocide had subsided in Nyamirambo. Bodies still lay rotting on the streets but there were few fresh killings. The daily battle for Kigali between government and rebel forces left many districts in a hiatus. Ernest became confident enough to pull Jean-Pierre out of his hole once or twice a week, always at night, and creep back with him to the courtyard of his house, where Jean-Pierre could pour water over his head and try to wash his body. He had lost weight. His stomach looked pinched and he could feel his hip bones through his trousers. He washed quickly in the privy and took a shit – he had become expert at controlling his bowel movements, though he was sure that the little he ate helped reduce the urge to go. He could hear Ernest on the other side of the door, monitoring the street outside through the gap in the wall. Leaving the hole was dangerous for Jean-Pierre but, in some ways, it was worse for Ernest, since he made many more trips up and down the alleyway. Ernest was vigilant, careful never to get into a routine, for fear that his movements would be noted by some sleep-deprived neighbour. For Jean-Pierre, this made it impossible to predict when the cover would slide off and the bucket on its chain would be lowered to him, nor when Ernest would suggest that it was a safe night for him to climb out for the twenty minutes they allowed for washing.

He cleaned as much of his body as he could with the bucket of water and the wafer of soap that he found wedged in a crack in the slatted wooden door. When he had manoeuvred himself back into the hole he would spend some time passing his hands over his face, breathing in the sharp, nettled tang of the soap that soured the back of his throat. It reminded him of his father's office at the hospital in Rutongo, near Kigali. When he was small, Jean-Pierre never went to another doctor; whenever something was wrong he walked along the green corridors of the hospital and waited to see his father. With his back turned, Papa Joe seemed to take for ever, methodically soaping and rinsing his hands to the point where Jean-Pierre worried his father would one day wash his skin off.

Muganga Joe. Papa Joe. The names were interchangeable, since they both described what Jean-Pierre remembered: a tall, elegant man with a ruff of hair and a white coat that billowed as he turned the corner from the hospital reception and walked to the gate, delving into the baggy right-hand pocket, pulling out his cigarettes, Belga Rouge, the first one lit by the time he passed the security guard. Feet in polished shoes that skilfully dodged the potholes and puddles, a right turn up the hill to the old colonial bungalow, perhaps stopping for a beer at the club, where Belgian miners gossiped amongst themselves, hunched over their imported Heinekens in frosted glasses, while Joe sat outside with a bottle of

Primus and listened to the *tsip-tsip* of bee-eaters and watched their housewifely bustle in and out of the dark curtain of euphorbia hedge that encircled the building, protecting it from prying eyes.

The hospital had expressed their deep disappointment when, in late 1993, Joe had let his colleagues know that he would be leaving them. He was in his late fifties, he told them – it was time to relax, cut down on his hours, try to enjoy life. He didn't tell them that the violence in the capital, just ten miles away, sickened him. The propaganda on the radio that chirruped in the background at the hospital had worn him down. He could not speak out against it: it was ludicrous even to respond to the allegation that the Tutsis were planning to take over the country, restore the *mwami* kingdom. It was true that the thwarted invasion by the RPF in 1990 had spurred a bilious, vile regime to further acts of violence against its minorities, but the murmured paranoia expressed by his Hutu colleagues and patients would be laughable if it were not so serious. Kibuye, the doctor hoped, was far enough away from the barked racism he heard on the streets of Kigali. Besides, the doctor had served his country well – thirty years of hard work in hospitals in Kigali, Ruhengeri and now Rutongo. Retirement beckoned, he told them, and with it were plans to build a bigger, more comfortable home.

Jean-Pierre had not managed to visit his parents since they had moved to Rubengera – a small village outside Kibuye – three months before the genocide began. But before the President's assassination his father had told him over the phone that the new house was coming along – walls, windows, roof all built now. Maize grew in the fields, which were larger than Joe remembered, reaching down almost to the Kibuye road. Soon they would be able to leave the old family house, and Jolie would have her new kitchen and a view from the window across the valley to the south and, if you craned your neck to the right, you could just see a splash of blue from the lake. 'Your mother will be very happy here,' Papa Joe had said. He paused. Long enough for Jean-Pierre to hear the fluted crackle of the line. When his father's voice came back it was louder. 'Of course,' Papa Joe said, 'I have been to the hospital here and offered to help out. Part-time, of course.'

Jean-Pierre had thought often about that pause of his father's on the telephone. It was so unlike his voice to catch like that, a half moment of uncertainty. The gruffness when his voice returned, reasserting himself. Perhaps the doctor had an intuition about what was about to happen to the country. Jean-Pierre rested his shoulders back against the walls of the hole and pictured Papa Joe standing at his front door, looking across the valley, ruminating on the best course of action. He knew his father would have paid little attention to Radio Rwanda (and certainly never turned the dial to the appalling Radio Mille Collines) advising people to stay inside. Papa Joe would have been decisive and quick. He would have taken his mother and his brothers and sisters north – along the edge of Lake Kivu – until they reached the border crossing with Zaire. His father had many medical contacts in Zaire and would most likely have made his way to Kisangani, the city where Jean-Pierre had studied, where he was probably already working in one of the local hospitals.

Burundi–Rwanda border, 7 May

At the border there was no protection from the sun. We baked on the wide expanse of tarmac that divided Burundi from Rwanda. The light felt over-exposed, as if a room had been suddenly illuminated by hundreds of tubes of neon. After half an hour in the heat we backed the car up to an old bent signpost and draped pieces of cloth between the car boot and the post. We sat in their shade on the roadside gravel, drinking tepid water.

Across from the rusted, red and white barrier, I could see Curic talking to the Rwandan border guards, who sat in their hut listening to him. Occasionally they would reach over and flick through the paperwork that Curic had presented to them. Our passports and letters of authorization from the Rwandan Ambassador in Burundi, whom we had visited late the night before, hammering on his door, demanding his signature.

Every so often, Curic walked back to our side of the border to explain what was happening. The guards were ringing headquarters to check, he told us. He wore an old creased shirt that was tucked into a pair of faded jeans. Trainers on his feet. A cross was tied around his neck on an old piece of leather. I tried to apologize – we were making him late. He waved me away and marched back across the road.

We had arrived in Burundi the previous day. The war between the Hutu government and the Tutsi-led rebel force, the Rwandan Patriotic Front, was a month old. The bodies that had begun to float, in their hundreds, down the Akagera river to Lake Victoria were the latest sign that the Rwandan government was orchestrating a genocide of all Tutsis as well as murdering Hutus who opposed the genocide. Much of the north had been taken by the RPF and large-scale massacres of Tutsis had been discovered by the rebels in many of the country's small villages they entered. But the south was still firmly in the hands of the extremist government and its soldiers. There had been little reporting from that relatively unknown part of the country, and few knew whether any of the large numbers of Tutsis who lived in the southern university town of Butare, and many of the other, more prosperous towns near there, had survived. The extremist government had moved too. The RPF was fighting a brilliant campaign and had forced the government army to retreat. We planned to drive north from Burundi, into southern Rwanda, and find out what was happening.

We had little idea how we could achieve this. We had witnessed the first, dilatory noises of international protest about what was taking place in Rwanda. So it seemed unlikely that the Rwandan government would welcome foreigners like us. But an aid worker who sat with us on the flight from Nairobi to Bujumbura told us of a priest she knew who had remained in Rwanda and was running food supplies from Burundi. A Bosnian. Or a Croat. She wasn't sure. But definitely from that part of the world.

I had stood in the dark reception of the Novotel in Bujumbura for more than an hour waiting for Curic. Groups of men sat about on sofas in the reception area. They wore crocodile-skin shoes and dark, double-breasted Italian suits and flicked their hands – but never looked – at the waiters with their ill-fitting black trousers and white shirts with dirty collars, two sizes too big, who shambled over to them, meekly listened to the order, never writing it down, and some time later returned with a tray of imported beer. Each bottle was opened with a silent, childlike intensity. The men drank and smoked and stared at the hotel guests – mainly Westerners in garish beach shorts and short-sleeved cotton shirts – off to the garden to lie under green umbrellas and watch their children scream and jump into a bright blue, kidney-shaped swimming pool.

The man that burst through the glass doors of the hotel was obviously Curic. He was small and wiry with a thick black moustache, matching the physical description the aid worker had given me. He wore jeans and a collarless shirt, and he was talking furiously with another man in heavily accented French. I stood close to them, waiting. He caught my eye as he shook the man's hand and began to make his way towards reception. I caught him up, introduced myself and tried to explain why we needed his help. I talked bad French as we walked. 'OK,' he said. He spoke in broken English. 'You bring your car. We leave at ten in the morning.' He looked at me carefully. 'If you are late – forget it,' he said. And then he turned away and began to speak with the woman behind the desk.

We found a car – a battered old Peugeot with two bald tyres and side windows that didn't wind up – and we were not late. And so, some hours later, I sat under the canopied shade at the back of the car looking up the road, into Rwanda. The heat was dense – a hot, smothering wetness. I looked at my bottle of water, which sat on the gravel. I thought I could see small bubbles inside – as though it had started to boil.

I heard the noise of the engine first. Before I saw it appear from over the brow of the hill. A white jeep that was hurtling down the road. When it drew near the border post it was forced to brake hard, almost to the point of skidding, to avoid hitting the barrier. It was the first car from Rwanda we had seen since arriving at the border two hours before. The driver – a white man – got out. Two guards emerged from the hut and began to circle the car. We could see the man following them, trying to show them his papers, but we couldn't hear what he was saying. The guards ignored him. They were peering inside the jeep. Then they opened all the doors. The man raised his voice. He was now shouting at the uniformed men, who seemed much more interested in the other people in the car. Eventually, one of the guards took the papers that the man was waving at him and began to flick through them. The second guard made his way to the passenger door and motioned for the person to get out. A tall, slim black woman emerged from the front of the car. She walked slowly round to the other side and lifted a small child into her arms. Two other children appeared from the car. They stood around their mother, holding on to her skirt, peering up at the guards.

Curic was now talking with the jeep's driver, who seemed to be demanding that the woman and children should get back inside the car. The priest's hands were on the man's arms, calming him. Then he spoke with the guards. It seemed as though he was acting as an interpreter. Two more guards appeared from the hut. They carried automatic weapons. I could hear the odd word shouted out by the man – 'Passport,' he kept saying. Curic took the man's documents and gave them to the guards. The men with the guns, meanwhile, had opened up the back of the jeep and removed a number of suitcases and cardboard boxes. The two older children had begun to cry. The soldiers opened the cases and pulled

WHEN THE HILLS ASK FOR YOUR BLOOD

out what they found. Then they turned their attention to the boxes and left the suitcases sprawled on the tarmac. It was much quieter now.

The driver had walked over to the woman and children and stood with them. Curic continued to talk quietly to the guard who was still leafing through the passports. It was extremely hot. My water bottle still sat on the gravel. I was very thirsty but I didn't move to pick up the bottle. Across the road, the guard walked with the family's passports into the hut. Curic waited outside. He was still talking, his gaze never leaving the guard. The armed men had finished with the boxes and now slumped against the jeep, watching the family. From the hut, the guard reappeared. He walked over to the man and gave him the passports. The soldiers levered themselves off the jeep. The man bundled his family into the car. Curic, meanwhile, had thrown the suitcases and boxes into the back and slammed the door shut. The man climbed in. A soldier slowly raised the barrier and the car drove through.

We waited for the man as he showed his passports to the Burundian guards on our side of the border. His back was to us but I could hear him breathing heavily. His shirt was soaked with sweat. When he turned back with his freshly stamped passports we moved gently towards him, carefully putting ourselves between him and the car. We asked him who he was. A biologist, he told us. On a year's secondment to Butare University from Italy. He had been to Rwanda many times before. It was where he had met his wife. He gestured to the woman who sat in the front seat. She appeared to have no interest in these people asking her husband questions. She sat quietly, staring straight ahead. The man was bearded and filthy, his hair straggly grey. He looked ill – as though he had a fever. He told us that he had been holed up for nine days inside his house with his family. Since they had heard the first screams of people being hunted down nearby and he had seen gangs of men roaming the streets with some official. They carried clubs and machetes. He had boarded up the windows and told the children to keep quiet. They had been careful about rationing food, but by the fifth day they were close to running out. Luckily it had started to rain the night before and he figured that this would drive the killers back to their homes. He ventured out – looking for food. He was right. The town seemed deserted in the downpour. Near the university he came across a trench. There were dozens of bodies inside. Most had been butchered with machetes, but some had been burnt to death – rubber tyres still around their necks. He found some food near the university refectory. On his way back to his house he passed the trench again. It was now also full of rainwater. Some of the bodies had started to float out of the trench and were being pushed by the floodwater down the street.

The man was raging now as he described what he had seen. His words flew out and his straggly hair flopped around his shoulders. He heaved great sobs as he talked about the trench. He had been told his family would not be harmed – the head of the department had come to visit him after the violence started and said he would personally vouch for their safety – but last night some of the students had come and hammered on the doors, screaming '*inyenzi*' – cockroach. They had stayed outside the house until well after midnight, taunting and frightening his children. His wife had an Italian passport – she was an Italian citizen, for God's sake – but he knew that it wouldn't matter. Everyone at the university knew that she was a Tutsi.

His children watched him as the pitch of his rant grew higher, their eyes blinking slowly, drinking in the foreignness of it all – their father lost and near deranged, a small group of white men and women peering into their car. Their mother still said nothing. The man got back in his jeep. 'It is madness back there,' he screamed, 'utter madness!' He slammed the door shut and jerked the car into gear. '*Coupé!*' he shouted at us, drawing his hand across his throat. '*Coupé.*'

The car lurched away. Curic came up with our passports. 'OK, they stamped them. We can go now.'

Odette

For Odette, the memory of life before their journey to Kibuye had dwindled into tiny needlepoints. She was sure that her exhaustion was shaped by a foreboding of imminent death. She tried to focus solely on the practicality of their situation, partly as a result of the demands of her children, but also as a means of blocking out the inevitability of her predicament. Whatever whiff of hope she might sometimes have was otherwise quickly extinguished by the certain knowledge that sooner or later they would meet soldiers or policemen or a gang of killers and she and her children would be murdered.

Trying to work out where they were proved to be a useful and welcome distraction. After leaving Kayenzi they had travelled north until they came to a wide river, which flowed past them, heading east. It had to be the Nyabarongo – which meant that they were north and west of Kigali. They followed the river west – away from the capital – for two days, drinking water from one of the many small streams that flowed into it. How long they should follow the river was decided after Mukaruziga came back from scavenging one night and told them that they were close to Nyabikenke, a small mountain town that Odette knew from the days when she had lived in Kibuye and had taken the bus home to Gitarama to visit her parents.

It was now late May. They had been on the road for a month. If they were to stick to their plan of making for Kibuye then, they reasoned, they ought to head south past Nyabikenke and then begin a slow climb westwards along tortuous hill paths towards their eventual destination. But Odette was unsure. Many of the fields they had walked through in this area had not been harvested. She knew from what her aunt had told her back in Kayenzi that many farmers had joined gangs of *interahamwe*. The national effort was directed at weeding out Tutsis rather than clearing the fields of ripe produce. Cassava, sweet potatoes, bananas – all lay rotting on the ground, providing pickings for the refugees. Water, too, was plentiful here. Much as she mistrusted the trail of other people moving alongside them, there was a sense of reassurance in numbers. Heading for the hills would deprive them of company and food. But their route so far had taken them past huts and villages, past the prying eyes of women shelling beans on their steps, their husbands standing just behind in the shade of the doorway. The wooded, sparsely populated hills further west would offer them some protection.

Odette drew some comfort from the increasing numbers of people who had taken to the road. She and the children had been travelling for over a month, since leaving the hospital in Kabgayi, and she noticed that there were people who passed them now who had travelled from much further east, escaping the advance of the Rwandan Patriotic Front. The Tutsi forces were making progress. On the outskirts of Nyabikenke substantial groups of refugees gathered in the late afternoon to buy food and trade news with villagers. Odette, walking past the fringes of the groups, heard the gossip, felt the faint ache of panic. 'The *inkotanyi* are advancing,' they said. 'They will take revenge for what has happened.'

Encouraging as the news of the rebel army's drive into Rwanda was, it was the reaction of the fleeing Hutus that drove Odette on. She kept moving not because she thought they could truly reach safety – it was by now unthinkable that Kibuye would be safer than any other part of Rwanda – but because if she stopped she knew they would be killed. To rest – even for a day – by the side of the road was to risk questioning and denunciation as a Tutsi waiting to be rescued by the advancing *inkotanyi*. The fear she sensed amongst those around her was fear of Tutsi retribution for what had taken place in their villages and on their hillsides since early April. The bewilderment in the faces of these people – simple farmers, some of whom had never left their *préfecture* before – could turn, she felt sure, to anger.

They turned west, climbing into heavily wooded hills. Mist clung to the sharp ridges above them. The streams that poured into culverts by the side of the road were icy in the morning. Cold draughts jagged at them, causing their heads to ache and the children to moan. They wrapped them up as best they could in their thin cotton shawls. The road plunged through cavernous granite gorges. At night, Vanessa was small enough to lie on Odette's stomach, cushioned by her breasts. But Sandra was bigger, two years old. One night it was so cold that Odette bound Sandra close to her, gripping her neck tightly like she was a dog, making her cry. The next day they decided to follow a road that would take them south, to where it was lower and warmer, and close to the main road from Kigali to Kibuye. And they would not stop, not for a moment, even though they knew nothing of where they were going.

Kivumu, 8 May

It had been nearly midnight by the time we reached Kivumu but we woke early the following morning. We followed Curic's advice and made our way down the pitted track out of his parish at Kivumu on to the road towards Kabgayi, which lay seven miles to the south. There was little traffic but the road was busy with people. Many pushed carts on which they had piled their belongings. The whole country seemed to be on the move. The car stuttered and choked its way up the hill towards the town of Gitarama, which we would need to negotiate before reaching Kabgayi. We arrived at the church of St André. It was set back from the road and there were at least a hundred people collected around it. The sky was military-blanket grey. The earth was the colour of rusted metal. The people who sat over small fires or lay draped in exhaustion on the church steps were the same colour as their surroundings. Clothes soiled red and grey faces, not black, silent and prone after days on the road. It looked like a sprawling yard of scrap metal.

We had seen none of these travellers on our journey into Rwanda the night before. It had been close to dusk by the time we had left the border. It was seventy miles to Kivumu but Curic had warned us that it would take several hours. There were many roadblocks. He told us to keep our car close to the truck and say nothing to the militia manning them, but just to show them the laissez-passer which we had procured from the Rwandan Embassy in Bujumbura the previous afternoon. Curic had been curt with us, understandably so, since our dilapidated tyres had suffered two punctures before we had even reached the border, delaying the priest's journey as we hurriedly made repairs. The broken side windows, he told us, were a liability.

We came to the first roadblock after twenty minutes. It was constructed of metal jerrycans and branches of eucalyptus spread across the road. I couldn't see a brazier, but in the fading light there were torches that flickered over the faces of the men who leaned in through the window to peer at us. They stank of booze and their eyes were bloodshot and curdled yellow. They all carried machetes. The one who took our papers chewed on a piece of meat as he read, then handed the documents to the others who pored over them. I counted six men in all. They were stocky, muscled and wore ragged shirts and trousers that had been cut off just below the knees. I wanted to get a better look at them but didn't want to lean out of the window. One man came back to our car. He spread his hands on the door. His fingers were thick and dirty, the skin on his knuckles scuffed like bloodied divots. His machete clinked on the metal edge of the window frame. It was dark, which made it difficult to tell if the stain that ran along the blade was blood. In the flickering light it looked black, like printer's ink. There were four of us in the car and none of us spoke. The truck started up its engine – thick snorts of diesel fumes filled our car. I asked for our papers and they were handed through the window as we moved slowly past the roadblock, the thin rubber tyres crunching over the dry eucalyptus leaves.

We encountered more than a dozen roadblocks on our way to Kivumu. Some of them were sophisticated – usually when we neared a town – with metal barriers, braziers, more men, some carrying rifles. At each stop we could hear Curic talking. He never left the cab of the truck, but sometimes we could hear his laughter. He spoke with a rat-a-tat rapidity, so fluently it hardly seemed believable that he had mastered what felt like such a complicated language to us. Six hours after we left the border, we arrived in Kivumu.

The next day, after leaving St André's church we continued through Gitarama. Steve sat up front with me. Tom and Monty squeezed in the back with Sam, an English newspaperman who had travelled in the convoy to Kivumu the night before. Most of the stores that fronted on to the main road were closed. There was no urgency to the people we passed. They shambled along the road and, if they weren't lugging carts, it was difficult to imagine what they were doing, since it seemed clear that the town had effectively been shut down. I watched in the mirror as they turned and stared back at our disappearing car. We climbed slowly up through the centre of town. Steve said, 'Well, it doesn't look bad here, does it.' It was quiet, like a dull provincial Sunday morning. Ahead of us, where the road rose to a small plateau, we could see a queue of people. It was an army roadblock. A soldier walked out and stood in the middle of the road, his hand raised up. We stopped. I showed him our papers. Another soldier had walked up to Steve's side of the car. He leaned in and asked him what he was holding. 'A camera,' Steve told him, 'a television camera.' The soldier looked at him. 'Television?' He reached in the car and tried to pull the camera out. Steve held on and shook his head at the soldier. 'No, that's my camera,' he told him. The soldier wrestled harder. Steve gripped the camera. Tom and I shouted, 'He thinks he's on TV, Steve, give him the bloody camera!' But by then the soldier had let go and was pointing his rifle into the car. The soldier with our papers ordered us out. 'OK, have the camera,' Steve said. Two other soldiers appeared. Both pointed their weapons at us. Tom spoke better French than I and started to reason with them.

We stood in the middle of the road. People watched us as they waited for their identity papers to be checked by the other soldiers. On the verge, there was a man on his knees. He wore a scruffy brown jacket. All his clothes were dun-coloured – muddied, I guessed, by years of farming. He was trembling. I could hear Tom behind me. '*Nous sommes journalistes avec la BBC. Vous comprenez? Nous avons l'autorisation de votre gouvernement pour travailler ici.*' Tom was working hard. The kneeling man turned and looked at me. Perhaps he had caught 'BBC'. He looked startled, his eyes full and black. There was dried blood down the side of his face. I could see now that he had been beaten. There were fresh bloodstains on his trousers and his left knee hovered above the ground, as though it was cut or badly bruised and any weight on it would be too painful.

The soldier who had grabbed the camera had large hands and they now moved over its dials and switches. Steve stood with Monty. Tom kept talking, but it was unclear whether the soldier understood French since he kept turning over the single piece of paper we had been given back in Bujumbura as if he couldn't make out what it said. 'Passports,' said Tom. He reached into his pocket. Mine was in the car. I reached into the back seat and grabbed my bag. The kneeling man had begun to shake. There was an overwhelming smell of human shit. Another group of men arrived at the roadblock. They all carried machetes. They spoke with one of the soldiers. The man on the verge began to weep. Not crying out or begging, but tears streaming down his face. I felt a bubble of air caught below my ribcage that expanded so that it became difficult to breathe. I could hear Tom behind me – he sounded shrill. The gang of men moved over to the kneeling man and picked him up. They walked off the side of the road to a copse of banana trees that lay thirty yards away, the man amongst them. His head bowed low. I looked at Sam, who shook his head. I said to Steve and Monty, 'They're going to kill him, don't watch.' But it was impossible to look away. The gang walked a few yards into the copse. They pushed the man over and began to hack at him. The man was partly obscured by the long banana leaves – the motion of the blades, too, was broken up by the undergrowth. The man made no sound and the blows seemed noiseless. I thought to myself, we are next. They don't care. I have been in enough places. *I know.* The bubble squeezed my chest so that my ribs ached. The men walked out of the trees and made their way down the road. Tom had stopped talking to the soldier. They knew who we were, they had our passports, they could let us go or they could kill us. I was sure they would kill us. Tom looked at me and

I think he thought the same thing. He lived in Africa. *This is sometimes how it is.*

A familiar white jeep appeared at the roadblock. Curic got out of the car and began to walk towards our little group. He ignored us and spoke to the soldier holding our passports. The soldier did not look at Curic. Curic kept talking. I wanted to touch Curic's shirt – thick coarse cotton that looked like the one that I had seen that morning through my little bedroom window, hanging on a line between two small acacia trees. If I could touch him, then I wouldn't be taken to the banana trees. That's what I thought. Curic talked. The soldier handed Tom our passports. Curic turned to me and said, 'Get in the car.' I could hear Steve and Monty climb in behind me. Tom closed his door. The sound of people outside became muffled. It was airless inside the car and when Tom said, 'Just follow Vjeko,' his voice was dense and flat. Fifteen minutes later we stopped at the entrance to what seemed like a college campus. Soldiers stood at a barrier. Curic got out and walked back to our car. 'You need military protection,' he said, 'otherwise you will face more of these problems.' That was how we acquired our new passenger, François.

That afternoon we began to thread our way along unpaved roads that connected the hundreds of small communities that stretched deep into the Rwandan countryside. The car skidded over the packed mud, the chassis grinding against the deep ruts that criss-crossed the track. François's rifle clanked against the dashboard with each lurch of the car. François was a soldier from the Presidential Guard. His uniform looked worn – years of endless pressing – but was clean. Light wispy hairs sprung from his upper lip and chin, and his eyes were soft, a gentle brown. He had joined us that afternoon from the compound we had stopped at in Gitarama. It had been a civil service college but now it was the headquarters of the decamped government. Groups of men and women walked slowly along the paved paths in the grounds, nodding politely as we passed. I could hear the *clack-clack* of typewriters from some of the brick bungalows that were nestled up against jacaranda trees. In one office we met with the Defence Minister, a man called Bizimana. He laid out maps on a metal desk and told us that Rwanda was in a bloody fight against an invading rebel force. Behind him there was a military camp bed. An AK-47 was propped up against the wall. An extremely fat man sat by him. This was Mr Niyitigeka – the Information Minister. They apologized for the problem at the roadblock, but the internal security of the country was a priority, they said. Mr Niyitigeka rolled his 'r's – *priority* was a word that he seemed to enjoy saying. Given the difficulties the country faced, it was no surprise that incidents such as the one we witnessed that morning were taking place. Soldiers had been instructed to be extra vigilant. They would do their best to ensure our safety – it was a *priority*; but this was *intambara* – this was war – and in war, people die.

In the car François and I made polite conversation. Where did he come from? The north. How long had he been in the army? Seven years. Did he like it? Did he see his family often? No, not for a long time. François gave a small, wistful smile. It was difficult to think of this man sitting beside me, with his gentle voice and shy manner, as a killer, but as a member of the Presidential Guard, he would have been at the forefront of the killings. It was those soldiers who, in the hours after the President's plane had been shot down over Kigali, had sought out and murdered liberal Hutus, political opponents and prominent Tutsis. Before leaving London, I had read reports that many of the Guard had participated in the attacks on Tutsis who had sought refuge in Rwanda's churches. The car trundled past a patch of adobe huts. Small children stared, half raising an arm in greeting. François said he wanted to go back home. He wanted to take over his father's land and farm.

After a mile we found ourselves in a small village. Many of the brick houses that lined the street had been abandoned. The doors had been removed. The window frames had been dug out from the brickwork. There was no furniture left, and what had been kitchens were now completely stripped bare. We stepped gingerly through the remains of one house, broken glass and paper littering the floor. I found an airmail letter, the sender's name and address half burnt away. Kimberley Fisch—. 1076 Ches—. —. Maryland. USA. Inside, Kimberley excitedly told of her decision to take Development Studies in her junior year at high school and that her family were planning a vacation out west, but she wasn't sure where yet. They hadn't decided. The letter was dated 12 February 1994.

Further up the street lay the corpse of a man. He had been beaten to death. His shoes were half twisted off his feet, his shirt hiked up over his chest. Two young boys kicked a wicker football past his body. A group of men emerged from a small store. Some carried machetes. One man held an old radio. Other than the group of men, the body and the two boys who had now stopped to stare at us, the village was deserted.

It was hot. A dry gust of wind kicked up pieces of old plastic wrapping. I could hear the chatter from the radio. The men stared at us. Two with machetes spoke to an older man who wore a grey jacket. Their machetes swung from their hands. The propaganda from the radio spilt out into the street. There were no televisions here, no newspapers reached these men who stood watching us. Just voices, spat out into an airless echo chamber. Exhorting the men with machetes to do their national duty. There were no pictures or printed leaflets to follow; the men could let their imaginations roam free. They could murder Tutsi children who kept American pen pals, loot and gut their houses, leave them like animal carcasses, their bones picked clean. Bludgeon to death Hutu neighbours stupid enough to object, or fanciful enough to protect a Tutsi friend.

François tugged at my elbow. 'We must go,' he said. I shook my head. 'No, we want to talk to those men.' Tom and Steve had walked up to some of the men and begun filming. 'Who was the dead man on the street?' Tom asked them. 'Who did the looted houses belong to?' The men looked blankly at us. 'Where are the owners of those houses?' Finally they spoke – asking us questions in turn, in Kinyarwanda. They pointed at the camera. Tom kept trying, but it seemed to me that none of them could speak French. The ones with machetes had edged towards the front of the group, which had now surrounded us. François tugged again. I pointed at his rifle. 'But you're in the Presidential Guard.' The boys had joined the group of men – their small faces peering up at us through the crooked elbows and machete handles. François shook his head and pulled hard at my sleeve. I could see sweat on his face. 'Let's go,' I said. Tom kept asking the men questions. 'We need to go, Tom.' Steve swivelled his camera round to the man with the grey jacket who began to shout at us. 'Tom, *now*!' Steve heaved his camera off his shoulder and we walked to the car. The men watched us but didn't follow. We backed slowly out of the village. François was breathing hard. 'They are very dangerous,' he said.

Back in Kivumu that night we ate a rich stew of pulses, and mopped our plates with bread. The rooms that faced the grass quadrangle were lit by single candles – what fuel Curic had for the small generator was to be saved for emergencies. We heard the groan of the metal gates opening and Curic's jeep crept into the compound. His sneakers squeaked on the cement walkway and we heard him chatter in the kitchen to the tall Rwandan who had served us our dinner, before he walked into the room holding a bottle of whisky and several glasses. Over many hours – that night and on successive nights that we stayed there – Curic sat with us and talked.

In a country with such poor roads, and with many houses tucked away in the folds of valleys and hidden in dense banana plantations, we wanted to know, how had the gangs managed to search out victims and kill so effectively? He explained that the administrative divisions were hierarchical and highly organized. A village – sometimes more than one – made up a *cellule*. Several *cellules* made a *secteur* which, in turn, formed a *commune*. The *commune* was headed by the *bourgmestre* who took his orders from the *préfet*, who ran the whole *préfecture*. The names and identities of the people in each *cellule* were known and recorded at the office of the local *bourgmestre*. Everyone in Rwanda was known. Even Curic would notice when people didn't appear at their doorways. He knew that since February some of the younger men had been leaving their *communes* for a few days. When they returned, people told him that they had undergone 'training'. Curic was certain that they had been prepared for the moment when they would be required to turn on their Tutsi neighbours. Ever since the RPF invasion nearly four years earlier, the extremists had slowly brought Rwanda to the boil. Propaganda against the Tutsi had been gradually piled on the Hutu peasantry so that women they had married or storekeepers they traded with had become, in their eyes, scheming and untrustworthy – fifth columnists ready to rise up, when instructed, against the Hutus.

For a month, Curic had been travelling through the south of the country – bringing in aid either through Butare or from Gikongoro. Everywhere he saw devastation. Farmers had not harvested their crops because they were busy killing Tutsis. At night they ate the slaughtered cows of the Tutsis they had murdered and got drunk on the beer that the authorities brought them. Not *urwagwa* but Primus – the good stuff that, usually, they could never afford. At roadblocks men complained about those who couldn't kill properly and needed to be taught how to. Curic paused. It was the propaganda that he marvelled at. The simple purity with which the extremists had turned obedient, ordinary people into killers – so that when the time came to begin the slaughter, it was less with a sense of inflamed retribution that they murdered but more the relief to be getting on with the job they sensed the government had planned for them all along.

Curic sat hunched over the oil lamp that flickered on the table. On the other side of the door I could hear his cook tidying away the dishes. The words poured out of the priest. Recently, on the road to Mbazi, near Butare, he told us he had stopped by a pile of bodies. The day before the road had been clear. Now he was forced to weave his jeep through a hundred people lying heaped on the road. His window was open and he heard a child crying. He climbed over the bodies and found a baby underneath its dead mother, unharmed. He turned his car round and drove to Burundi with the child on his lap, waiting until it slept before throwing his coat over it, crossing the border and delivering it to an orphanage in Bujumbura. Another day, near the frontier, he had been hauled out of his jeep by *interahamwe* who accused him of being a spy for the *inkotanyi*. They took him down to the river to shoot him, but he told them that he was a priest and if they killed him they would have to answer to God. He laughed when he told us that they had walked away and he had sat there, being sick into the river. The week before he had hidden three people under the truck and smuggled them out of the country. That was dangerous. There were too many children standing around at roadblocks who were small enough to look under a truck. It had worked once but it was too risky to try again. He pulled maps from the shelves and explained how the RPF were sweeping south and west. He told us about the camp at Kabgayi and showed us which way to go to avoid the major roadblocks. I looked at Curic, animated, unstoppable. I thought to myself, you're enjoying this.

We got up before dawn the next day and drove to Kabgayi. We found the field, which was perhaps ninety yards wide and just over a hundred yards long. A series of yellow, dirt-stained brick buildings marked one end. Wooden paling and strings of barbed wire ran along the lengths and eucalyptus trees fringed the bottom of the field. The trees that lay closest to the fence had been stripped of their branches and stood like ancient radio masts. A layer of smoke hung low, thick enough to obscure the hills behind and transfigure the people who lived in the field into grey ghosts. There were eight thousand of them packed into the camp. Curic had told us the field used to be pasture for the Bishop's cows. Now it was churned mud, foraged until it looked blasted. Every corner of the field was occupied by huddled groups of families or friends or impromptu gatherings of men, sitting back on their haunches, murmuring quietly to themselves.

We pushed our way through the wire-mesh gate and the crowd of people who had pressed their faces into the metal when they had heard our car arrive. It had been cold when we left Curic's compound. It was still cool – the soldiers by the gate stood hunched in thick jerseys, shivering in the grey murk. Inside, the camp steamed. Sweat and ordure. The crush of people. Some still lay where they had slept, shivering under blankets, old jackets and shawls or matting. Most were awake. A few aimlessly threaded their way through the camp, sometimes disappearing into dense smoke from the few small fires around which old men, blankets draped over their heads, squatted. The camp gave off a low hum – punctuated by the cries of small children. Human turds littered the ground. Women with babies breastfed, rocking their children. Toddlers stood around, apathetic, their eyes glutinous with smoke and conjunctivitis. Older children moved around the camp – their quick, confident limbs side-stepping people. Despite the crush of people I could see the tiny pathways that had been created, which the children followed. When an army truck started its engine on the other side of the wire the children slowed down, dropped their heads, hardly moving. They looked old, their faces drooping, their small bodies sagging and they seemed to melt into the mass of rags around them.

A hand grabbed my wrist and a man in his twenties pulled me to the side of the sheds. We made our way towards the entrance to one. The wooden door had been ripped off for fuel or protection from the rain. He said that they had little food or water. People were getting sick and there were no medical facilities. Inside the shed were cow byres. People lay huddled on the concrete floor. The man said that those who were really sick were brought in to the sheds. There was a strong stench of putrefaction. He pointed to the holes in the roof at the back of the building. Grenades, he said, thrown by soldiers several nights before. We took ourselves off to a corner – where his English didn't have to strain so hard to be heard above the noise of the sick. Two weeks earlier he had been woken by the sweep of headlights from an army truck. Soldiers kicked through the gate. He heard the screams of a young woman as she was dragged out, past the wire. There was shouting and he saw two men he knew running towards the gate. 'Then there was shooting,' he said, 'that was very loud.' No one moved until the truck had long disappeared. In the morning they wrapped the bodies of the two men in blankets. The girl was never seen again.

People in the camp were sick. The man explained that they did the best they could, collecting the dead each morning. Near the sheds was a makeshift morgue. Feet protruded from the ends of several parcels of rolled-up papyrus matting. Pairs of tiny feet. The young and the very old were most vulnerable, he said. Through the mass of people I could see the soldiers standing on the concrete wall close to the gate, their green uniforms and claret berets vivid against the wash of brown. Until a month ago these men spent their days checking identity cards, throwing the occasional slap or kick, but people could normally walk past them unscathed to resume their lives as teachers, farmers, businessmen. Now, with thousands of people captive, herded together, these same soldiers could push the bounds of their own imagination. This wasn't a training exercise. They could do whatever they wanted.

Tom came over. He looked as white as a sheet. He had found people from the International Red Cross who staffed a building across from the camp. 'They say the soldiers are murdering people every night,' he told us. 'They won't talk on camera because they will be killed for it. All they can do is pick up the bodies.' Beyond the camp I could just make out the cathedral tower and the Bishop's quarters. When he took evening Mass he would be able to hear the people down here, below him. If he walked to the far edge of his gardens he could smell them. At the gate, the man who had guided me through the camp stood in a crush of people. Children stared through the wire mesh, their small fingers curled around the rusted metal. The man asked us to help them. They would die without help.

We walked the few hundred yards up the path to the Bishop's quarters and waited outside Thaddée Nsengiyumva's office. We were led into his garden with its neat hedges and rectangular patches of clipped lawn. It was cooler here, away from the crush of people. The Bishop greeted us with a grave face. He wore a carefully pressed tunic with red trim at the collar. We asked him to explain what had happened to his country. He clasped his hands together and said that he was struggling to understand that himself.

'People are being killed,' Tom said. 'Thousands of innocent people are being butchered. We have witnessed it with our own eyes.'

'Exactly,' the Bishop said. 'How can it be possible for these things to happen?' A pause before he added, 'It is confusing, in this time of war.'

'This isn't a war. At least not in Gitarama. There are no soldiers fighting here. What we saw were civilians murdering their neighbours. The International Red Cross are calling it genocide. The United Nations has condemned your government for actively pursuing a policy to eradicate Tutsis.'

The Bishop blinked slowly. 'We have to pray for our people. We must all pray to God that this madness will end.'

Below us, just out of sight, was the camp. Could the Bishop guarantee the safety of the people who had taken refuge here, Tom asked. Nsengiyumva replied that he was praying for his people and he hoped that God would answer his prayers. Then he excused himself and we watched him walk slowly back to his quarters.

The next day I was accused of being a spy. It was my mistake. That morning I had driven to the military camp to pick up François. I chatted at the barrier to the soldiers who were now used to seeing me pick him up and later, in the afternoon, drop him back. I took photographs of the soldiers as I waited. They posed with their guns. Behind them I noticed a caravan. It was painted in vivid colours and sported a large aerial. As I clicked away, it dawned on me that the caravan was a mobile radio station. Perhaps this was Radio Mille Collines. A government minister emerged from the gatehouse. He was furious, demanding to know why I was taking pictures. 'I am a journalist,' I told him. 'No,' he spat back, 'you are a spy!' I told him I worked for the BBC. 'British? Then you are spying for the Tutsis,' he screamed. The Rwandan government distrusted Britain and its long ties to Uganda, from where the RPF had invaded a month earlier. The minister shook with rage. I was taking unauthorized pictures. This was treason. I would be tried and if found guilty, I would be imprisoned or shot. He pointed his finger at me and ordered the soldiers to arrest me. 'I am a journalist, not a spy,' I said. 'I am here reporting for the BBC.' The man was triumphant: 'Yes, you work for your government.' The pitch of his scream intensified. 'You are a spy!' I lost my temper. I was frightened by his threats and I was angry at his imputation. 'The BBC does not work for the British government,' I yelled. 'I don't give a fuck about the pictures I've taken. Here.' I ripped the spool of film out of the camera and handed it to the soldiers. François arrived. I said, 'Look – this is our military protection, given by your government. Your Defence Minister authorized this man to protect us.' The minister seemed surprised by my outburst but he was still seething. He said something to the soldiers and they stepped back. 'You are not welcome here any more,' he said, in a quiet voice. 'You are not trusted.'

That evening Curic advised us to leave. He was apologetic, but the government was paranoid and our presence was endangering his efforts to ferry supplies into the country. We left the next day. Curic came with us. We stopped in Butare at a Jesuit centre run by the Poor Clares. Curic told us to wait in the car; he needed to check on some people inside. After forty-five minutes Curic reappeared. We drove for the border. Curic negotiated us through the dozen roadblocks we encountered. Daylight made the men on these roadblocks seem more normal, but it may have been that I had become inured to the sight of illiterate killers with bloodied machetes standing by the side of the road demanding to read documents they couldn't decipher. By dusk we were in Bujumbura.

CHAPTER FIVE

Jean-Pierre

When Jean-Pierre ran his finger over the roughened ridge of the heel of his foot it felt the same as the edge of Sandra's cup – the frayed plastic, grated by her small teeth. He could see her. She was sitting at the table. Her eyes looked up over the rim, still drinking her milk, a phlegmy breath echoed into the cup. Another look, he saw her put the cup down, dewy milk clinging to her upper lip. Jean-Pierre paused. They couldn't kill babies, could they? He was sure they would not. To kill babies was stupid. But Ernest had whispered that his neighbour Kayotani had been cut down, and he was over eighty. If old men were seen as a threat then babies were just as dangerous.

The darkness in which he lived felt like a heavy gas that had settled inside his head, blocking his mental processes, polluting memories with thoughts of death. He felt stymied by it; pushing through the black to grasp the fragments of a story that he could piece together made him worry his brow with his knuckles.

He was exhausted, worn down by nearly two months of

darkness, by the constant repetition of the only thing he understood. They were shooting Tutsis and hacking them to death with machetes and knives and clubs until, he surmised, there would be none left. When he thought like this he realized that he was tired of sitting in his hole for no reason. If they were killing everybody, then what was the point of being here, trying to stay alive, he thought. He decided that it would be better to die. He had tried hard to stay alive, but with no end in sight he felt he had survived long enough. He would leave the hole and walk down the alleyway towards the roadblock, just fifty yards from where he sat. He imagined the faces of the men as they watched him, pointing at him, picking up their clubs and machetes. Just beyond the roadblock he would see the main road. A few people would stop to watch what was going to happen next.

He felt the cool earth press against his arms and back. He thought about being cut to death, lying on the dirt road, listening to his own blood leaving his body, watching it catch in the cracks of the concrete before it drained away into earthy pockets and sank slowly into the ground leaving a wet, muddy stain. He did not want to be killed by a machete. He thought he could cope with being shot, but to climb out of his hole to face a machete seemed impossible.

He stretched his arms out and touched the walls again. His mind was shutting down the pathways that might lead him out of this hole. He didn't care. All that existed was here, a barrel, a pail and a cup. When he bumped into thoughts of his life before the hole he saw himself from the outside, detached, like viewing drawings in a book. He saw himself walk up the bumpy hill from his parents' home in Rutongo, he saw the pair of shoes his father had lent him. He was going to meet a girl called Agnes. He was nineteen. His father said, 'Jean-Pierre, you cannot take Agnes out in those shoes of yours! Borrow a pair of mine.' Up the track in his father's shiny black leather slip-ons, so new they nearly made him lose his footing. He could see the shoes but he had no memory of his father's face that day, let alone of Agnes. There was no picture of her that he could conjure up. Was she small? Or pretty? Where did they go? Did they dance? He didn't know. Nothing mattered. Agnes was surely dead. His father must be dead too.

At dawn a sharp crack of light seared across his eyes like solder – Ernest had been sloppy and had failed to close fully the cover after he had lowered Jean-Pierre back in the night before. Jean-Pierre had lost so much weight that Ernest now had to help pull him out of the hole and keep a tight grip on him as he dropped him back down. His legs were skinny. They dangled into the empty space, the tips of his toes wriggling, groping for the solid touch of the metal barrel.

He took out the roll of money that he had kept in his pocket for more than a month. Eleven thousand francs. He held it up to the light. The face of the former President stared out on to distant Rwandan hills. The general wore his military uniform. He looked younger and leaner. Stern, under his dark eyebrows. His lips were thick and wide, his nose broad, hair crammed under his peaked cap. A symbol of Hutu superiority. Jean-Pierre had kept the money because he was worried that if he gave it to Ernest his friend would use it to go and buy food for him. The money was not for food. He counted out the grubby notes – a mixture of five-hundred- and one-thousand-franc bills. The money would, he had decided, pay for his death. There was something fitting about Rwanda's assassinated President being involved in this transaction. Jean-Pierre's thumb rubbed the notes – gently enough to feel their indentations, the curl of the signature. The money was his insurance that when it was time for him to die he could pay for a quick end. It was not much money – no more than his day's pay from a client whose books he kept. But for a killer in Nyamirambo it was a sizeable sum and would, he hoped, guarantee a bullet rather than a machete.

A bullet on Rue du Lac Mihindi. Near where he drove Papa Joe one day. 'Wait for me,' Joe had said. 'I am going to this place.' He pointed to a house. 'Who lives there?' Jean-Pierre asked. 'A friend.' 'How long are you going to be?' 'An hour, maybe two.' Jean-Pierre waited. He heard a muezzin and saw men walk to Friday prayers. The sun was lower now and the car was hot. He reclined the seat. Where was his father? What was he doing? He slept a little. When he woke the car was in shadow, the light was fading. The street was blue. He saw his father. A woman at the door. When Joe climbed into the car, Jean-Pierre said, 'Papa, she is not as beautiful as Mama.' His father put his hand on his shoulder and smiled. 'I don't expect you to understand. But I wanted you to know.'

He was tired. He was sick of this hole. His world had fallen slowly into dark close-up. He had no answers. He wanted to die.

CHAPTER SIX

Curic

By the end of May, the north of the country was firmly in the hands of the rebel army, the Rwandan Patriotic Front. Large parts of the capital had also fallen to them. The districts of Kigali that remained under government control were embattled, bloody areas that sucked in troops, allowing the RPF, under the command of Paul Kagame, to intensify its swoop southwards. This prompted thousands more Hutus to flee their homes in advance of the *inkotanyi*. The diocese of Kabgayi, including the town of Gitarama, the temporary seat of government, became a way station for streams of villagers who had fled their smallholdings in the east. They tended to settle in the former homes of Tutsis or in schools, where they collected in the corners of abandoned classrooms like dust. The women set their backs against the adobe walls, faces like stone, and cooked. The men picked at their broken sandals and wondered at the way things had turned out. In March they had moaned with their Tutsi neighbours about the rain and the chances for the harvest. In April they had slaughtered them. And soon after they had killed everybody they needed to kill, they were ordered to gather up their things and leave. Pots, plates, mattresses, blankets, pictures, crucifixes, old hats, new shoes – they loaded them all up. Sacks of rice and bundles of clothes. They stripped the metal sheeting off their roofs and bound their farm tools together. They piled it all on to their bicycles and carts and walked away from the fields they had cleared and dug, sown and harvested for generations. They had trekked west along hot bitumen roads and pitted mud paths and now they lurked in the doorways of gutted houses and stared at the confusion all around them. They stood almost motionless, like children in a new playground, hardly daring to move, their eyes swivelling and tracking the strangeness of their surroundings. The afternoon rain, once the gripe of every planting season, fell unnoticed.

By now, Vjeko Curic was making three trips to Burundi every week – running supplies to the refugees in Kabgayi as well as to feeding centres close to Kivumu and the nearby town of Murambi. He had dollars, whisky and food to negotiate his way through roadblocks. He and his two drivers had worked out several different routes to ferry aid from Burundi. Poring over his maps, armed with the latest intelligence on the status of roadblocks and where fighting had broken out, he could switch from the quicker main road through Butare to the more circuitous routes via Cyangugu, which lies at the bottom of Lake Kivu, almost the furthest point west in the country. Back in Kivumu, his cook Oswald was a safe and reliable pair of hands. The Catholic charity that was funding Curic deferred to his judgement. And most critical of all, the fluid and malevolent chaos, the sheer scale of the lawlessness in Rwanda, which had stupefied the international community, was the ideal environment in which the Bosnian priest could operate, and meant he occupied a unique position in a country that now existed in a political vacuum.

As a parish priest Curic had had little direct business with the government. The Bishop's offices – with all the implied power that his high-ranking party membership carried – had always been the one who dealt with the low-grade flunkeys who sat in Gitarama's stagnating local-government buildings. But now, with the central government holed up in their temporary digs in the town, AK-47s propped up against the walls of their offices, Curic had become influential. Rwanda's ministers were stymied. They had lost large parts of the country. Hemmed in, they had to scrounge rationed fuel to leave their own compound. They were denuded, cut off from an obsequious bureaucracy that had served them in Kigali and might still have been doing so now, if its members hadn't fled or given up work some weeks ago. Telephones were useless. They had to beg the military for use of their satellite phones if they were to find out what was going on in their department or district, or even where their families were.

In this boiled-down universe, Curic possessed the two things of most importance: the means to travel and the technological ability to communicate. In his white jeep bouncing down dilapidated roads, fuelled by aid-agency money, Curic worked across government and rebel front lines throughout southern Rwanda. He had come to know many of the roadblock leaders and, head poked out of the car window, was as confident talking to them as he was sitting across the table and negotiating with politicians. He could leave the country, regularly and with near impunity – not something that a politician would risk doing. Using his satellite phone to glean information from journalists and the handful of aid agencies positioned on Rwanda's southern border, his maps were patchworks of arrows and squiggles that identified new roadblocks, flows of refugees, alternative truck routes, military activity. Government officials began to seek him out since his information, gained from his travels on Rwanda's roads, was often better sourced than the news they were receiving. Curic was careful to protect his neutrality, and the intelligence he gathered was channelled into refining and improving the mission of delivering aid, but his notoriety emboldened him further than he could once have imagined possible.

For several years Curic had felt his parish duties becoming a burden. The connection that he had felt with the rural poor when he first walked across Rwanda's hills had been lost under the weight of his priestly responsibilities. The building work and the creation of a new school and health centre were at the centre of Curic's life as parish priest, but too often he felt encumbered by the politics and petty rivalries that accompanied his plans. Now, however traumatic the circumstances, he was truly following his calling again. It was a shame, he decided, that Sebastijan Markovic was not here to see what it meant to be a Franciscan – living with the people. Markovic might have pointed out that St Francis would have advocated suffering alongside the refugees in the dirt of the camp in Kabgayi or staying to give daily Mass to his parishioners in Kivumu, rather than battling through roadblocks and negotiating with *génocidaires*; but it would be churlish not to acknowledge that Curic's exasperated rants over the last few years at the pettifoggery of parish life had been far from his mind since April, and his presence in southern Rwanda was keeping thousands of people alive.

He felt leaner and sharper and increasingly certain that he was right to have remained in the country and engaged with the catastrophe that had befallen it. He had spoken to friends in Uganda over the satellite phone a few days earlier. 'It is devastating but I am staying, whatever happens,' he had told them. They told him he sounded well and he said he was. In fact, the clarity with which he had explained what he was doing – his words sharply delivered into the night air outside his room – had electrified him.

It was this sense of mission that saw Curic, on 5 June, driving south in a larger than normal convoy towards the Rwandan border. Sitting with him were three Rwandans. All were Franciscans – at differing stages of their training. All were Tutsi. For once, Curic was not leading the convoy but had deferred to another vehicle which also contained a Franciscan. All four Tutsi priests had spent the last six weeks in hiding, three of them at the Poor Clares' convent in Butare. No one in Curic's jeep spoke. They were watching the car ahead. Its driver was a major in the Rwandan army. Everyone was aware that Curic's opportunism in having a senior officer – a Hutu – chaperoning several Tutsis out of the country could seriously backfire. Curic kept close to the other car. At each roadblock they sat idling nose to tail. He wasn't sure what he would do if the officer betrayed them, but he was sure that the man would be less inclined to renege on the deal if the priest remained large and vivid in the soldier's rear-view mirror.

Some days earlier, Curic had heard that the government

was stepping up the killings in response to the speed with which the rebel army was taking the country. In Butare, the moderate Hutu *bourgmestre* had been shot and replaced by a man with greater zeal to eradicate the remaining pockets of Tutsis. The university town had not escaped the massacres but its liberal traditions and distaste for the extremism of recent years had encouraged many locals to take a step back from actively engaging in the slaughter.

As teenagers, four Tutsis whom Curic had recruited for the priesthood – Aphrodis, Florent, Aimable and Joseph – had dragged the timber and mud bricks, alongside Curic, up the steep hills of northern Rwanda to build a new Franciscan house. When Curic had fallen into a deep ditch and injured his back, it was Aphrodis and Florent who had carried him to the hospital.

Now, some years later, and close to finishing their training, the priests had been living in a friary house outside Butare when the genocide began. On 18 April, three of the friars – Joseph, Aimable and Florent – had managed to get to the convent in Butare. It had been a traumatic journey. A day earlier, Florent had attempted to enter the town with two European priests and another novice, George Gashugi. They had been stopped at a roadblock and George had been pulled out of the car, marched a short distance up the road and murdered. It was a vicious and senseless killing – acted out in plain sight of the other priests. George was a local man and known to be fully Tutsi; Florent, on the other hand, had Hutu relations and survived. The group turned back and rested that night at the friary. Isolated in a small village, with no phone or means to contact the outside world, the priests felt the least worst option was to try again the next day.

Only Aphrodis objected and decided to remain at the friary house. The following morning all three Rwandans and two Europeans made it through the barricades to Butare. The traumatized European priests left for Burundi the next day. No such option was open to the Rwandans and they remained with the Sisters at the convent. For more than a month they survived by supplying the local *interahamwe* with food. As long as they were quiet and kept their gates shut to outsiders, the killers told them, they would remain unharmed. Back at the friary house, Aphrodis spent days hidden in the loft to elude the killers who occasionally searched the building.

Curic had few qualms about the fact that food he delivered was being divided up between the friars and the Hutu militia since the transaction was keeping his priests alive. He knew that trying to evacuate the men from the country would result in their deaths. But on 3 June the *interahamwe* warned the Franciscans that a new cadre of militia would be arriving in Butare in the next few days. They came from the north. They had orders to kill all remaining Tutsis.

Curic had been asked by the *préfet* to help transport a number of Hutu orphans from the town to a refugee camp just inside Burundi. He had guessed that some of the children were the sons and daughters of military officers, since a Rwandan army major by the name of Jean-Didier had been with the *préfet* at the time. Curic agreed to help. He told the *préfet* that he could provide fuel for the truck carrying the children and escort them to the border, provided Jean-Didier also accompanied them. In passing, he mentioned that he would be travelling with several of his Franciscan brothers.

On the morning of 5 June a truck carrying two dozen children arrived at the Poor Clares' convent. Jean-Didier joined them later that morning in his own military jeep. Curic was determined that at least one of the priests should travel with the major. The risk of being exposed at a roadblock was far greater if the officer travelled alone. With one of the priests, Florent, in the car with him, Jean-Didier was now part of the deceit. The convoy left at two in the afternoon. It made a short stop at the friary house, where Curic collected Aphrodis, and then began its journey to the border, twenty miles to the south. To Curic's surprise, Jean-Didier had seemed unbothered by the presence of the priests; perhaps Florent's mixed ethnicity had helped reassure the soldier. It was only as they neared the first roadblock that the army officer fully comprehended what was taking place. The dozen men at the barrier were *interahamwe* – not the local band of men who stood most evenings at the convent gates waiting for food, but from the Hutu heartlands in the north of the country. The men sprang towards the convoy and engaged Jean-Didier in animated conversation. Several circled the jeep, peering into the back, checking its number plate. There was none of the bored insouciance that Curic had seen from some units of militia, worn down by the relentlessness of their roadside duties, nor the meek shuffling of peasants ordered off their fields to do their afternoon shift. These men were proud of their identity and nomenclature: *interahamwe*, 'those who stand together'. They were diehard members of Hutu Power – an extremist political movement with a vanguard of several thousand young men who had been ferried to villages and towns across Rwanda where they cajoled and, if necessary, bullied and threatened their fellow Hutus into accompanying them to hospitals and schools and churches to kill with undiluted ferocity. The men who were now scrutinizing the convoy were the bloodied, blunt means to a political end.

It would have been in February that Curic had first driven past groups of young men like these, starting to gather in Kivumu. They chanted songs and danced. 'What are you doing?' he asked one group he knew. 'Why are you not at home helping your fathers?' Few waved back and he disliked what he saw. There was a formally dressed man whom Curic hadn't recognized – clearly an out-of-towner – who stood at the centre of the circle addressing the youngsters, but he instinctively distrusted him.

Rwanda was changing. Curic had noticed how there was less and less land for farmers' sons to cultivate food for their own families. The country had suffered an economic collapse; there were few jobs in the towns either. People were hungry. The war in 1990 had frightened farmers – what land they had was not safe from invaders. Bored and idle, the boys from the back country fell prey to the extremist Hutu political parties that emerged from the fledgling democracy movement. 'You have an ethnic problem in this country,' Curic had told Aphrodis. 'When I came here you were one people, but now you are lots of different groups.' It exasperated him that the poor, already downtrodden, should have their roots exploited by a manipulative, incompetent leadership that had placed the country in such economic and social peril. Curic challenged his acolytes to see themselves through the prism of their faith. 'How can you be Tutsi or Hutu when you are all baptized in the same name?' he asked them. 'Stay out of politics,' he warned.

Now Jean-Didier had got out of the car and was walking over to Curic. He looked pale. He leaned into the white jeep and, in a low voice, told Curic that he knew that he had been tricked. His breath was sour. He looked into the back of the car, scouring the other priests' faces. 'They are all T—,' he started, the last word dropping away as some of the *interahamwe* approached them. He was breathing heavily. The man was trapped: he could step back and denounce Curic and the priests to the militia, but then the shadow of suspicion would fall on him too. Why was he with these *cockroaches*? In the man's fear Curic saw how Rwanda had careered off a moral precipice. The country was in the hands of the mob. A senior army officer carried less political weight than the ragtag group of men that had gathered around the car. There was one in a baggy suit with large lapels, who looked like a civil servant. Next to him, a teacher perhaps, with his dusty jacket and split plastic shoes. The two men with sandals were farmers, he was sure of that. The frayed shirts and muscled forearms gave them away.

For an instant Curic found himself back in a small bar just outside Mostar in Bosnia the previous summer, when he had been stopped by the Croatian army. They warned him that he would be killed in the crossfire between Croats and Serbs if he tried to cross the river Neretva. He sat for several hours trying to decide what to do. Suspended in the corner of the bar, a television showed the news. It was difficult to decipher where the report came from, but what he remembered were the images of armed men in civilian clothes standing on a road next to a row of small houses. It could have been anywhere in Bosnia. The men were mostly in middle age, a little stout, wearing cheap nylon tracksuits and flat leather caps and smoking cigarettes. They carried rifles which they brandished at the cameras. He had been curious about how these men, who could have been neighbours of his parents, had turned into venal thugs – but he was more surprised by how little he felt for their bellicose defence of their village. He felt far removed from their world – as if the screen were a puppet theatre. He'd finished his beer, turned the car round and driven away.

In the rear-view mirror Curic saw that Joseph and Aphrodis stared at their hands, fearful that they would catch the eyes of the men who surrounded them. He remembered what he had told them earlier that morning. He had known them for years. From shy beginnings, they had grown comfortable with each other. Joseph had an infectious, high-pitched giggle; Florent, a dry self-confidence. Aphrodis was the most sensitive; his deep empathic voice felt like sugar sliding off a spoon into a cup of dark coffee. But that morning the men had hardly spoken. Their steps had been tentative as they emerged from the walled existence that had kept them alive for nearly two months. They moved like the very elderly, with great care and deliberation, fussily adjusting their seatbelts, tweaking their clothes. Before they left the convent, Curic had reminded them that to remain in hiding would mean certain death. They would be discovered and they would be killed. This way, at least, they stood a chance. As the men settled themselves in the jeep, Curic saw on their faces something other than fear. In the muffled intimacy of the car interior the men seemed isolated from each other, alone in the darkness of their own thoughts. He twisted his body round to face them, the plastic squeaking as he moved. 'This is my country too,' he told them. 'If I die, I am going to die with Rwandans.'

Curic shoved his door open, forcing Jean-Didier back-wards, and told him to show the militia the orphans in the truck. He walked up to the man with the oversized suit and explained that he and his fellow priests were accompanying the military orphans to Burundi. He spoke quickly, looking directly at the man. He was on official business for the diocese, he told him, sanctioned by the military authorities in Gitarama and Bishop Nsengiyumva of Kabgayi. It was already late and he knew there were several more security checks to pass through before they reached the border. He was concerned that further delays would mean the children were unlikely to reach their destination before nightfall. Unless there was a specific problem, then he would like to continue with their journey. Through the windscreen the priests watched Curic, hands on hips, square up to the road-block leader. The man stared back at the Bosnian before the return of Jean-Didier from the rear of the truck distracted him. Curic remained motionless. Silence fell over the two men and those who stood nearby watching the encounter. The banter that had typified Curic's roadblock negotiations since April was absent. It was as though, finally, the priest had exhausted his lexicon of unctuous flattery; as though the insult of offering words to inflate this man's preening self-regard in return for the lives of men whom he had known and loved for years was too great, not just for his faith but for his entire being. He had nothing more to add. The man must work things out for himself and Curic would play no more part in the decision. A long time ago, back in Yugoslavia, his car had been stopped by the police and for more than an hour he had been interrogated on the side of the road. Where was he going, the policeman had asked. To Travnik, he had replied. Why was he going there? To talk to a man about becoming a missionary in Africa. You're a *priest*, the officer had spluttered. Why would you want to be a *priest*? Curic lost his temper and had spent several hours in a police cell for tipping the man's cap off his head and throwing it on to the road. But Curic was older now. He brought one hand up and looked at his watch. The man grunted and turned away, but the priest did not move again until he saw the militia open the barrier to let the convoy pass.

A mile later Curic flashed at the major's jeep ahead to stop. He got out and walked over to Jean-Didier's door. The soldier was still seething and swore at the priest. 'You have tricked me,' he fumed. Curic ignored the rant and handed him an envelope with seven hundred dollars inside. It would be enough to buy his silence for the dozen further roadblocks they encountered before they reached the border. At each barrier, Jean-Didier left his car and walked to the truck, standing by the children, leaving Curic to explain to the *interahamwe* who the men were who sat in the jeeps. The twenty-mile journey to Burundi took four hours. In Bujumbura, Curic deposited his priests at a parish house. The next morning he loaded up the lorry with sacks of food and crossed the border back into Rwanda.

Odette

The village of Mukura lay at the southern edge of a large national forest reserve, a few miles north of the main road to Kibuye. There was an abandoned school in the centre of the village and it was here that Odette, Mukaruziga and the two children found themselves, exhausted and starving, in the first few days of June 1994.

Three days earlier they had left the chill of the mountain paths and dropped down on to the main road, heading west, joining a column of thousands. Their plan – if it could be called a plan – was to stay on the road until they reached Kibuye, twenty miles away. The road was packed with people and, for the first time in several weeks, Odette allowed herself a tincture of hope that they might survive. The talk was of the surge by the *inkotanyi* and the imminent defeat of the government. The mood was one of gloomy unease. These people had packed up their belongings, as they had been told, and set off westwards. No one spoke about the crimes they had committed and the evidence that had been left rotting in the swamps and fields near their villages. But they bickered about their crops that lay unpicked and fretted that their homes would be destroyed or, worse, invaded by others. Wives cold-shouldered the men, leaving them to push the carts alone. The unspoken fear of these people, Odette guessed, was that they would never return to their villages. Odette and Mukaruziga, Sandra and Vanessa, joined the throng. Two worn-out women on the road with two young children – as hungry and desperate as everyone else.

When they heard that there was a military roadblock ahead, Odette decided to get off the main road and find an inconspicuous place to settle and wait. With no identity cards and the laissez-passer long since softened in her pocket into an indecipherable mush, it would be pointless to risk a roadblock confrontation. The village of Mukura was close enough to the road to attract plenty of other refugees but, she hoped, far enough away to avoid any attention from wandering militia or army units. It was a relief to stop. The children were emaciated and exhausted. They had been on the move for more than a month. Odette was unsure how long they would stay.

The weeks on the road had been frightening and uncertain, but she realized that little separated them now from the Hutu refugees and they were probably in less danger than she had first thought. Their weary plod had left no impression on the land and as the earth ground its way into their clothes, bleaching the patterns, softening the cotton until it frayed, their identity had slowly drained away as well. Through fields and down paths, unremarked and unnoticed, passing like shadows. They stank like beasts.

They settled in the corner of a field close to the school. Mukaruziga scurried around the village looking for food. They cooked over a fire – just like everyone else. Vanessa stared into the smoke, unbothered by the treacly film that filled her eyes. Her once stout legs had become spindles, propping up a stomach that was as tight as a drum. Her head seemed huge – the lower jaw, a teak-coloured prehistoric mandible, the skin pulled back, winnowing her lips to thin curls of clay. She stayed close to her mother, glazed and vacant. When she cried Odette noticed that her wail, which used to swell with indignation into a full-bellied roar, had been replaced by a dry, anguished bleat that made the tendons on her neck bulge with the effort of forcing the sound out of her sharp-boned body. The mother ran her hand down the side of her daughter's head. The hair had stiffened into tight, light brown curls as if it had been scorched.

When they were on the road she had thought only about the route they would take that day, the village they would have to avoid. At Mukura they sat quietly, their physical selves fading as quickly as the memories of their lives before. They were malnourished and seriously ill. This much Odette now knew.

Odette had trained as an accountant. She had never been intimidated by numbers nor by dense columns of print. She'd never let her emotions cloud her judgement. She understood that she and her children were dying, and she balanced the risks of staying in the village against the risks involved in resuming their journey to Kibuye. One alternative was to return to the main road that would take them directly there. She looked at the other figures nearby, hunched over their fires. There was none of the fear and hatred here that she had experienced back in April. The ennui was overwhelming – as though the country had collapsed with exhaustion from its violent convulsions. Wherever she looked she saw decay: schools had been abandoned, land lay idle, people were listless. It was true that the men on the roadblocks might still have the same feral enthusiasm for killing, but the risk of running into such men no longer seemed incalculable. Rwanda had ceased to exist as an entity, and she doubted anyone cared now where you came from or who you were, and if she was unable to produce identity cards, she doubted people would care about that either.

That night Odette gazed across a field at the huddled shapes of families lying prone on the earth. A few small fires still smouldered. Faint plumes of smoke. A child's grumbling, tubercular cough. Bodies stirred restlessly on the hard ground. She looked at her children – indistinguishable now from the hundreds, probably thousands of Rwandans who were drifting aimlessly across the country. She thought about the day she married Jean-Pierre. He had looked so smart in his new suit and elegant leather shoes. She had loved his certainty, his belligerent confidence in his Tutsi lineage, the roots that reached deep into Rwanda's past. They would build a family, he had told her. This was their country too.

Odette and Mukaruziga left before dawn, having decided to take the main road to Kibuye. The people who had settled by the track were either still asleep or watched them silently as they slipped by. Later that morning, a military truck thundered past and stopped thirty yards from them. Soldiers clambered off and walked back through the refugees traipsing along. Odette tried to push past but one soldier stopped her and asked her where she was going. To Kibuye, she said, where her father-in-law lived. He shook his head. The area was unsafe, he said, it was still with the government. He spoke softly and it took Odette a few moments to understand that she was talking to a rebel – Tutsi – soldier. She explained that they had left her family in Gitarama six weeks earlier. He looked back up the road and sucked air through his teeth. Well, she could go back to her home now, he said. The government had fled. To the south mainly – along with the army. Odette uncoiled Vanessa from her back and placed her on the edge of the road where she sat, baking in the dust. After the soft pathways Odette had trodden, the tarmac was excruciating, burning her feet. She and her children had been on the road for more than a month. Was there any transport? The soldier shook his head. Could the soldiers take them back? No, she would have to walk.

It was strange talking to this man. There was no sense of relief. She felt only foreboding. She looked back up the road. Weariness swept over her. An ache that spread across her neck and shoulders, as though a heavy burlap sack had been lowered on to her. It was still early and, looking east, she could see the road disappear in an angry yellow glare. She looked west towards Kibuye. The soldier watched her. 'They're all dead,' he said.

Jean-Pierre

Jean-Pierre looked at the small metal bowl next to him. He brought it close to his face and sniffed but the food was cold and odourless. He had lost his sense of taste. The bowl had sat there for two days, untouched. Ernest had come earlier that night to retrieve it but Jean-Pierre had shaken his head and his friend, looking puzzled, had crept silently away. In the darkness the faint glow from the metal rim of the bowl and the fuzziness from the outline of the food was all Jean-Pierre could see. He stood up and stretched his hands across the span of the hole so that his fingertips touched the earth on both sides. His trousers hung from his hipbones, sagging in the middle by his groin. His elbows were sharp, knotty points that left indentations in the earth. When he levered himself back on to the drum he grimaced at the effort. He could feel the hard edge of the metal through the flattened pillow and his thin buttocks.

Ernest would be back again that night asking for the bowl or perhaps bringing more food. But Jean-Pierre had not decided when he would eat, or if he would eat at all. He thought about how Ernest would have prepared the food for him, portioning out a spoonful from the pot that sat in the corner of the yard, growing cold whilst Ernest ate and waited for darkness to fall. He ran his finger over its contents and felt the stub of corn, the floury cassava paste. Perhaps he would not eat ever again. He could wave Ernest away and after a while the cover would stop sliding back and he would not have to watch the bowl being lowered into his hole. He could end his nightly geometry sessions as he tried to work out whether the guns he heard had moved since the night before. He could stop the struggle to remember his children.

He would not have to be pulled from the hole by his friend. He would not have to listen to his friend gasping with exertion as he shouldered him out of the alleyway and through the gate of the house. He would not have to feel guilty for the risks Ernest was taking on his behalf. He could curl himself into a tight ball at the bottom of his hole and listen to his heartbeat.

The anger he felt at his predicament was not new. He remembered the letters he had received three years earlier when he still worked at the Chamber of Commerce in Kibuye. He knew that there were men and women who were jealous of how quickly he had risen. He was sure that the letters from Kigali informing him that his work had fallen short of acceptable standards had been instigated by two of his colleagues. The letters – inside small, yellowed envelopes that sat on his desk – were badly written and the allegations unsubstantiated, but he was powerless to defend himself against them. Odette had suggested he quit but Jean-Pierre liked his job. He knew all the businesses in town – sometimes it took him thirty minutes to walk the short distance to his house from the office because store owners held him up to talk. So much government red tape – they knew Jean-Pierre could fix it. He had steeled himself for the moment when he would receive the final letter, but he had been surprised by the hurt he still felt.

Jean-Pierre looked at the bowl. Its rim seemed to glimmer as if there were grey filaments hanging over it. If he picked it up, his fingers would dip into the cold food and he would squeeze the cassava into baggy pouches, and when he was done he would lick the metal surface with his tongue. Or he could leave it there. It was his choice. He closed his eyes.

The grey light from the bowl shifted into a different shape and turned into a small figure. When his elder daughter had just been born he could balance her in the palm of his upturned hand. She was so small it made him laugh out loud. Her back would rest against his wrist and her tiny calves dangled over the tips of his fingers. Later, when her hair grew, her mother wove tightly sprung plaits that hung from her head like large black caterpillars. In the morning he would stand by the door and watch her sleep. Under the mosquito net in the thick grey light she seemed to hover between the sheets and the air around her. She giggled if he rolled a ball to her. She liked honey.

Jean-Pierre picked up the bowl and began to eat.

CHAPTER SEVEN

Rwanda, 3 July

The roads were deserted. Normally, people – even killers – filled these roads on their walk to the local store or their fields. The fields were empty too. There were no farmers hacking away at the bush or children dropping their ball of twigs and chasing our car. We passed whole villages and saw no one. Not a soul. The land was empty, a human deforestation. We drove past a line of one-room mud-brick houses. Three had been burnt out. *Tutsi* had been scrawled with white chalk on the walls. The propaganda on the radio had warned Hutus that Tutsis were preparing to take back the country. Did they really mean these people, I wondered. This was a remote corner of Rwanda, a day's walk from the nearest town; Kigali was not so much a capital for people here as an imaginary place – a glittering citadel half suspended between earth and sky.

All of the capital was now in the hands of the rebel army. Those of the regime's soldiers who had not surrendered or been killed had fled west. Most of the country had been wrested from their hands. We were corralled in the Christus Centre, a series of pale brick buildings that had been run by Jesuit priests before the genocide as a Catholic retreat. On the morning of 7 April, an hour after the President's assassination had been announced, soldiers from the Presidential Guard entered the compound. They shoved the nineteen Rwandans into a small bedroom and put the handful of Europeans under armed guard in the dining room. In the early afternoon the Europeans were released. The Rwandans – including eight young women from a Catholic order and the Centre's cook – had been executed. Apparently the Centre had been targeted because back in February hundreds of refugees had fled there for protection after the unrest that had followed the assassination of one of the leaders of the new political parties. The bodies had been buried but the room had been left untouched. On the walls there were brown smears of dried blood and bullet holes. Torn pages of a Bible fluttered about on the floor amongst the shell casings from the automatic weapons. Our room was next door.

The Centre was close to the Amahoro Stadium where several thousand Rwandans had been protected by the meagre UN force that had remained in Rwanda. Next to the stadium was the UN headquarters. The head of the mission explained what was happening. He was a Canadian general called Romeo Dallaire and in April he had watched most of his force leave the country, after the Security Council deemed Rwanda not fit for help. He looked exhausted. The rebel Rwandan Patriotic Front, the general said, had defeated the Rwandan army and his best estimate was that more than two million Hutus had fled their homes. This we already knew because Kigali was, more or less, empty. Those who had survived gathered at feeding centres that had been set up around the city. There was little food elsewhere, but even if there had been, people would have come here. They were reluctant to leave, preferring to camp close by. 'They feel vulnerable,' the general said. 'They don't know if the killers will return.'

I tried the only number I had for Curic. His phone rang but no one picked up. I phoned the aid agency that had supplied his convoy with food and fuel. They said he was running aid supplies into the south-west of the country where there were several refugee camps. He spent little time at Kivumu; once RPF soldiers had liberated the camp at Kabgayi three weeks earlier, he had shifted his focus to the south-west, to Gikongoro – a town just to the north-west of Butare – where thousands of other Tutsis had fled. The agency understood that the friary was empty; the cook, Oswald, had left when the rebels had walked into Gitarama. Curic reportedly was unsure where he had gone, though he suspected he had headed west, like other Hutus who feared Tutsi reprisals. I rang the Red Cross in Kabgayi. People had left the camp and returned home, they said. Bishop Nsengiyumva had been arrested along with an archbishop and bishop. A few days later, in early June, several RPF soldiers – allegedly seeking revenge for the deaths of some of their families – had murdered them. The government had fled Gitarama and was now holed up in Bukavu, just across the western border in Zaire. I had heard of Bukavu. It was a pretty town – a weekend retreat for politicians, UN officials, generously budgeted aid workers – with guesthouses that looked like Alpine chalets and gardens stuffed with bright red bougainvillea that set off the dazzling blue of Lake Kivu to perfection.

That evening at the Christus Centre a journalist who often appeared on television explained to me that in situations like these, an interview with the new leader and an emotional human story kept the news desk happy. To that end, he had talked to the new President, and that afternoon he had been pleased to discover, at a local hospital, an abandoned ward of mentally handicapped children.

We left Kigali at dawn on 6 July. We were now a new team. My cameraman, Greg, and I were recently back from the Middle East, where we had been covering the return of Yasser Arafat to the Occupied Territories, in between our Rwanda assignments; Robin, our reporter, had arrived from London; Trevor, the sound recordist, had come up from South Africa. We drove east for three hours. Then we followed a small sign that pointed us on to a dry dirt track. The car bumped and groaned and in places strained to push its way through the bush that had been left untended for three months and which now toppled into the track. After thirty minutes of this we rounded a corner and saw the church – built by Rwandans for the Belgian clergy sixty years earlier. It was blunt and industrial-looking. The façade had narrow oblong windows that would let little light into the nave. Above double doors, mounted on a plinth, was a statue of Christ, arms outstretched. To me, it felt like a church for devout Walloon coalminers to trudge to every Sunday, along damp, flat-faced terraced streets. Here, set against the acacias and giant albizias over which it towered, the building seemed an imposter, a livid, brick-red bully.

We parked in the courtyard. The sun had baked the mud. Gusts of hot wind made the trees sway and the leaves shuffle.

The courtyard was a mess – there were rags and clothing scattered everywhere. The heat made me slow down. I walked to the boot of the car and reached for my small backpack. Our Rwandan translator leaned against the car, his arms crossed, staring at the church. There was another sound – a faint buzz. I walked towards the building. On the steps leading up to it there were more rags. The rags were bodies. They had shrivelled into bundles of bone and sinew and dried-out skin. Tufts of hair were still attached to their skulls. The bones had cracks in them or were chipped like old china. The skin was yellow and had peeled off like desiccated leather. Some of the skulls were nearly severed from the bodies. Near the main doors the feet of one man had been separated from his legs. His arms were stretched towards the church. He had been a tall man – a tall *inyenzi* for the killers to cut down to size. He must have died as he struggled to reach the building, leaving his feet behind. There were bodies in the flowerbeds that were arranged around the church. Some had been killed close to the windows; perhaps they had leapt out to try and escape the killers. Inside, the tall, narrow windows allowed a weak, shabby light to fall across the pews. Several people had been praying when they had been killed and, by the altar, a long elongated shadow seemed to undulate down the altar steps. Behind the sacristy a group of children had been hacked to death and lay in a pile, fine skinless fingers, perfectly formed bones stretched out over each other. The heat was oppressive.

Around the church were a series of further courtyards fringed with single-storey buildings. Clothing, glass and bodies lay twisted together. I had counted fifty dead in front of the church, but there were more bodies all over these courtyards. I tiptoed through the grass but it was impossible to walk without treading on people. Across one courtyard were convent classrooms. Air and smell were indivisible. I walked through moist clouds of sweet decay. I stuffed a handkerchief in my mouth. Greg did the same. I looked back and saw our car parked in the distance. What had likely happened, I surmised, was that the killers had herded people away from the church and pushed them into a more confined area where there was no possibility of escape. Flies erupted as we reached one classroom door. It was almost dark in here so the bodies were still bloated, although some had begun to split and burst through their stretched clothing. There were small windows that threw a dim yellow light into the rooms. My eyes began to grow accustomed to the low light and I could pick up details. The people were different sizes, men and women, thick-tongued and bloated, yellow cardigans and patterned dresses, leather shoes, children, all squeezed and wrapped around one another as if semi-suspended. We walked through three classrooms. At the back of each room the bodies reached the height of my waist, before tapering down to the doorway, where they rose to just below my knees. Greg said, 'I can't find focus. It's too dark.'

This is what took place at Nyarubuye parish ten weeks before our arrival.

A few days after the assassination of Juvénal Habyarimana several thousand Tutsis and Hutus who lived in this remote corner of south-east Rwanda had fled to what they hoped would be the sanctuary of the parish church. No one knows the precise number that reached it. On 15 April a local politician, Sylvestre Gacumbitsi, arrived at the church in the middle of the afternoon with a convoy of vehicles carrying local policemen and *interahamwe*. Gacumbitsi was well known. Before political office he had been a teacher and a bank manager. For much of the previous week he had incited local Hutus to murder Tutsis, whom he accused of being accomplices of the invading rebel army. He also distributed weapons – rifles, grenades, machetes – around his district. When he climbed out of his car at the church, a local man, a Tutsi called Murefu, approached him. It was not clear if the man knew Gacumbitsi but people reported that he had walked up to him with confidence. Gacumbitsi killed him where he stood. This was the signal for his accomplices to move forward into the crowd of refugees. Using a megaphone, Gacumbitsi instructed any Hutus to separate themselves from the Tutsis. Once it was clear that those who had wanted to comply had done so, the politician ordered the gang of men to begin the massacre. As they killed, they also raped. By nightfall the killers were exhausted and left. The next day, Gacumbitsi returned with his men and a local judge called Rubanguka. This man was reported to have used a spear to stab bodies that he walked past. The men spent the day finishing off any survivors they found and looting the parish. On 17 April they returned again and did the same.

It was dusk when we left. The afternoon breeze had died. The trees stood rigid and still and the church had become a silhouette – a series of dark, perpendicular lines cut against the deep blue sky. We talked about where we would go next and agreed that we needed to head west, to the border with Zaire, to where the killers had fled. We stopped talking. The car pushed its way through the bush. The tall grass, pressed against the side windows before it sprang back across the track, was briefly illuminated by the red tail lights, and then disappeared into darkness.

Jean-Pierre

'Wake up, Jean-Pierre. Let's go running.' Jean-Pierre buries his head in his blankets. Papa Joe is drunk. 'Dad, it is two in the morning. There is school tomorrow.' 'So what, come on, let's go,' his father says – a dark shadow in the doorway. 'No, Dad, leave me alone.' His father walks past Jean-Pierre's bed. 'Mukassa Joseph!' He leans over his son and shakes him awake. 'Come on, Mukassa Joseph, come running with me.' Jean-Pierre's brother lifts his head and groans. 'Are you coming, Jean-Pierre?' 'Forget it, Dad, it is late and I don't want to run at night.' Mukassa Joseph gets out of bed. His brother is only twelve. Jean-Pierre is angry. He watches him get dressed and leave with his father. He lies awake. He cannot sleep. Thinking about where the two Josephs have gone running. They are running through dark streets. It is crazy and dangerous. He lies flat on his bed, tracing the cracks on the wall with his finger. He knows he was right not to go. But now he wants to hear them again, hear their breathing heavy from their running, see their shadows at the door, hear his father saying to Mukassa Joseph, 'Shush, keep quiet, you will wake Jolie.'

Later, he wakes when they get back and his father says, 'I will give Mukassa Joseph a cow, but I am not going to give *you* a cow, Jean-Pierre.' 'Fine, don't give me a cow. I don't want your cow.'

In the morning Jean-Pierre goes to the bedroom where his father is waking up. 'Hey,' he says, 'don't forget to give Mukassa Joseph a cow, like you said. You owe him a cow.' His father says, 'What cow? I never said anything about a cow.'

Jean-Pierre watched the sharp oblong of light drift down the wall of the room before it slipped on to the floor like a drunk sliding off a chair. The day grew and light bleached the room. His eyes hurt and he shifted his body on the mattress so that he faced the wall. He didn't know how long he had been lying in the room but he remembered that he had woken once before, when it was dark. He had panicked and shouted, which only confused him more because his voice seemed different – lighter, airier. His words had lost their earthy clamminess. They no longer pressed into his chest or hung suspended in his mulch but seemed to fill the sharp corners of the space around him. He lay there breathing heavily, unsure of where he was.

Later, when he woke and it was light again, he recognized the mattress. His finger traced the pattern – scraping across the stitching. He had brought the mattress to Ernest's house when he moved in. Ernest had put Anny and the baby in the back room and pulled a chair to one side in the main room so that Jean-Pierre could lay his bedding down by the wall. He remembered that he and Ernest had sat outside in the courtyard where they had roasted maize and discussed what was going to happen. That was in March.

He lurched in and out of sleep. Each time he opened his eyes the light was different. Sometimes the room was green but when he woke up later it seemed to glow, catching tunnels of dust in sharp beams. He could half close his eyes and splodges of different colours would swirl in front of him. He watched the oblong of light on the wall. His head rested close to the floor. Across the room a sharp crack of light protruded from the bottom of the door to the courtyard outside. He remembered watching Ernest close the door. Just before his friend left he had reminded him where there was food, but so far Jean-Pierre had been too tired to move from his mattress.

When Ernest had pulled him from his hole for the last time – two months and sixteen days after he first crept into it – and dragged him to the house, he had explained that he was taking Anny and the baby and they were leaving. The road-block nearby had been abandoned. The *interahamwe* were moving out. The RPF were close to Nyamirambo, Ernest explained, and there was panic everywhere. Even though he was Zairean he had decided it was too dangerous for him to stay. He was Francophone, he had survived unharmed, he worried that suspicion would fall on him. His mother, who lived nearby, was too old to leave and had decided to stay. Jean-Pierre should go to her when he felt strong enough.

Jean-Pierre crawled over to where food had been left and pushed some cold beans into his mouth but the effort made him retch. He thought to himself, why am I bothering to eat. He felt worse than he ever had when he was in his hole. In the hole, he felt contained. Out here, he felt he was dissolving. Everything that had made him survive had become nothing. He could feel himself shut down. There was no memory, there was only him, and that him was draining away. He rested his head on the bare floor and listened to the street outside.

When he woke again he heard nothing. He lay on the mattress for several hours. He slept. The next time he woke he sensed the same emptiness from outside. He decided he would leave. It was difficult to stand because his legs were weak. He managed to open the door into the courtyard and crawled to the gate. When he got to the street he saw the remains of someone lying in the gutter. Then he passed out.

'How come this one looks like a Tutsi?'

Jean-Pierre came to. He was lying on the side of the road and a soldier was staring down at him. He was too weak to pick himself up. Two soldiers threw him on to the back of their truck. The truck moved off. He lay on the floor at the feet of the soldiers. They watched him.

After a few minutes the men shouted to the driver to stop. He heard rifles clatter as two of the soldiers jumped off. The ones who had stayed on the truck shouted down to them. 'Get me a Fanta,' they said. Jean-Pierre's throat was parched. The metal panels burnt the skin on his arms and feet. He wanted water. I have done my best, he thought to himself. I've done all I could.

'It's OK to kill me. Please shoot me.'

The soldiers ignored him and drank their Fantas. The truck moved back on to the road. Strips of sunlight flashed into his eyes. He could smell diesel. He tried to swallow but his throat was jammed. Then the engine died and he was grabbed and pulled upright. The soldiers shuffled him to the back of the truck. He could see a church. It was called St André. He knew this place. It was a church and a school and a health centre. He felt himself being pushed off the tail-gate. He dropped into the arms of two soldiers who carried him across the road and propped him against a doorway that looked like a hole in the wall. He heard the men talking to someone and then he watched them walk back across the road to where the truck was parked. It seemed to shimmer in the heat – as though it was a mirage. He was hauled to his feet and taken to a room full of hospital beds, where a nurse attached an intravenous drip to his arm. It was only later, when he asked if there was a place where he could wash himself, that Jean-Pierre accepted that he was safe.

Rwanda, 7 July

We drove north-west, towards Ruhengeri – a traditional Hutu stronghold – where a few loyal remnants of the Rwandan government army were defiantly withstanding the RPF. Hundreds of Hutu refugees had taken to the road and were heading further west, for the border with Zaire. They were late leaving their homes. Most people had left weeks ago. These stragglers must have clung to the hope that somehow the rebels would be defeated. They staggered under the weight of their sacks of food and clothes and cringed as trucks carrying the victorious Tutsi rebel army thundered past them. Some soldiers had stopped to celebrate. They told us Ruhengeri had fallen – or was about to fall. It didn't matter. The war was over, they said. We found their commander. He sat in his jeep, one boot drawn up on to the dashboard, watching his soldiers singing war songs nearby. They had stomped the grass flat by the side of the road with their dancing.

'Is the war over?' we asked.

'The war is not over. There are killers and we must catch them.'

The colonel spoke slowly, plucking words in the same way that he picked at the small tufts of beard that sprang from his chin.

'There is blood. The bodies. The children.' He paused – almost lost in the words that he had uttered. 'The blood. There must be justice.'

The genocide was at an end. Paul Kagame's rebel army had defeated the extremist forces of the so-called interim government. The story of how such a crime could have happened was emerging and with it came calls for justice. The testimonies of those who had survived would prove crucial for the liberating army – soon to be government – in their quest to enlighten a world that had, until then, largely averted its gaze about the scale and depth of the crime. In time, these testimonies would form the core of the country's efforts to move beyond the slaughter. But for now, piecing together the collective memories of what the survivors had seen and endured would prove, indisputably, how Rwanda had been in thrall to a handful of men who, fuelled by a powerful and toxic racist ideology and expertly schooled in Rwanda's administrative culture, provoked mass murder in their countrymen for the purpose of political domination.

When the death of their President was announced on national radio on 7 April, the plan by Hutu extremists, begun four years earlier, to stoke the fires of racial hatred and fear to a point where they could confidently imagine a country free from all Tutsis – and Hutu opponents – had been realized with precision and enthusiasm. The justification for their campaign – and what became their rallying cry –

was the invasion in 1990 into the north of the country by the RPF and the subsequent fear amongst the ruling elite that new, multi-party elections would result in their losing power. Extremists inside Rwanda's government began to differentiate between trustworthy, normal Rwandans and *ibyitso* – those they deemed accomplices of the rebel army. The latter group included, obviously, all Tutsis, but also any liberal-minded Hutus who supported a government that reflected the ethnic mix of the country. A new radio station, Radio Mille Collines, broadcast splenetic propaganda that characterized the Tutsi as untrustworthy, subhuman, *inyenzi* – cockroaches. The extremists formed a political movement, Hutu Power, which crossed political lines and lured the young, the unemployed, the poor and the disenchanted into its ranks. Between 1990 and 1993 several thousand Tutsis were deliberately massacred, fuelling the sense of a country on the brink of ethnic collapse, defending itself against an alien threat from the north. The ruling party created a civilian militia in 1992, the *interahamwe*, so named after a popular pro-independence song and meaning 'those who stand together'. Thousands received military training and were readied to defend the country against the rebel army and any opponents that threatened the state. Truckloads of arms – rifles as well as machetes – were imported into the country and distributed to the militia.

The extremists entrusted the initial task of mass murder to the army and gendarmerie, backed by a ravenous militia. They were confident that the state's moral authority would mobilize ordinary Rwandans and that the powerful bureaucratic structure would ensure an efficient and comprehensive approach to eradicating the Tutsis from Rwanda.

And so it was. Across Rwanda massacre sites were being discovered and survivors told similar stories that pointed to the deliberate planning of the genocide. On a map it didn't matter where you looked – what road or track your finger followed – there were atrocities to be found everywhere. To the east, in Mukarange, shortly after Radio Rwanda announced the death of the President, soldiers and gendarmerie placated those who had gathered at the church and encouraged more to congregate there. Three days later, the police threw grenades into the compound buildings, before the *interahamwe* entered them and began to hack the wounded to death. The killing took several hours. Each morning, for several days, the militia returned to ensure that everyone was dead. In the marshes of Nyamwiza, local people joined in the daily hunt for Tutsis who had escaped from the schools and churches where they had initially fled. Those reluctant to join the killing spree were physically intimidated by the *interahamwe* who had been brought in to police the operation. People killed quickly so that they could get home to do their chores, although they were often rewarded with beer and meat brochettes – making killing more productive than farming. A woman in the village of Musha admitted killing her neighbours' children – an act of generosity, she said, since the parents were already dead and Rwanda was no place for Tutsis. They didn't cry out, she said, because they knew her. At Kibogora hospital killers were helped by medical staff to identify Tutsis who had attempted to hide. Those who ran to Rukara Maternity Clinic on 12 April, convinced that a maternity ward would offer them protection against the killers, were shot by soldiers. Hospital staff allowed the *interahamwe* access to the wards so that they could machete the newly born. Everywhere political leaders – *préfets, sous-préfets, bourgmestres* – organized the killing, provided the weaponry, the gathering places for killers, the disposal of bodies and the schedules for ordinary Rwandans to arrive and finish off any remaining survivors.

We drove towards the border. We stopped at abandoned villages and peered into the dark, muddy interiors of people's empty houses. We met only dogs that sat in the shadows of the huts, their eyes slits against the sun. When we picked our way through fields and across ditches we walked into clouds of decaying, moist air. Each invisible cloudburst told its own story, but in the silence the deaths felt connected.

Jean-Pierre

Medical supplies were limited at St André, and Jean-Pierre was quickly taken off the drip and moved from the ward to a small house at the back of the health centre. He didn't mind. He had begun to feel restless, pinned to the mattress. But when he walked across the small patch of grass he felt faint. There were others who were recuperating in the house. One man told him that he had to be careful not to eat too much or too quickly otherwise he would die. It was the kind of advice that he might have paid careful attention to in the past, but now he felt differently. When food was offered he ate methodically and without stopping. With one of his thousand-franc notes he bought sugar, which he heaped into his tea, ignoring the exasperated sighs of the know-all. He sat outside the house, his back wedged against a wall, and watched patients, wrapped in grey blankets, pick their way past other survivors who sat or lay, exhausted, flat on the grass. He felt he had changed. In the hole, he had often thought that he could be killed easily, that he would die at a moment not very far into the future. But sitting against the wall at St André, he felt stronger inside. He thought, if someone says to me, I will kill you, then I will handle it differently. I will not just accept it.

On 11 July he borrowed a car and drove to Gitarama. There was little traffic on the road. For a while the novelty of passing empty villages helped distract him, but the strangeness of the landscape quickly became familiar and he was left heavy and drained by the burden of what lay ahead of him. At St André he had listened to the telling and retelling of stories from survivors, the ceaseless roll-call of the names of the dead, updated each day, as more evidence of the scale of the slaughter was uncovered. He knew that he must make this journey to Odette's family home because it was his duty to check that no one was there. It was an undertaking that seemed sharply defined and he understood it. But when he contemplated that his responsibility went further – that he must find out not just whether his own young family had left, but whether they were dead – he struggled. The task became shapeless and indistinct. It was as though a dark stain seemed to spread through his body.

The government soldiers and *interahamwe* had long gone, but Gitarama still felt like an unruly and lawless border town. Stores had been looted, houses burnt. Survivors from the camp at Kabgayi who had not yet dared to make the journey back to their villages drifted through the streets as aimlessly as the smoke from the fires that others crouched over. Boys snapped their sticks at goats. It was quiet. The town smelled of wet smoke and human shit.

The metal gate to his father-in-law's property was closed. There was no sound from behind the high walls that protected the house. He tried the side door, next to the gate. It was open. He walked inside. The cow byre was empty. It was clear that people had camped here. Rubbish was strewn across the rectangular yard. He stepped over rusted cans and plastic containers, piles of half-burnt wood and torn clothing, and went down the small passage on the right, which led to the house. He saw the upstairs window of the spare bedroom where he and Odette had stayed after the wedding ceremony. The roof tiles were intact. It seemed to him that the house had not been looted – at least from what he had seen so far. A bee-eater perched on the top of a banana tree. Its head cocked sideways, watching him, as he made his way towards the door. The door was closed. As he ventured in, his eyes took a few moments to adjust to the dark. All the furnishings were gone, tables, chairs, plates that had sat in a row on shelves, a calendar that had hung on the wall. His feet scraped in the dirt of the concrete floor. He was thinking how empty the house was – of furniture and people – when Odette walked into the room.

Jean-Pierre stood and looked at his wife and thought to himself simply, you didn't die. She stood half in shadow so he could see only one side of her face. Her skin was grey and taut, her jaw sharp. She seemed half hidden, hostile, her head only partially turned towards him. He worried that if she took a step away from him she would slip back into shadow and then she might disappear altogether. That made him want to move closer but he decided to stay where he was. Odette had not moved either. They stood, a few yards apart.

'Where is Sandra? Where is Vanessa?'

Odette glanced over her shoulder and Jean-Pierre walked through the darkened doorway and saw his daughters sitting on the floor, playing. He watched them for a few seconds and then came back into the living room, walked up to Odette and put his hands on her shoulders. Neither spoke. He moved towards her – into the space that had always been hers, where the air grew thick and there was no need for words. He bowed his head so that his brow rested on the top of her forehead and he felt her breath on his chin and her pulse on his fingers. He could hear his daughters next door – the clink and clank as they played. His eyes had grown accustomed to the dark and he could see that Odette had swept the room and had hung clothes across the windows, perhaps to dry or perhaps to hide herself from anyone who wanted to look into the house. Part of Jean-Pierre knew that he should say something, but he was thinking about himself and what he thought was, I have found my wife and I have found my children and they are alive.

After a while he told her that they needed to leave. Together they packed a few things, put the children into the car and left. The journey should have taken an hour but took less. There was no traffic, of course, and he drove fast and the countryside flashed by. Jean-Pierre looked across at Odette, who sat in the passenger seat, holding Vanessa and Sandra. He was content not to talk and relieved to find that Odette was preoccupied with pacifying the children who were anxious about being in a car. One thought circled through his head – again and again: this was why I didn't die. So I could find them.

Nyamirambo was empty. Jean-Pierre and Odette carried the children into Ernest's house and closed the door behind them. They didn't leave for two days. There was enough food only for the children, but Jean-Pierre and Odette were content to watch them eat. He told Odette little about the last three months of his life, preferring to ask her questions. She explained how twenty miles from Kibuye they had been turned around by RPF soldiers and told to walk back to Gitarama. It had taken a week to reach her father's house, and she had found it ransacked and deserted. Mukaruziga had returned to her house nearby. There was no hint of what had happened to her parents. Most of the townspeople had fled, but there were some families who had not participated in the killings who had decided to stay. A week after she had returned one of the remaining neighbours told her what had happened. A few hours after Odette left for Kabgayi hospital back in April, the local politician who had protected them fled west, to Gisenyi – fearful of the invading Tutsi rebel army and what they might do to a man in his position. Odette's family lost the protection that had kept them alive until then. That same evening her father, Bernard, and a son-in-law, Bosco, were taken from outside their home and walked to the end of their street where they were hacked to death. The gang then returned and dragged Odette's mother, Joséphine, and grandmother, Euphrasie, to a nearby house. That night of 18 April, Joséphine was raped by several men, before she and her aged mother were murdered the following morning.

Jean-Pierre didn't know what had happened to his own

parents but he had heard at St André that Tutsis in Kibuye had been targeted with equal ferocity by extremists. When he thought back to his journey to Gitarama, he realized that even though part of him had been unsure what he would find, there was a strong sense that Odette and his children would be alive. Why else would he have survived nearly three months in a disused cesspit? But when it came to thinking about his father and mother, no such instinct existed. Kibuye seemed far away, a lakeside town separated from the rest of Rwanda by unforgiving mountains and cold white mist. He knew that if killers had come to the door of his father's house he would have walked out to meet them and told them that he was a doctor, that he'd been born in this village fifty-seven years before and he had returned to Kibuye to work at the hospital and help the sick. His father was dead. Jean-Pierre knew that now.

He watched Odette and his children sleep. He did not know what would happen next. But this is what he thought: I am still here; you have killed my father and my mother, and you have tried to kill me, but I am still here. I am Muganga Joseph's son and if you want to kill me, remember I have children and one day they will have children too.

This is my country.

PART II

2004

'And so I came back
You did not know, did you
That one can come back from there.'

Charlotte Delbo, *Auschwitz and After*

CHAPTER EIGHT

Goma, Democratic Republic of the Congo

His name, he tells me, after we had established that we were
to be friends, was François-Xavier. I ask him for a business
card. He takes my pencil from me and writes, slowly but
neatly, in firm block capitals, in my notepad.

CIRIMWAMI BUHENDWA FRANÇOIS-XAVIER.
HÔTEL DES GRANDS LACS. GOMA. B.P. 253.

He had caught up with me on the veranda, where I sat on the
rusting springs of an old, cushionless garden chair, just by
the crumbling front steps of the hotel. There was a gleam of
sweat on his handsome, oval face, despite the shade that we
stood in and the pillowy, cool draughts of the early morning
that were trapped under the awning. Motes of dust and
small flies dipped and flared as they bounced between the
shade and the muted, oblique sunlight. I stood up awkwardly
as he scrutinized me. Half an hour earlier – just before
dawn – I had crossed from Rwanda into Congo, the former
Zaire, and walked through the front gates of the hotel. I

had wandered into the decayed foyer, the porter asleep on a blanket behind his desk; I had moved down empty corridors, preoccupied and detached – rather like a visitor who has slipped, unplanned, into an art gallery – mooching slowly through each space, a half-critical eye sizing up each room, each dark corner.

François-Xavier explains that he is the hotel manager and that I have been seen acting strangely. (In this part of Congo everyone is watched.) He wants to know who I am. Do I want a room?

'No. I just want to look around. Not to stay.'

His face baulks. A deepening frown like a spoilt schoolboy's. Behind us, the janitor pushes old crackly leaves into a corner of the steps – only a few tufts remain on his battered broom. The veranda furniture is as I remember it. Rusted chairs, sprung with rigid metal bars. A few still have plastic seat bottoms and backs, but they are ravaged – the plastic split, the foam spilling out. The paint on the gable above the entrance is flaking away. Inexplicably, some of the foot-high Gothic letters of the hotel's name have been rubbed out.

ÔTEL DES RANDS ACS

The janitor wanders off, up the steps, his broom dragging behind him, a faithful dog with a bad case of mange. I try to explain.

'I was here,' I tell François-Xavier. 'Ten years ago. I spent many days living in this hotel.'

He pauses – counting the years back. *'Le génocide?'*

I nod. François-Xavier smiles. Crinkles spread around his

eyes and mouth and, for the first time, I see that he is a much older man than I had first thought. He tells me that he was here then. Just an assistant manager in those days, of course. He looks keenly at me. So I had really stayed here?

'Yes,' I tell him. This had been my home. *'Mon réfuge.'*

It was at this point that we had introduced ourselves and he had written his name down for me. We begin a tour of the hotel. Down dark corridors and tiled floors to the inner courtyard – a small square patch of grass – on to which the rooms of the two-storey building open. Wild, blood-red roses cling to the tatty plaster and wind themselves around concrete pillars, the paint distempered, patches of damp smudged on every wall. We sit on a step.

He is lucky to still have the hotel, François-Xavier tells me. Most of Goma had been destroyed by *'la catastrophe'*. He shakes his head slowly and begins to draw circles with his finger in the dust. This, I guess, is a reference to the latest disaster to befall Goma. A vast river of lava that, two years earlier, with almost embarrassed decorum, flowed from the Mount Nyiragongo volcano twelve miles west through Goma before it slurped, vanquished, into the deep waters of Lake Kivu. When it arrived at the outskirts of town the lava flow had paused, as if unsure which way to go, before opting for the main street, through which it slid, coyly, engorging cars, shops, the post office, the police station and the Catholic cathedral, but leaving the little gabled hotel, and the wide boulevard that runs down to the border post, untouched. 'There is little electricity and water these days,' he says. 'But we make do.'

My companion brings out a stack of toothpicks. He offers me one – 'no, thanks' – and begins quietly to work away, sucking air tightly through his teeth. Was I here when the Hutu came? I nod. He shakes his head again. 'That was the beginning of the end for this town,' he says.

Finally, François-Xavier draws himself up, explaining that he has work to do, but that if I want good coffee I should go to the Masques Hotel round the corner. Lebanese-owned, their contacts with the local authorities mean they get a dependable water supply. He shrugs. They have better coffee beans, too. At the entrance he stops and, spotting the pile of dust and leaves left earlier on the steps, shouts for the janitor. I sit back against the pillar, wedging my shoulder blades against its narrowness. Insects hum across the courtyard. Outside, the high-pitched drone of motor scooters. A new day. I place my palms flat on the cool stone steps and close my eyes.

The night before, in Rwanda, on a hill overlooking Congo, I had imagined this moment. The sun had set quietly, with little fuss, behind Goma – just a few hundred yards away. I could see the border post. Soldiers were draped over the barrier, smoking. The sun weakened. The shimmer over Lake Kivu faded and the waters subsided into darkness. There was nothing, I told myself then, that was forcing me to make this return journey. Nothing, either, that suggested it would make any difference.

Sunlight creeps slowly into the courtyard; sharp lines across the faded paint, a negative-positive of light and shade. I can hear François-Xavier's echoed, tetchy reprimands to the janitor. If I close my eyes, the memories of the events here swirl into vague and comfortable fragments that swoon and then disappear amongst the prickles and translucent splodges of light almost as quickly as they have arrived. But with my eyes open, I am forced to unpick what happened, frame by frame, a stream of still photographs, each with an accompanying set of notes detailing time, place and person. Exhibits for a courtroom. Glints of light catch in my eyes. Soak them. Kaleidoscopic colours refract and shift in front of me. Reds, yellows, dark greens. And voices.

This is what happened.

We decided that we would leave Rwanda, and on 11 July 1994 we crossed into Zaire in anticipation of a large number of Hutu refugees who were now on the run. Goma was quiet. The cool, lakeside town – a popular retreat for President Mobutu and his cronies from the corrupted stench of Kinshasa – seemed to be holding its breath, bracing itself for the rumoured arrival of an unknown number of Rwandans.

We – that is, Robin, Greg, Trevor and I – checked into the small Hôtel des Grands Lacs, decrepit even then. It sat next to the main road that we guessed the refugees would have to walk down once they had crossed the border. It was a wide boulevard – perhaps fifty yards across – with a generous and well-tended grassy strip down the middle. We sat around, drank coffee and waited. Wondering just who and how many would have made the decision to flee northwards to Goma rather than south, to the bottom end of Lake Kivu, to Bukavu.

By then, the genocide in Rwanda was at an end. Massacre sites – such as the one we had seen at Nyarubuye a few days earlier – were being discovered throughout the country. Western politicians gravely pronounced that the architects of the genocide would be found and tried, at an international criminal court, for the extermination of the Tutsi people.

Except the Tutsis had not been exterminated – Western governments were wrong about that, just as they had been wrong about pretty well everything else since the genocide began in April. People had survived. Thousands were beginning to emerge from their hiding places, from under floorboards and behind eaves in the *secteurs* of Kigali and Butare, from the cesspits and sewers of Ruhengeri and Byumba in the north, from the stinking swamps around the Akagera river, from under the shadowed canopy and damp mulch of the Nyungwe forest, and from behind the barbed-wire encampments in Kibuye, Cyangugu and Gitarama, where they had sat like hemmed-in cattle. Now, they had begun the slow, numbing walk back to their homes.

Perhaps as they neared their towns and villages they would breathe in the clouds of dust left by the thousands of Hutus who had fled only hours before. The exiled Hutu government boasted that the great swathe of people charging for the Zairean border would soon reconstitute and, along with the surviving elements of the army, ready themselves for a victorious return. But I didn't believe it. For three months these people had immersed themselves in wholesale slaughter and they knew the extent of their crime.

I could see it in the faces of the first straggle of refugees who arrived early that afternoon in Goma. There were fifty of them. They pushed wooden carts and wheelbarrows, piled to mountainous peaks with their belongings. Men were balancing rusted sheets of metal pulled from the roofs of their houses or pushing bicycles – so many bicycles. Children, dragged from their hillside villages, were hauling jerrycans and sacks of flour on wooden carts. Mothers were carrying babies wrapped – front and back – under filthy shawls. These people had packed for a long absence. They pushed forward, refusing to be distracted, staring rigidly ahead. There were no longing looks back towards their homeland. They looked fearful, close to panic, and were consoled, I wilfully imagined, only by their collective guilt over what they had left behind.

No one paid us any attention. The power and arrogance of only a few weeks earlier, while manning their roadblocks, the insouciant violence as they battered away with their machetes. All this had gone. They were desperate to escape their past and leave it in what was now a foreign country.

By three o'clock, the early straggle had become a stream and then a deluge of dirt-stained humanity. It was difficult to estimate how many had passed us, but for two hours now we had watched a crush of refugees traipse from the border, and there was still no end in sight. The road and its grassy strip had disappeared from view. The weight of people had even bent metal signposts to the ground. The pace slowed, from a steady plod to a weary shuffle. A journalist standing next to me muttered as he wrote in his notebook.

'Killers.'

The killers that I had seen in Rwanda were the army, the police, thuggish young men at the roadblocks. Not old women, who walked past us now on gnarled sticks, children bound on to their backs with tattered cloth.

'Not all, surely.'

'Well, if they didn't actually kill, then they're accomplices. And they're just walking away from the scene of the crime.'

The sun burnt. Bright, white light beat down on this zombified mass. I had a metallic taste in my mouth. The atmosphere graduated from crushed acceptance to murmured

disgruntlement. The afternoon heat, the terrible slowness –
many were dehydrated. Some dropped to their knees where
they were knocked and bashed by those behind them.
Children were crying. A woman dangled, hopelessly, a dirty
cup at us. Eyes lowered, back bent, she begged us for water.

We plunged into the river of people. The smell and heat
were overpowering. We were swept along, arms flattened
against our sides in the crush, our cameras cracking into
heads, widened, bloodshot eyes turning on us, yelps of surprise. The problem – the cause of this crush – lay just ahead.
Zairean soldiers had arrived and were beating the refugees
with wooden canes, pushing them away from the avenues
that led into town towards a narrower road that by-passed
Goma.

Two hundred thousand people were now massed on the
road, from the border to the main roundabout a mile away,
where the Zairean army stood with their sticks. Two hundred
thousand people shuffling along a single road, hemmed in
on either side by angry Goma residents – who warned off
intruders with guns and axes – and then forced to slow to a
grinding shuffle by vicious, cane-whirling soldiers who lay
waiting for them. In the hour that we walked with them,
we moved no more than a hundred yards from the hotel
driveway. As the bottleneck grew (by now it must have been
close to four in the afternoon) we heard the throat-clearing
growl of diesel engines. The noise grew closer. Behind us a
number of large green trucks loomed up. The convoy sounded
its horns and revved its engines, bullying and goading the
refugees to stand clear. These were the remnants of the
defeated Rwandan army.

Until now there had been a kind of meek, bovine momentum to the refugees' progress. But when they heard the shouts, the blasts of whistles, the crackle of gunfire from behind them, they began to panic. The problem was that there was no room. All they could do was bump and crash into those walking right next to them. The mass on the road started to sway and lurch dangerously as thousands struggled to avoid the vast army trucks that churned their way through.

Dozens of soldiers clung on to the sides of the lorries, others sat on the engine hoods, waving Rwandan flags. They screamed at the people below them, a furious, feral, drunk, beaten and humiliated army, forced to flee in front of their own people. The closer they got to the bottleneck, the more they had to slow down. This just made them angrier. Zairean forces were supposed to have disarmed them at the border, but many Rwandan soldiers still carried AK-47 rifles which they now used to beat people out of their path. A man, too weak to push his cart out of the way, was felled by a rifle butt, the cart crushed under the massive tyres of a truck. The soldiers who sat on top thought this was hilarious. An old woman tripped under the wheels of a lorry – her family was driven on, unable to stop for her. 'I can't get the camera on my shoulder,' Greg shouted, clutching it in a bear hug amongst the crush of people. The heat and mass of the crowd boiled around us. I grabbed at shoulders and arms to keep my balance. Sweaty faces loomed in front of me and then lurched away. Foul breath. A few shots rang out. Then more – as soldiers fired their automatic weapons into the air in an act of defiance; a pointless, infantile demonstration of power.

Peering through the bodies I saw a small boy – perhaps nine years old – pick up a hand grenade. I moved Greg away and felt the crack of a knuckled hand on the back of my head. A soldier was shouting at me from a truck, his eyes creamy-yellow. Drunk and angry and stoned. The soldier's truck drove on, bouncing people from its rusted fenders, but he was still looking back and pointing at me, still screaming, '*Anglais – FPR! Anglais – FPR!*' The diesel engine revved furiously. The truck barged its way forward, the soldier's voice finally drowned out as the lorry disappeared.

A loud metallic clang and then screams. We squeezed through the crush. I couldn't see Robin any more. Trevor – big South African forearms – grabbed my collar and hauled me past the body of the little boy. He had lost most of his head. It lay flattened, like a rubber mask, dripping into the gutter. Three other people lay on the ground. 'Move!' Trevor shouted. We were swept up in the dense heat, the ordure. I could see a gap on my right, saw Greg and pulled him over with me – crashing into people, carts, wrestling past children – head bowed, the edge of the road close now; I rammed forward and caught a woman square on her chin with my elbow. Her head snapped back. She dropped her plastic water container as she cried out. And then she was gone, before I could turn, disappearing. I followed Greg as he threw himself out of the road into a small garden. He had scratches down his chest and his shirt was torn.

'I can't get any decent shots. I need some elevation.'

I said, 'Forget elevation, we need to follow the Rwandan soldiers.' When we reached the hotel we found an expatriate Frenchman who lived in Goma. He lent us his VW van and a driver. I sat in the front, next to the driver, who was called Anicet. He wore a khaki safari shirt and tattered shorts. Robin sat on a single seat just behind him. He pressed his face into the window. Behind him sat Greg and Trevor – Greg clutching his camera to his chest, Trevor curling his sound cables into a neatly bunched circle that he could Velcro to the side of his recorder. Anicet trembled as he gripped the clutch – an old-fashioned lever that came out horizontally from the dashboard. His feet pressed frantically at the pedals. The car shuddered and leapt forward out of the hotel entrance, bumping into people. I shouted at the driver to turn right but we were hemmed in by a crush of refugees. Anicet tried to move off, but his clutch control was terrible and he lurched forward, throwing the car at the crowds that swarmed around us. I yelled at him to stop. Faces peered at us as we sat there, our car washed up by this human tide.

'This is pointless. We'll never get through. Let's find a back road.'

Then the rear door slid open. Two soldiers jumped in. My door, too, was thrown open and I found myself being pushed towards Anicet who stared past me, his hands frozen on the steering wheel. A woman, soaked in sweat, had joined us in the front and was sitting in my seat. I was jammed between her and Anicet. She drew a large pistol and pointed it first at Anicet, screaming at him to drive on, and then at me, where it remained. She wore camouflage. The red flashes on her shoulders identified her as FAZ – Forces Armées Zaïroises. Anicet had begun to shake and the woman yelled at him again. I tried to put my hand on Anicet's but she screamed at me and waved her pistol – so close now that its snubby foresight and greasy barrel were out of focus. 'OK, OK,' I said. I watched Anicet grind desperately through the gears. We passed Corinne, a photographer I knew. She was surrounded by angry Rwandan soldiers who had clambered off their truck. She was wearing the red kitten heels that I had teased her about. Two of her cameras were slung around her shoulders, the third pointed at several more soldiers who were striding towards her, raising their weapons. Then she was gone from sight and we had veered off the main road.

Anicet drove very badly. The van lurched with every gear change. This made the FAZ woman even more furious. She shouted instructions at him and we drove out of town, away from the swarm. I looked behind me. One of the soldiers was staring at Greg and his camera. The other seemed to be in a trance. He had his thumb hooked through the loop of a hand grenade and was sliding the firing pin out of its hole, back and forth, back and forth.

Luscious ovals of sweat had formed on the woman's top lip – we were squeezed very close together – and her eyes were bright and very red. She reeked of alcohol. Robin was grinding his back teeth, rigidly staring out of the side window. Greg and Trevor sat together, looking at me. Trevor grimaced and gently began to shake his head. We drove into green countryside. On either side of the road lay thick bush.

I turned and tried to talk to the woman. She wore vivid scarlet lipstick, creamily smeared on to her mouth. My attempts at conversation seemed to amuse her and she threw a comment behind her for the two soldiers. In the mirror I could see them blink slowly, their eyes glazed. '*Uhhh*,' they said. A stoned, low murmur. Anicet stalled the car again. More screaming from the woman. Anicet began to weep. 'Don't worry,' I told him, 'everything will be OK.' He looked at me as if I were mad. His whole body shook.

We emerged from the forest and found ourselves on a road that hugged the shore of Lake Kivu.

The woman turned towards me. 'You are journalists,' she

said. It was more of a statement than a question. But then she asked where we were from. This was difficult. Zaire had long sympathized with the Hutu regime in Kigali. Britain had not. I didn't want her to misunderstand. 'We are the BBC,' I told her, 'not the British government.' She turned and stared at us. 'English?' she asked. She had a tight bun of rich sleek hair, scraped back and shiny, and her mouth, I noticed, if you could get past the lipstick, was wide and sensuous. It seemed, to me at least, that the further we drove down this road, the more important it was to try and make some kind of connection. I told her my name and asked for hers. 'Elizabeth.' I tried another question – so many people, what did she think. She ignored my question and asked her own.

'*Vous aimez le Tutsi?*'

'No, no,' I said. 'We are journalists. We don't take sides.'

Elizabeth looked at me and translated what I had said for the soldiers in the back. '*Uhhh*,' one said again. The other carried on sliding the pin of the grenade in and out.

We cornered sharply – Anicet late into the bend again – and Elizabeth shouted for him to stop. We lurched violently to the right and stalled. Plumes of dust clouded us. We were on a small road. Thick bush on either side. The van sat, exhausted, its engine still creaking. In the mirror I could see Robin grinding his molars. The side door was violently wrenched back. Elizabeth snapped at the soldiers and they jumped out. She was struggling with the latch on her door. I reached across. My bare arm rested on her camouflaged thigh, which was soaking wet.

As she climbed out she shouted – not at her men, but into the bush. Three soldiers emerged and greeted Elizabeth.

They stood on the road looking back at us as she spoke. They talked among themselves for some minutes. Then they all began to walk away.

'Do you think we can go?' asked Greg, as we watched them move towards the bush. His voice was a surprise. None of us had spoken for several minutes. His face was completely white.

Robin squinted at the backs of the soldiers. 'I think we were just a taxi.'

We carried on watching the soldiers walk into a bank of green vegetation, slowly dissolving. Good camouflage, was what I thought.

Greg was not sure about leaving. 'If we try and drive away, they may just open fire. I mean, they didn't say, "You can go."'

The engine *tick-tick-ticked* in the silence. I could hear Anicet breathing heavily. Our feet scraped noisily on the metal floor as, for the first time in this journey, we felt able to move. Trevor shifted his sound gear into the boot, swearing quietly to himself. I gazed into the dense undergrowth looking for Elizabeth, her wide, libidinous mouth. But we were entirely alone now.

'I agree with Robin. I think we can go.'

That night, back at the hotel, I sat on the floor of the corridor with Corinne, my photographer friend. Outside, refugees had given up walking and had sat down on the road. Gunfire crackled around us. We agreed that it had been a bad day. I complained that I was sick of Rwanda, the violence and the fear. She told me how in Sarajevo she had broken down one day, taking pictures after a bomb had exploded in a marketplace. A photographer friend had run up to her and said, 'Corinne, stop crying, look down your camera lens and just do your job.'

At dawn we joined the heaving torrent that had picked itself up and resumed its wearisome walk into the Zairean bush. A Red Cross official stood counting the refugees – sixty thousand, he thought, were passing every half-hour. Robin began to stop people and ask them why they were leaving, where they were going, would they return. They looked bewildered by his questions; poor, ill-educated peasant farmers staring into a camera, struggling to understand this *umuzungu*.

The crowd around us grew larger, curious about this gaggle of men and television equipment. They edged in on us. Three men – who were armed with a rifle and machetes – elbowed their way to the front. I recognized their type from Rwandan roadblocks during the genocide. They were unemployed, brutish, semi-literate young men who had sat, angry and listless, for years, in Habyarimana's Rwanda. But for the planners of the genocide they were ideal blue-collar murderers.

Now we were the ones being asked questions. 'Journalists,' we said. 'BBC.' '*Anglais?*' they asked. Behind the group of three stood a small boy. I smiled at him. He looked back at me impassively.

'*Anglais? Eh? Eh?*'

Each *eh?* grew louder, more insistent. The men pitched on to their toes, leaning forward. There were now perhaps thirty people around us. The questioning became more theatrical. The three began to play to the crowd. It was as though they were back in Rwanda again, back on their roadblock, all-powerful. The people around them sensed that too, listening quietly to the performance.

'BBC? *Eh? EH?!*'

Behind them a man shouted something into the din. One of the three turned round and spoke angrily to the new arrival. It stirred the crowd into a debate – the murmur among them grew louder, other voices chipping in with their opinions. I wondered whether the man was speaking on our behalf, but he might just as easily have been encouraging the three at the front. Robin tried to talk but was shouted down.

'*Vous aimez le Tutsi? Eh? Eh? Inyenzi? Les Anglais? Vous aimez FPR?*'

The murmurs grew louder and the men's barked questions became more frenzied. They were stoking themselves up. The crowd moved back: if a debate had been going on about us, it was over now. The man who had spoken up had been silenced by the force of the three men who jabbed their weapons at us.

I looked across at a newspaper journalist, Chris, who had come out with us on to the road. He was a small, pale man but now he seemed almost ghostly. He caught no one's eye and said nothing, staring out through the crowd at an illusory middle distance. He seemed to be disappearing in front of my eyes – disassociating himself from us. His eyes said, these guys with their TV equipment and their chat are going to get killed but nobody will see me. I am going to survive. The small boy had pulled out a wooden stick and pointed it at me, squinting down it as though it were the barrel of a pistol.

It didn't seem possible for the confrontation to last much longer. The men's anger was sharply honed, uninterrupted, channelled directly at us. The audience seemed expectant. They had lost interest in us. They just watched the three men to see what they were going to do next. Inside my chest I felt the now familiar sensation in my ribs, as if a bubble of air had been trapped inside, pressing urgently on me. But when I opened my mouth I couldn't release it. It remained anchored in my chest, squeezing the breath out of me.

Next to me, Trevor reached into his pocket and pulled out his passport. 'No, no!' he shouted. 'I am South African. *Sud-Africain.*' The three stopped barking. Trevor waved the passport in their faces. '*Sud-Africain.* Nelson Mandela, Nelson Mandela!' He reached his arms around our shoulders, pulling us together. His beefy white forearms were spotted with insect bites. 'Friends. *Mes frères.*' I tightened my grip around his waist. The men looked at his passport and laughed. 'Mandela,' they shouted. 'Mandela!' The crowd gathered closer, peering in at the passport. They looked at the three men and laughed and shouted, 'Mandela!' We raised our fists, Mandela style. 'Mandela!' we all shouted. 'Mandela!' Then the three walked through us and were gone.

It took less than a minute for us to get back to the hotel. The other journalists had left. A mortar had exploded close to the border post. Many refugees were said to have been killed. Robin flagged down a jeep that was on its way down to the bombsite. It was blue, with a small cab and an open, flatbed back. 'Let's go,' he shouted. 'Where will we all sit?' I asked. 'One in the front, three on the back,' he replied. I felt my head shaking but Robin had already turned and was helping Trevor put his sound equipment in the rear of the jeep.

'No, Robin,' I heard myself say. 'This is too risky. Up front is OK, but the guys in the back are just sitting targets.'

'It's fine, David. Don't be silly.'

'No, it's not. It's not fine. Anyone could take a shot or lob a grenade in.'

'No one's going to do that. We'll be driving fast. Come on, let's go.'

Robin turned again and began to get into the front of the car. I hadn't moved. Out on the road I could see the heaving refugees trudge past.

'It's not safe. We need to find another car which is covered – which we can all sit in. We can't go in this.'

Robin's teeth were grinding as he climbed out and began to prowl around the back of the flatbed. Greg and Trevor stood and watched us. This was no longer a conversation; we were having an argument.

'This is ridiculous. Come on. We need to go NOW!'

'No.'

'Look, OK. I'll get in the back and we'll squeeze two in the front.'

I looked out at the road again. I had a strange sensation, of my vision clouding, darkening at the edges. All I could now see was this jeep and the four of us. And the driver – the Frenchman who had lent us Anicet and the VW van the day before – who had begun to shout at us to get a move on. Robin muttered and continued his prowling. Greg looked at me. Come on, his look seemed to say, make a decision for us.

'We'll wait for another truck, we can just wait—'

'There are no other trucks, David. We have to leave now, now, *now*!'

Robin helped Trevor on to the flatbed. Greg climbed up as well. Robin got in the front. He leaned out of the window. 'Come on,' he said to me, 'get in.' But I was no longer with them; I was wrapped in a cold layer that left me shivering, an early morning chill. I shook my head. My words seemed musty and stale, sour-tasting. They began with imperatives, *we have to . . . we must . . .* but they tailed off, dwindling out of shape.

'Are you coming with us or not?'

I told them I wasn't. I told them it was safer if there were only two on the back, not three.

Robin turned and told the Frenchman he could leave. The truck drove out of the hotel driveway into the road. Robin stared straight ahead. The truck nudged into the swarm of refugees. Trevor busied himself with his equipment, but Greg stared back at me, watching me, until his face disappeared, absorbed into a thousand other faces, blurred and, then, gone.

A man from the UN came up to me. I had stayed, rigidly fixed, to the spot where Robin and I had argued. The man was talking about the crisis: no resources, no water, no shelter. I had no idea what I was saying in response. I could feel my mouth moving. It may well have been a normal conversation; I had no way of knowing because I couldn't hear anything I said. But he must have been happy with the answers that I was giving because he kept talking to me.

I walked to my room and sat on my bed. Then I got up and tried to splash water on my face but I had forgotten there was no water. My hands were twisting the rusted taps of the basin, but in my head I was watching the truck drive away, seeing Greg's face looking back at me.

I found myself walking back out of the hotel entrance – it might have been fifteen minutes later, it could have been an hour, I had no way of knowing – to see a Red Cross jeep hurtling out towards the road. I screamed at them to stop and bundled myself into the back. It tore down to the border post. In the back were three medics, trading drips and syringes between their bags. The driver was called Marc. He crashed the car through the crowds, horn blaring, until we arrived at the spot where the mortar had exploded.

Most of the dead – perhaps forty – had been laid out near the road, close to the border post. The refugees must have been terrified of going back towards their former country and, in their panic, had run in the opposite direction, across a small field of maize. At the far end was a broken-down wall. At its foot lay more bodies – at least sixty – of those who had been the first to arrive at the wall but were then crushed into the rough stonework by the hundreds who had followed them. The pressure of the people had caused the wall to collapse partially. Back at the mortar site, many of the injured were still being treated. A woman was propped against a tree, legs heaved up, as if giving birth. Her pelvis protruded out of her, a shiny white bone, indecently clean against her muddy red shawl. Beside her, a young girl sat staring at the medics. The medics tried to move the woman, but she shrieked in pain and blood rushed out of her wound, pouring down into her lap. There was a brief conversation. One medic lifted the little girl up and carried her to the jeep. The girl's chin was propped on the nurse's shoulder – she stared back at the woman by the tree but she didn't cry out. The other medic bent and gave the woman small sips of water. Ten feet away lay a small papoose, the kind that mothers wrap their babies in before tying them to their backs. It lay abandoned, adrift amongst the lost belongings and torn pieces of body. I called to the medic and we walked slowly over. The cotton was old and soft, frayed at the edges. I looked back at the dying woman by the tree. She was staring at the papoose.

'I think this belongs to her.'

The medic looked first at me and then towards the woman by the tree. She was young, the medic, with a strand of fair hair that had fallen loose when she bent over the bundle of cloth. She kept trying to hook it behind her ear. We knelt down, rocked back on to our haunches. 'I'll look,' I said. But her hands reached over to the loose flap of cotton and she gently lifted it up. A small face looked up at us, bright black eyes, that blinked, unfocused, a mouth pinched into a tiny 'O' of surprise. She ripped off the cloth, her hands moved quickly around the boy's body before she scooped him up and ran to the truck. The woman by the tree watched as the baby was wrapped in a blanket and placed inside the truck. The medic yelled to me. Did I want a lift? I told her I would walk.

There were fewer people making their way up the road now – most, I guessed, had already crossed the border. I joined the last few hundred or so. Some came up to me, shouting angrily. I felt strong, almost invincible – I took giant powerful strides. Hands grabbed at me. I ripped them away. I roared at those who challenged me, 'Back off, you fuckers. *You fucking fuckers!*' In this way I walked the mile back to the hotel.

Greg and Trevor were sitting on the veranda. Robin had gone to my room, Greg said, and wanted to start editing the footage. He got up and asked if I was OK. I told him I was absolutely fine. Trevor sat at a small table, staring intensely at his sound cables, wiping the mud from them with an old cloth. They had only spent ten minutes down at the mortar site filming, Greg said, before heading off down the lakeshore road. There was a rumour that a whole battalion of Hutu soldiers were readying themselves for a counter-attack. But they had been unable to find any evidence of the soldiers and, after an hour of fruitless driving, had returned to the hotel. They had got back fifteen minutes ago. Behind Greg, I could see Marc, the Red Cross driver, and two of the medics sitting at another table. A waiter arrived at Trevor's table carrying two cups of coffee.

'I'll pay for these,' I said to Greg.

'No, you're all right, mate.'

I struggled with my backpack to get it open, my hands wrestled with the junk inside, scrabbling to find my wallet.

Greg waved me away and handed the waiter a few notes. Trevor had finished cleaning his cables. He leaned forward in his chair and began to take small sips from his cup.

'How are you, Trevor?'

'I'm good.'

It was the first time I had heard him speak since dawn, when he had raised his fist and shouted 'Mandela!' at the armed men. He drank his coffee quietly. Now that he had leaned forward, I couldn't see his face properly.

'Trevor, I just want to say—'

'Yeah, what do you want to say?'

Greg came over to me. 'You're fine, mate. Really. Don't worry about it.'

Across from us, I could see the blonde medic and Marc were sharing a joke, her head tipped back in laughter. Trevor turned and watched them, still sipping his coffee. Greg put a hand on my shoulder and smiled. I turned and walked up the steps of the hotel – my back to the road, where the last few refugees were struggling past – towards the dark corridor and my room.

The coffee at the Masques Hotel is as good as François-Xavier said it would be. A fan whirrs above me, keeping the lounge uncomfortably cool. Two Uruguayan UN officers sit nearby – their table awash with documents, their Zippo lighters and tax-free cigarettes placed strategically, as paperweights, against the fan's downdraught. The arrival in 1994 of a million Rwandan refugees into what was once known as Zaire, but became the Democratic Republic of the Congo three years later, was a precursor to a war in this country that has left more than two million dead in the ten years since the genocide, and Goma still acts as a way station for the international force that attempts to mediate – mostly ineffectually – between the warring factions.

The Uruguayans' uniforms have been carefully pressed, the creases sharp. My father would approve. As would my stepfather. Both had been naval officers, spending half their lives in submarines, shadowing the Soviet fleet – warriors of the Cold War. When my stepfather returned from sea he used to sit on my bed and read to me – Kipling's *Just So Stories* were our favourite – his skin pale green from weeks of living without daylight, his body still reeking of engine oil despite the long, deep baths my mother had drawn for him. He never talked about his time at sea. His journeys were secret and the code he lived by was strict. Duty and responsibility to Queen and country acted like a thermostat on his emotions.

Not long after my mother remarried, we went on a camping holiday to Devon. We swam in a freezing river; at least, my stepfather swam. I clung on to his back, my skinny six-year-old arms gripping his shoulders, my fingers digging into him, crab-like. From the bank my mother called anxiously to us as we steamed slowly off towards a deep pool in the middle of the river. 'It's *fine*,' I remember my stepfather saying, a note of exasperation in his voice at my mother's fussing, 'he's all right.' His back seemed vast – a great slab of white, like the deck of an aircraft carrier, on top of which I was perched. And I *was* all right. There was not a moment when I didn't feel completely secure. I had no doubt that if the river turned into a raging torrent, sucking me downwards, his great bearish forearms would pull me to safety, long before he had any thought for himself.

In Goma, the morning sun warms my back as I leave the Masques and begin to walk down the long road that leads to the border. A few bicyclists, a woman hurrying with an empty basket towards the market, otherwise it is quiet. The lamp posts – back then, bent double by the deluge of people – have been replaced. A half-hearted attempt has been made to repair the wall where the refugees had been crushed. The mortar site itself is overgrown, a scrubby patch of tufted grass. A few Congolese shout out to me. I wave back at them and carry on walking. I draw near to where Trevor had pulled out his passport. He is dead now. The new South Africa that he had proudly proclaimed to the thugs that day had, apparently, been too confusing for him and he took his own life a year later. Greg is God knows where, and Robin I see occasionally. We reminisce – but he never mentions that morning by the hotel and neither do I. An impotent, blank space exists between us.

I reach the shore of the lake. It shimmers in the brightening heat. I sit on a crumbling concrete step and look back across at Rwanda. I think of Vjeko Curic – how he remained defiant throughout the genocide while so many in the West, including me, had not. At first it had seemed easy to forget about him: for a few short days, in a place a long way away, I had known him a little. But perhaps, too, it was more convenient to disengage with the past. When I finally left Rwanda that summer and returned home, I probably mentioned him to a few people – a strange priest who defied the *génocidaires* and saved the lives of thousands of Rwandans – but I didn't linger, preferring to shrug off Curic and the memories of Rwanda like a dog shaking water off its coat. Then I heard the news of his assassination – shot in 1998 in his beloved white jeep on a Kigali side street. It had been a shock. Curic had seemed indestructible.

The dawn mist, which had curled around the hills like steam swirling off a coffee cup when I walked across the border earlier this morning, has gone. And now, even though it is still early, the heat has begun to bleach out the fields – the crumpled, green-shadowed softness ironed into a hard, flat yellow by the sun. I wonder who killed Curic and why. In the intervening years between the end of the genocide and his death, Curic would have walked the same paths and ministered to the same people who, back in '94, were part of a world that had become morally inverted. Back then, he had been a potent figure – empowered by the scale of the chaos and his belief that he could change people's lives. What he experienced in those few months would not have left him, and I need to understand how Curic coped in this new Rwanda, magnetized, as he was, by what he had endured. The past, I had begun to realize, is always with us, and even as it recedes in time, its presence deepens and grows stronger.

*

Jean-Pierre is waiting for me across the border. He sits solidly on the bonnet of his Toyota and looks at his watch, shaking his head. 'You're crazy,' he says. 'Wandering into Congo like that.' I climb in. 'Did you find the hotel?' he asks. I nod. We skirt around the shore of Lake Kivu. A group of small boys plunge into the water – their skinny bodies gleaming, kicking water cruelly at one boy, who stands alone, shielding his face, as if in prayer. I tell Jean-Pierre about my morning. That it had felt as though I were back in 1994.

'Everything was the same. In my head, too.'

Jean-Pierre nods. 'Of course. Everything is still here. Everywhere.'

We say the last word – *everywhere* – together and laugh. The Toyota slowly climbs into the hills above the lake. I can still just see the boys – small pencil drawings, dancing and jumping, knee-deep in the water. Behind them, the low, splattered sprawl of Goma. Glints of sharp, metalled light reflect off corrugated roofs. Ahead, a long grey curve, and then the lake, and the town, disappear from sight.

CHAPTER NINE

Kigali

We rattle down the road through Kacyiru, swerving past overladen *mutatus* which lurch stupidly out from their lay-bys – gobs of diesel exploding from their back ends – and put some distance between ourselves and the hotel. Past the Gisozi Memorial – its grey roof barely visible through the thick cloud – and south-west, down towards Nyabugogo and the city gates. Stalled traffic by the Apex Hotel, which lurches over us like a smashed wedding cake, the balconies strewn with washing from its semi-permanent guests – *Gastarbeiter* road crews, away from the city right now, thirty miles north, their lean refulgent bodies smeared in tarmac. With the Gitarama turn-off in sight, we sweep past a building site. A gaggle of pink-pyjamaed *génocidaires* hang from its wooden exoskeleton, sharing a smoke. They loom up in my cracked side mirror, pinned to their scaffolding.

Out of the city. Five miles following the Nyabarongo river and then upwards, climbing for twenty minutes, from the valley's cold, grey murk, before we reach the summit and a sharp prism of afternoon light bounces different colours through our windscreen, blinding us as we plunge into a new valley, its green wedges of undergrowth seared red by the thick earth of the newly ploughed terraces. I turn to Jean-Pierre and clap my hand on his shoulder. It feels good to be leaving Kigali.

All morning I had sat in the hotel and watched black roiling clouds loom up, enveloping the hills to the east and throwing a malevolent shadow over the city. It had, I felt sure, added to the numbing discontent that had overtaken me. Sharp, bitter gusts had blown through the covered patio, sending the waiters scurrying after paper cloths that flapped off the tables like angry seagulls. I sat, drinking lukewarm coffee, waiting for Jean-Pierre, feeling niggardly and irritable, unable to concentrate. The usual jauntiness of the patio had evaporated; it was gloomy, and smelt like an underground car park – unwashed, pissy. Alcoholic. The oversized lights, encased in stained globular teardrops, emitted a dull yellow glow – the colour of old teeth. The weather seemed to have confused even the *insinzi*, which, fooled by the darkness, had erupted at midday and had hurled themselves into the blue neon bulbs where they crackled and died, their charred bodies spat out on to the cement floor.

It was, I knew, my trip with Jean-Pierre the previous day that had provoked this dark mood. It had been my idea. But Jean-Pierre had agreed. He told me that he rarely returned to the district where his friend Ernest had lived before the genocide.

Nyamirambo clings precariously to the southern flank of Kigali – a chaotic spider's web of paths and unpaved roads, through which cars, scooters and bicycles slid and skidded helplessly through the mud that had yet to dry from the early morning rain. We abandoned the car and decided to retrace Jean-Pierre's journey from Ernest's old house to the cesspit that had become his sanctuary. The path between the houses was dark. Overcrowded with rubbish and open drains. For a big man, Jean-Pierre moved with surprising elegance – I was breathless, trying to keep up.

We stopped outside a series of small one-storey brick dwellings that lay on a side street. Jean-Pierre walked towards a house that was mostly obscured by large rusted metal gates. Spikes protruded from the top of the gates and broken glass had been cemented on to the walls on either side. This was where Ernest lived, Jean-Pierre told me. Where he had stayed for the first three nights of the genocide. The house was twenty-five yards from the crossroads where the militia roadblock had been set up. When he crept out of the gates in the early hours of 11 April 1994 the militia were asleep.

'But there was no way I could walk past them. If they had woken, they would have cut me.'

We walked up the street to the next house. The woman who answered our knock recognized Jean-Pierre. She led us down a narrow alley. Rainwater streamed down from the walls on either side and collected into a narrow gutter that ran the length of the alley. There was an overpowering smell of shit. I followed, cursing that I had not chosen to wear my boots that morning, and wedged my shoes into the right angle made by the wall and the gutter. Jean-Pierre was ahead of me – an oversized Fagin, skittering down the alleyway. Fragments of shouts from small boys and a slosh of water being thrown from the other side of the wall. Jean-Pierre stopped and stared at the wall. He was breathing hard. 'I don't remember this wall,' he said, tracing his hand along the rough bricks. The alley we had stumbled down was eighteen inches wide and thirty yards long. I could now see that two buildings made up its left-hand side. In the gap between the two was a small, perfectly bevelled cesspit. 'This isn't it,' Jean-Pierre said. He pointed to the building that began on the other side of the hole. 'This house is new,' he said. I gestured at the cesspit. 'Has this been here a long time?' I asked. The woman shook her head and pointed to a line of broken concrete that ran along the edge of the alley and then disappeared under the new wall. 'This was the old cesspit,' she said, 'but it was filled in when they built this house.' 'Yes,' Jean-Pierre said, 'here it is – you can see it. It's much bigger.' He seemed relieved. Had the woman lived here during the genocide, I asked. No, she replied, she came after.

We walked back to the rusty gates of Ernest's old house and a young girl answered our knock. Several faces peered out from behind her. Jean-Pierre explained who we were. She called over her shoulder and another woman came to the gate. No, she didn't know where her neighbours were. Yes, we could come in. But she was due to go to work so we could not be long. We walked into a small courtyard. Jean-Pierre explained how it had looked back in '94, but his answers to my questions were short, abrupt almost. The women watched him as he prowled around the small yard. Jean-Pierre asked if I had enough information. 'I think so,' I said. Would he like to go now? 'If you want,' he said.

As we were walking back to the car, a man approached us. He started to ask us questions. His tone was enquiring. I heard the word *umuzungu*. I asked Jean-Pierre what the man wanted. 'He wants to know why we are here, what I am doing here with you.' Jean-Pierre reached into his pocket for his keys and resumed walking slowly towards the car. The man was still asking questions and had moved closer. There was suspicion now, haughtiness at Jean-Pierre's apparent lack of courtesy. One or two people turned their heads as they walked past. 'What is he asking you now, Jean-Pierre?' 'He wants to know who I am, what my name is.' The questioning from the man was calm, but his doggedness betrayed his sense of superiority, his assurance at his absolute right to be asking these questions. The glasses on his face – thick-rimmed, old-fashioned spectacles – kept slipping down his nose, forcing him to flick them back up. When we reached the car, Jean-Pierre turned quickly on the man – his balletic feet again – and shouted at him.

'Don't talk to me. Get away. Who are you to ask me questions? I can go where I like. Go. You.'

His finger jabbed violently at the man who had now stepped back, surprised by Jean-Pierre's vehemence. Jean-Pierre's voice got bigger, challenging not just the man but all the silent stares of those who had stopped to gawp.

'Who are *you*? Where were *you*? *I* was here.'

The man walked away, defeated. Motorcycles buzzed past. Three small boys guilelessly peered up at Jean-Pierre, intrigued by his outburst. Gently, he moved them back, opened the car door and climbed in. When I got in the other side I saw that he was shaking. I put a hand on his shoulder. Big, meaty shoulders, wide enough to throw his youngest daughter up and have her perch there, like a baby crow. When Jean-Pierre climbed out of his hole on the morning of 27 June 1994, he weighed less than six stone. His bones were so weak that he could hardly stand.

He took off his glasses and wiped his eyes, the dust on the back of his hand smeared wet.

'Sometimes, I see people and I think, who are you? Where were you in ninety-four? Are you a killer?'

He stared out at the street. 'I was in my hole when my parents were killed,' he said. And he explained what had happened. It was only a few days after 7 April but he was unsure of the precise date. One morning, a group of men had arrived at his father's house, in the village of Rubengera, just a few miles outside Kibuye. They had come on the orders of the *préfet*, looking for Muganga Joseph. He was to accompany them to the hospital. He left Jolie and the children at the house, walked down the path to the car that waited for him and climbed in. After driving two miles in the direction of Kibuye they stopped at a bend in the road. They walked Joseph from the car up a small path, where several of the men hacked him to death. They threw his body in a ditch.

Jean-Pierre pressed his fingers into his eyes, squeezing out small trails of tears that ran down the side of his face. The *préfet* was a doctor too, but he had never liked his father, he said. He was probably jealous of him because Joseph had worked in many hospitals and was a better doctor.

'When the men came and said the *préfet* wanted him to come to the hospital, I think my dad knew that he was going to be killed. That he would never make it to the hospital. I think he left the house quickly so that my mum and the kids would be left alone.'

The killers came back for Jolie and the children who were still living at home later that day. She was killed outside her house, probably by a machete. Jean Mugabo, Job Munguhanacoyo and Jacques Muhire were killed next to her.

Two of his sisters – Jeanne Nors and Donathila Uwamahoro – were murdered in Kigali. Joseph Mukassa had fled to Butare but died there. Aimée Nyiramatama was killed in Gisenyi, where she'd gone on holiday. Of the ten children, only Jean-Pierre, Joseph Binego and Didier Nors survived the genocide.

Jean-Pierre bends his old Toyota for more than an hour around the steep, well-graded road. Old dead Habyarimana had this road built in the eighties – to connect Kigali with Rwanda's second city, Butare – in a deal with the Chinese. We pass a small memorial – a plinth erected in memory of fallen Chinese road workers.

Over the last two months Jean-Pierre and I have become friends. I am here producing a feature film about the genocide, based on a story I wrote with a friend, which tells of a young Western aid worker's dilemma over whether to stay or leave Rwanda as the genocide erupts. Jean-Pierre got the job of organizing all the transport for the production. It is stressful, time-consuming work. He is constantly battered by requests from the Western crew. His easy manner and gentle humour have endeared him to everybody, but I know that he is struggling to keep up with the demands of the filming. I feel protective towards him. When he learned that I was in Rwanda during the genocide ten years earlier, he told me that Odette, his wife, had been not far from Kivumu, when I was there, staying at Curic's friary. Perhaps it was a connection that was bound to happen; after all, many of the Rwandan members of the film crew are genocide survivors and someone was bound to have relatives who lived close to where I had been in 1994. But I had always felt comfortable talking to Jean-Pierre, and when I explained that I wanted to look into what happened to Vjeko Curic, he said he would be glad to help – drive me around, do some interpreting. I knew already, second-hand, a little of Jean-Pierre's own survival and was surprised, initially, at how readily he talked about his experiences. Jean-Pierre was, I discovered, still searching to understand how and why his parents and siblings had died and how he, even ten years later, could live with that knowledge. So, I had come up with the idea of taking him back to Nyamirambo. 'Perhaps we both need to retrace our steps,' I'd said.

The pine resin that I smell as we drive, searching for a turn-off, is what tells me we're close. I recognize it, embedded as it is in my childhood: the phalanx of Scots pine below my grandfather's house where I used to watch Archie, the gardener, cut and slash through the undergrowth, the diesel from the tractor mixed with the pines' gluey resin – a dark, dense inner sanctum of the garden, away from my grandfather's looming austerity and heavy right hand. This part of the garden, with Archie, was always a good place to be, and now the smell, in this second haven, is doubly familiar. Sure enough, I soon find the small, sandy track that branches off from the main road, through the bank of evergreens.

We drive slowly towards the church and what had been Curic's living quarters. Little seems to have changed in the ten years since I was last here. The vegetable garden – neat rows of sweet potatoes and beans – and the rooms for acolytes set around three sides of the grass square. It is peaceful, tucked away, just as it was when, in that spring of '94, we used to swing our battered old Peugeot, coughing and wheezing, off the main road – leaving behind, in the rear-view mirror, the figure of a man holding a machete, head turned back, watching us, suspicious, monitoring our progress – and drive up that lane, disappearing into the bank of pine trees. Then, finally, we could hear ourselves breathe. Sour breath, slowly exhaled. Sucking in fresh pine. Vjeko just up ahead. Safe now.

With a small gesture – the palm of his hand facing me, twitching a quiet 'no' – Jean-Pierre elects to remain in the car. The courtyard is quiet and I can hear each tick of the engine – precise semiquavers in the midday heat. A few Rwandans stare at me, frowning at my mangled greeting. They stand by the wall, half slouched, bodies twisted, heads lowered, like old-fashioned anglepoise lamps, but eyes looking up at me. It is exceedingly hot. I walk quietly towards the church, squinting; the inside looks cavernously dark against the glare of the sun. I stare up at the sun. The heat has made the air thick, suffocating. Untrustworthy. An insect lurches past me, swings back on itself and meanders past again, forcing me to swipe at it. A young girl giggles at my buffoonery. Her laughter echoes around the courtyard. She whispers to her friends. My hearing feels amplified, my head hazy, menaced by something indistinguishable. If someone asked me a question I'm sure I would lie – a strange sense of deceit still lingering.

The girl's laughter still echoes behind my eyes as I head for the church. The thick rubber soles of my boots crunch noisily on the gravel in the courtyard. Nothing seems to have changed from ten years ago, but in fact everything is different. The staring, the whispering, the half-suppressed giggle; they all stir a collective memory from another time, long past, where whispers and stares existed, only then there was no return on them; falling, as they did, into a moral vacuum, like stones down an empty well.

An oversized grave sits next to the altar. It is covered in cheap white tiles, like those in a shower room at a municipal swimming pool. A photograph of Curic is propped up against the cross. I sit wearily on one of the wooden pews. My camera knocks against the cement floor, the noise resonating around the chapel. My head hurts and my mouth is dry. Curic's photograph stares back at me – a broad, generous smile under a Fuzzy Felt moustache, his surplice impossibly white against the sea of black faces that surround him. On 7 April 1994, after the news of the President's assassination broke, Curic took evening prayers in the small chapel next to the friary's sitting room, his voice rising above the hum of the single strip light that stuttered above him. It was the first Thursday of the month. Psalm 29 followed by Psalm 31. A reading from St Peter. A concluding prayer:

Lord God
you give us the moon to illuminate the night,
and to dispel the darkness you bring in the light of the day:
grant that during this night
we may elude the grasp of Satan
and in the morning rise to give you praise.

It was dark when they left the chapel. Their footsteps echoed as they returned, in silence, to their rooms. The radio had told people to stay at home and wait – and across the valley there was no sign of life, not a sound, a cry, a flicker of light.

I leave the church and make my way to the friary. The

driveway leads me through a pair of gates, swung wide open. A chained dog pants under a piece of corrugated iron. The metal doors of the small, neatly bricked rooms that surround the quadrangle of grass are freshly painted and locked. A young man crouches on a step, washing old pots, their bottoms tarred black with age. He smiles briefly and leans his frame out of the doorway to let me past as I step into the kitchen. It is scrubbed clean – the same soothing antiseptic sheen on the old wooden surfaces by the sink. Next door is the cheap table where we sat late at night gratefully drinking whisky. Sitting there, with his back to me, is a white man in jeans and an old cotton shirt. Opposite him is a Rwandan. They are talking quietly to each other. My tongue feels slow and thick as I lurch through an introduction. The white man has a cross hanging from his neck and a wide, open mouth topped with a bristling eighties-style moustache. His name, he tells me, is Ivica Peric. He is the priest now at Kivumu and he resembles, unsettlingly, Vjeko Curic. Like Curic, he too is from Bosnia – a Bosnian Croat, to be precise. He says he knew Curic. They were friends. He carried his coffin, six years earlier, in 1998. The man opposite him is called Gatete. He stretches across the table and shakes my hand.

I lay my hands flat, palms down, on the table. The room smells like the pages of an old book. Peric pours me some black tea. A fly is caught between the folds of the old yellow curtain and the window. It bumps angrily against the panes. The walls are unpainted brick, which I remember well. But the picture of Christ and his Apostles that hangs prominently from the wall is new or, at least, I don't recall it. Peric tells me that he is discussing some new building work in the parish and Gatete is the builder – down from Kigali for the day. He tells me that he has been here for six years. The explanations end. At home this sort of void would be quickly filled – probably by me, words gushing out to avoid the social pitfalls of any unfortunate silences. But here I am happy just to sit. Peric gets up and opens the window for the fly, which careers off into the courtyard. When he sits down again he pours me more tea and, after what seems like a long while, asks me why I am here.

I begin to explain that I stayed here during the genocide and witnessed how Curic defied the extremist militias and saved the lives of thousands of Rwandans. I say that I think, most probably, he saved our lives too. I feel my throat start to ache as I describe his courage. It is an effort to speak. I try and explain that, on one particular day, towards the end of the genocide when I was over the border in Goma, things didn't work out the way I wanted. A grand muscular struggle is taking place in my face and eventually I give in. Peric puts his hand on mine and leaves it there. 'It's OK,' he says. Gatete has brindled grey hair and a generous, beamy forehead. He smiles at me. I wish the fly was back in the room, blazing away.

Peric gestures to Gatete. 'Well, you have a brother now.'

Gatete explains that Curic saved his life in April 1994. There were many roadblocks, says Gatete. Many many roadblocks. Vjeko was a very brave man. We sip our tea and Peric shows us the hole in the door when men came to kill Vjeko. I laugh when I tell Peric that I had never met a priest who drank whisky and swore until I met Vjeko Curic. And when my face crinkles the tear stains make my cheeks feel as if they have been lightly varnished.

Some time later, we walk to the car. It sits in shadow now,

the heat of the day has passed. Jean-Pierre dozes in the rear.

'I am back,' I tell Peric, 'because I want to understand how Curic found the courage to stay when everyone else had left.'

He tells me that he and Vjeko knew each other well at college.

'He was a big man. Not big, like big.' Peric stretches out his arms to demonstrate. 'Big as in strong. He was a fighter. A Croat,' he says, as if that explains everything.

I tell him I need to find out why, years after the genocide, Curic had been killed. Peric smiles broadly and shakes his head. 'Be careful', he says. 'This is Rwanda. So many secrets.'

I had heard that few Franciscan priests left Bosnia and of those that did, only a fraction went to Africa as missionaries. Peric nods but tells me that Vjeko was different. He points his index finger at his right eye. 'You could see it there,' he tells me. 'There was fire. If he thought something was wrong he would fight to make it right. I think whoever killed him was frightened of that.'

In a nearby field a man pitches a large thicket of maize on to his shoulders and slowly walks down an old track. In the trees that surround us, there is a faint trill – a shiver of wind. Across the courtyard, into the doorless, dark church, the afternoon light catches the corner of Vjeko's tiled grave, an equilateral triangle against the dark recesses of the church. The man with the maize reaches the bottom of the track, his tattered shorts still flapping in the light breeze. Peric tells me that I look tired. He gestures towards the small rooms in the quadrangle. 'Come back here if you want to,' he says. 'There is a room for you. Any time.'

I walk back alone to the church. A few goats are pat-patted past me by a small boy, a stick in his hand, worn-out rubber flip-flops on his feet that are white with dust. The children from earlier have drifted off. The goats trot past. Brisk, dainty hooves skidding as they negotiate the corner. I sit again on one of the pews that are fixed to the floor. Ten years ago hundreds of Tutsis gathered here during the first few days of the genocide. The church was a magnet for people terrified that they were going to be killed, unaware that they were doing exactly what the killers wanted. The man in the photograph understood this and chose to help. I wonder where he found the courage, which failed me, and so many others.

The day will not end. We get back to Kigali and the city is broiling under a late afternoon sun, the stern morning gloom burnt off. We pass high brick walls fringing the highway, topped with razor wire, sentry posts and large signs advertising security companies. 'INTERTEK – WHERE SAFETY COMES FIRST!' Behind lie vast newly built mansions, preposterous-sized villas, with blue-uniformed guards standing at the gates.

'These are homes for the new returnees,' says Jean-Pierre.

'You mean, "new Tutsis"?'

'The people who come back now – many years after ninety-four. You know? They fled in fifty-nine, when the Hutus seized power. They lived in Uganda, New York, London – all over the world. Now, they are back and get the business.'

Jean-Pierre has his arm crooked out of the window; the small wooden blue, yellow and green cut-out of Rwanda that hangs from the mirror flutters in the breeze.

'Many of us who survived were traumatized. Business wasn't important for us.'

We drive on in silence. Jean-Pierre did not survive just the genocide. He belonged to a Tutsi family that did not flee the pogroms of the early sixties. Newly independent, the first Hutu government targeted the Tutsis who had been favoured by the Belgian colonialists. Thousands were killed as decades of Hutu resentment against the Tutsi minority burst out and swept through the country. Many Tutsis ran for the borders. Some south to Burundi, but most to Uganda, where they sat in well-organized refugee camps, schooled their children and planned for their eventual return to their homeland. While many Tutsi émigrés grew rich and educated, those who had remained – like Jean-Pierre and his family – continued to suffer under the Hutu regime that had held unequivocal power since independence. I ask Jean-Pierre why his father did not leave when the Hutus took control of the country.

'He was a doctor. He thought he would not be in danger.'

Halfway down the Boulevard de la Paix we park and I walk down the hill examining the lamp posts. What I know is that on that day in January 1998 there were two men in the jeep here with Curic, and eyewitnesses reported seeing a struggle. Then people heard shots and Curic's car went out of control as it came out of the roundabout and headed down the hill, before it crashed into a street light. The two men ran from the car, leaving Curic slumped over the steering wheel.

A motorbike narrowly misses me. The passenger's head turns back and he stares at me as he speeds away. Other people watch me from the battered stalls on either side of the street. All the lamp posts are bent, plastered with graffiti and old posters, rusted and broken. I wipe the grime from my mouth. It is still hot. In fact, it feels hotter – the sun is lower but seems closer. The heat makes me want to burn the details of Curic's last moments on to my memory – like a branding iron on an old piece of flesh. It feels shoddy to say, 'Well, it was one of those lamp posts, but I don't know which one.'

I look back at Jean-Pierre who is sitting on the bonnet of the car watching me. He waves at me – shooing me on – before turning to answer a man who is shouting down to him from one of the stalls. The tarmac is sticky under my feet; it feels as though the smog is trapped, unable to escape the heat which, even though it is getting late, is intense, crushing every colour and smell into burnt yellow.

At the roundabout a man comes up to me and asks me what I am doing. He looks young – perhaps in his early twenties – and listens carefully as I explain. He takes my hand in his and tells me that I am looking in the wrong place. We walk together back up the hill, edging past the roundabout. Antoine is a student, he tells me. He is a small man, neatly dressed and carries a weather-beaten brown satchel over a bony shoulder. We drop down a small escarpment, my feet slithering in the fresh mud. The cars are above us now, at head height, and we are walking through a clutch of small huts. Children peer from the doorways, dirty with brown snot, big eyes staring vacantly at us. Antoine has neat little feet – his smart, black pointy shoes seem to play hopscotch over the open drains and rubbish-strewn paths. I galumph after him.

'Did you know this priest?'

Antoine asks this as he stops at a low brick wall that surrounds a small pointless-looking muddy space. It's a wall that seems to have no purpose, dividing nothing. In the middle, wedged between the bricks, is a collection of little artefacts.

There are some dirty plastic yellow flowers, a wooden cross and a photograph of Curic.

'Yes. Ten years ago. Look, why is this here? I've been told that Curic died in his car on the road by a lamp post.'

Antoine says nothing and we stand by the wall looking at this little memorial. I am baffled. Curic had never worked in Kigali, and any impromptu memorial should surely be up on the road. I look at Antoine. He has a flattened brow and close-cropped hair that sits only fractionally above his wide-set eyes. He shrugs – the sharp angles of his shoulders reveal his smallness, the undernourished body that his trim clothes have tried to disguise.

'Maybe people who live here ran to the road when they heard the shots. Maybe they were there when he died. He was famous.'

Antoine frowns when I ask him if he knows who killed Curic. I follow him back up to the road. He stands watching me as I thank him and climb into the Toyota. He puts his hand on the open window of the car.

'I am a student at KIST. But it is very expensive. You see, to stay at school. I have to pay. Do you have any contribution?'

Jean-Pierre's glasses flash angrily as he overhears Antoine. He barks at him, his hand flicking him away. Antoine ignores Jean-Pierre and asks me again, this time more insistently. '*Monsieur*, please, *s'il vous plaît*,' he says. Jean-Pierre's irritation drowns out much of what Antoine is saying but I catch the words *twenty thousand*. About twenty pounds, for a term at the Kigali Institute of Science and Technology. I easily have that much in my wallet. I can hear Jean-Pierre mutter, sucking in air through his teeth, his small squeaks of disapproval, as I hand Antoine five thousand francs. He looks at it and his sharp shoulders shrug again as we pull away. In the wing mirror I can see he is still staring after us until we have disappeared round the corner.

'It's a lot of money, *eh*? Five thousand. He did a good job for you?'

'He can go to school now, Jean-Pierre.'

'And he can beg, too. We all become beggars now.'

Traffic is thick and the Kiyovu roundabout is in chaos. The law has just changed: now cars arriving here must behave like the rest of the world and give way rather than just hurtle into the mêlée. But it's taking time.

The hotel speed bumps – designed to slow down 4×4s – grate the undercarriage of Jean-Pierre's small Toyota. As I gather up my old blue knapsack, he puts an arm across me and asks me to wait. His large frame leans forward as he struggles to pull something out from his back pocket. He thrusts a piece of paper into my hand and asks me to read it. 'Not now. Later.' His eyes blink behind his glasses and he starts to stammer. The liveried doorman waves at us to move on. Behind us a white 4×4 cruises up and sounds its horn at us. I can make out a few words at the top of the paper. '*Cher Jean-Pierre . . .*' The driver of the car behind pokes his head out of the window and begins to shout, distracting me from what Jean-Pierre is trying to say. He grips my arm, clutching the letter. I lean out of the car.

'Could you just wait, please.'

Jean-Pierre is stammering, leaning over me and opening my door.

'It's OK. Go. But t-t-t-take it. *Eh?* R-r-r-read it.'

Jean-Pierre looks behind and waves at the driver who has his hands up, palms upturned – *what?* – and gently pushes me from the car. I am not ready to leave. I hear the man in the car behind still shouting. Then the horn goes again. It has been a long day. I lean out the window.

'Will you *fuck* off!'

'No, David, it's OK. Just r-r-r-read the letter. He is in Kibuye. I don't know what to do. Should I meet him?'

I watch the old white Toyota drive away, a sharp *crrrp* as it grinds over the speed bumps. The writing on the letter is neat and curly and reminds me of my daughter's early efforts to join up her letters. '*Je m'incline . . .*' The passengers from the car behind swing open their doors and I am forced backwards towards the hotel reception as three men, dressed impeccably in dark suits, climb out of the 4×4, stare at me curiously, and walk into the hotel.

I watch one of them turn back and look at me – my filthy jeans and sweat-stained T-shirt. He mutters something to his friends. Through a gap in the hotel gardens I glimpse Jean-Pierre's Toyota crawling gently out into the stream of traffic to begin its journey back to his house in the cluttered mass of Gatenga.

It has turned cold on the veranda. A few Rwandans traipse along the road, hunched in their thin cotton clothes against the brisk wind. Kigali sits high up – more than a thousand feet above sea level. The chill seems to accentuate the difference between nine-tenths of Rwanda – or as close to ten-tenths as it is possible to get – who walk past the lush gardens of the hotel, oblivious and excluded, and the small minority who sweep in off the highway in their shiny-bumpered 4×4s, which glide past the neatly drilled platoon of palm trees, the bottoms of their trunks painted white like soldiers in spats – and deliver their hefty deposits of the seriously rich. Middle-aged women who struggle grumpily in the gusty wind to control the folds of their *igikwembe* – the brightly coloured length of material they are swathed in – and lumber slowly inside like Elizabethan galleons, flicking away their drivers, faces set like spoilt children; vast iridescent ships off to anchor in calmer waters, to eat ice cream and plough through bowls of greasy *frites*.

Cher Jean-Pierre,

Je m'incline et vous demande pardon, j'ai participé aux tueries de votre famille, j'ai reconnu mes crimes et j'ai demandé pardon, je sais très bien combien c'est assez dur de vivre après ces tragédies de 1994. Pourtant votre père était un collègue que je connaissais depuis longtemps. Encore une fois je demande pardon à tout ce qui vous reste comme famille et à vous-même.

Merci et bonne compréhension et je sais que c'est dur après ces événements macabres.

Nkubito. M

The casualness of the words – his backsliding – leaves me breathless. 'I would like to ask for your forgiveness . . .' Clear then, what he wants. More opaque is what he did. 'I participated in the killings of your family.' Not, 'I killed your family,' but a vague unspecified position at the crime scene. He is unsteady, this murderer – flinching in the face of blood spilt and his equivocation makes things worse. '*J'ai participé.*' He has reanimated the crime, taken us back, unwittingly, to that day and forced us to re-examine the sequence of events. A group of men cornering a woman, who is backing into a doorway, sweeping her children behind her; their faces peer upwards from around her skirts. A doctor pulled from a car on the bend of a road and led to a ditch. There would have been a moment when time stood still for the killers, for Nkubito. At the house he would have heard the stutter of a small motorbike from the road below, a shout from a passer-by walking to the health centre, the last half-breath from the woman as she watched the men, her arms braced backwards, wrapped around her children. At the ditch the eyes of the doctor are levelled at his killers'. The stench of sweat, the air thick and metallic, the men gone now, just a grey shapeless mass. Then a shift – an insolent tremor through the men – and the first blow, a brittle clang. For a moment there is nothing to see. The killers hesitate and look foolish. Then the skin unzips, deep to the bone, and blood pours like milk from a jug. Quickly now, a flurry of blades. '*Je sais très bien combien c'est assez dur de vivre après ces tragédies de 1994.*' The penship is artful, the sentiment – empathetic. 'I know how hard it has been to live since the tragedies of 1994.' An invitation, then, to the survivor – to share with him the hardship of life since the tragedy that befell both him and the people that he killed. The 'tragedy', he calls it – casually reclassifying the brutal murder of five people. I can see Nkubito, squeezed into a corner of the steaming prison in which he now sits, formulating the words, balancing responsibility against abrogation, each sentence carefully weighed against the next, carefully distancing himself from the crime. He knows the letter will be a deep and painful intrusion into the life and memory of the man whose parents and brothers and sisters he killed, so he elects to claim a share of the pain along with his victim. Together they can bemoan the hardness of life. He, too, is suffering the loss of Joe. 'Your father was someone I had known for a long time.' One more demand for forgiveness – he is becoming a nag now – and then a final whine: 'life has been tough since the macabre events'. The killer has moved on from 1994. Surely, he says, it is for the best that Jean-Pierre does the same.

I have heard about these letters. Two years ago, Rwanda began a new system of justice in an effort to reduce the number of men and women languishing in prison who have either been found guilty of genocide or are still awaiting trial. Partly, too, it is an attempt to heal the divisions between Hutu and Tutsi. Tens of thousands remain incarcerated and the justice system is gridlocked with cases. *Gacaca* is an inimitably Rwandese criminal justice system, where killers meet the families of their victims in village courts to confess their crimes and ask for forgiveness. Prisoners who confess fully are released back to their communities, once they have spent several weeks in a re-education camp. For many prisoners, writing to a surviving relative of their victims is viewed as a means of seeing their prison sentence reduced, or for those facing a *gacaca* court, the letter is a useful piece of evidence to present to their peers that they have already begun the process of seeking forgiveness.

Beyond the city the hills are in gentle shadow, overlapping each other into the distance, turning green to blue to milk, as they disappear. It is early evening and a few generators rattle into life across the valley – where the well-to-do live – and lights blink, spitting like fireflies. But the people who live below us, in their wooden squats, remain in darkness. Jean-Pierre told me that soon they will be gone, relocated, to make way for a new city zoo. It is, apparently, an acknowledgement that the elephant and water buffalo that had previously roamed across the gentle savannah in the north-east of the country are no longer there. Both armies, it is said, ate them all back in '94. So now the animals will be flown in from South Africa and protected by steel bars in this new, peaceful Rwanda.

The letter sits by my half-eaten supper. It is a cold, peremptory invitation, full of self-pity and wheedling pseudo-empathy. The killer offers no explanation for why he did what he did, disassociating himself from murder. In the new Rwanda, the President wants Jean-Pierre and thousands of other survivors to meet with the killers, but I wonder what that would resolve.

Earlier that day Jean-Pierre had told me that he has returned to his father's village several times, looking for the remains of Papa Joe. He has walked the road and searched the ditches for signs of a shallow grave where his father might have been buried. He asked local people and they told him where they thought a doctor had been killed, on the bend of the main road heading to Kibuye. He wept as he told me that he had crawled on his hands and knees, digging the earth, searching for evidence of where his father might lie. He had found nothing. For a while we sat in silence.

'When the killing began, my father told a neighbour that he knew I would have been killed straight away. He said I would have fought the killers and they would have cut me to death.'

'You did the right thing, Jean-Pierre. You know that, don't you?'

'Of course. But I can't tell my dad that, can I?'

Dusk has gone now, all is dark. I angle the letter, squinting at the inked letters in the yellowish hotel light. Nkubito sits in his jail, surrounded by thousands of others guilty of the same crime. They killed together and they were imprisoned together. Conjoined, they plot how best to extract forgiveness from their victims. Their lives now are driven by simple absolutes that offer them comfort and perhaps even absolution. With a shrug, Nkubito tells Jean-Pierre that it was 'something macabre' that befell them all.

There are no such easy solutions for Jean-Pierre. Each morning, just before dawn, as Odette rises from the bed, he wakes and hears her pour water from the well into the metal bucket and place it on the fireplace at the end of the path by the corner of the house. In an hour she begins her half-mile walk to the bus stop where she will take a *mutatu* to her office at the Electricity, Water and Sanitation Authority. Sunlight filters through the cracked windows of the minibus. She watches a young girl next to her pick away at the peeling window sticker that proclaims: 'God is One'.

By the time Odette has reached her office, Jean-Pierre is up and warming a pan of milk for the children over the fire, staring at the bubbles which begin to form a ring around the liquid. Work as a driver and translator for visiting journalists is haphazard. In the years that immediately followed the genocide, when much of the north-west of the country remained dangerously unstable, Jean-Pierre was kept busy with foreign journalists, who came to report on the murderous incursions from Congo into Rwanda by remnants of the defeated army and gangs of former *interahamwe*. He gained a reputation as a reliable and companionable 'fixer'. By 1998, the RPF had driven the militia back across the border and work for Jean-Pierre became less predictable except, that is, for the few weeks leading up to the commemoration of the genocide, when to this day Jean-Pierre is a favourite among foreign television crews. The money is good and the work is easy – carting dumbfounded foreigners from massacre sites to presidential press conferences. But April is a bad month. Memories that usually lie buried under the weight of work are ignited by the endless talk of 'Ninety-Four' from journalists fresh to the country, their questions blushingly pressed, asking Jean-Pierre to explain his own story.

The memory comes quickly, a pressure on the front of his brain. It feels almost like a physical force, inhabiting a space between the flame that warms the milk and the prone body of his baby boy lying just behind him. Some days it lasts several hours; other times he can flick the memory away – back into his subconscious. But the memory never disappears. It is not some dim, distant fragment. It is hot and viscous, sticking to all surfaces inside his head. It is volatile too. Given air, it burns directly behind his eyes, a dark flame, staining his vision brown. Turd-brown. And then he is gone – back to the hole, his only light a small crack above him where the metal covering had warped away from the edge of the concrete cesspit – far from his wife and children, dead to his father.

The creases in the paper are deep – Jean-Pierre must have unfolded and refolded the letter many times. Big-toothed, red-clawed, Nkubito has wrestled his way into Jean-Pierre's life, staking a claim over memories that my friend believes are his. Nkubito reassures Jean-Pierre that forgiveness is the correct remedy for the troubles that exist for all of them. Forgiveness seems far away for my friend right now. He is still trying to work out how to survive.

CHAPTER TEN

Slavonski Brod, Croatia

In November 1997, a few months before his death, Vjeko Curic flew to Nairobi to meet with another Franciscan, Tomo Andic. It was already dark by the time his taxi pulled into the driveway of the Sisters of Mercy convent, where both priests would stay for the few hours they were in town. The two men embraced, but it wasn't until they had walked under the porch light that Andic could see the dreadful state of his friend. He looked exhausted. Curic explained that he had cadged a lift on a Russian cargo plane and had been stowed uncomfortably in the back of the aircraft, wedged between pieces of industrial equipment. But Curic seemed more than tired – he was agitated and distracted. There were dark creases under his eyes like smears of brown boot polish. He had put on weight. His face was pale and doughy. Twenty years earlier, Andic had sat across from Curic listening to his friend's excited chatter about a life in Africa. It was true that they were men in their forties now, worn down by the physical effort of mission work, but even during the worst of times (and God knows, his friend had seen plenty of those)

Curic had never been one to brood. Now, Curic said nothing and their footsteps echoed as they walked down the darkened convent corridors.

Tomo Andic tells me this as we sit in the restaurant of a nondescript roadside hotel just outside Slavonski Brod, the border town between Croatia and Bosnia. A waitress brings us coffee. We are the only ones here. He is a good-looking man with a grizzled beard. When I arrived he asked me a number of questions about my interest in Curic but now, his interrogation concluded, he seems happy to talk. We stir our coffee. It is still early in the morning but outside I can see a queue of cars forming at the border post. 'Black market,' Andic says and winks.

Tomo Andic and Vjeko Curic had met as teenagers at school in Visoko, a large town in central Bosnia. The Franjevacka Klasicna Gimnazija was the most rigorous Catholic boys school in the region – famous for its academic prowess. It took in over a hundred boys each year, thirty of whom were separated off and trained as priests. It was a tough regime – a quarter of all students dropped out after the first year. Tomo and Vjeko thrived and became firm friends. Later, they trained together as novices at the Sarajevo Theological College. Three years after Curic left for Africa, Andic followed, to a mission in Uganda. Over the years he often travelled to Rwanda, where the two priests would visit their favourite bars in Kigali. 'It was good to drink a decent beer after too many months in the Ugandan bush,' Andic jokes.

When Curic rang in November '97, suggesting they meet, Andic was not surprised. Curic's optimism in the days following the genocide had, over the years, dwindled into resignation and even despair. His hopes that the new regime would back his plans to bring Hutu and Tutsi together had foundered. The government was secretive and mistrustful of him and his work. There was clear evidence, he said, that many Rwandan Hutus in his parish had been victims of revenge killings at the end of the genocide by the RPF, yet he believed that none of the murders had been properly investigated. He knew he was watched and had been for several years. His responsibilities as the bursar of Kabgayi, the richest and most established diocese in Rwanda, had become an immense pressure. Hundreds of thousands of dollars were flowing into the region from Catholic NGOs eager to pour their aid budgets – inflated by public donations ever since the genocide – into reconstruction projects. But the backstabbing was appalling. Curic had begun to mutter darkly that life had been simple during the genocide: there were victims and there were killers; now Rwanda was a seething mass of local jealousies and ethnic rivalries. The end of the genocide had prompted a stream of Tutsis to return from Burundi and Uganda, to develop land that had been theirs before they fled the first pogroms thirty years earlier. Curic often found himself in the middle of arguments between these, often wealthy, former exiles and an enraged group of Tutsis that had remained in Rwanda and survived the genocide and now expected these arrivistes to reward them with lucrative building contracts. Seeing most of the returning 'new Tutsis' settle in sparkling new properties in Kigali only fuelled the notion amongst survivors that they were, once again, second-class citizens.

There was, Curic noted, little of the small-town corruption that had bedevilled the old Rwanda but everywhere there was violence. Each night shots crackled in the hills around Kivumu and Gitarama. Towns and villages reeked of revenge. The dead in these conflicts were usually Hutus – some were those who had stayed after the genocide but had since been denounced as killers. Others were recent returnees – Hutus who had fled the RPF to camps in what was now the Democratic Republic of the Congo. Recently they had been forced out of their camps by invading RPF soldiers and told to return home – only to fall prey to a vengeful Tutsi minority. There were reports that some of the returnees were *interahamwe* and that they were responsible for some of the new deaths themselves – exacting revenge on Hutus who had remained in Rwanda and whose loyalty to the old, defunct Habyarimana regime they doubted. More perverse still, some Hutus who had remained in Congo sent relatives back into Rwanda to defend their properties from any Tutsi interlopers, with predictable results. No one knew how many had been killed, Curic had told his friend, but macheted bodies were dumped in front of Kabgayi hospital or the Gitarama offices of the Red Cross most mornings. The government paid little attention to the evidence uncovered by human rights investigators that the number of dead was far greater than anyone was publicly admitting.

During that final meeting in Nairobi, Curic talked and would not stop. He had no one to talk to in Kivumu, he said. It had been days since he had been able to speak. So he kept talking, the words whirring like a model train on a single circular track. He was worried about the reconstruction project he was managing. In his parish they had built several thousand houses for Tutsis with Catholic NGO money but they needed more. Hutus, too, needed houses. He had to fly to Canada and Germany – that was where the money was. He was worried that his planned orphanage in Kivumu would not be built. Thousands of children in the district were homeless and without families. They would starve to death. No one in Kigali cared about them or, even if they did care, there was no money. Curic moved quickly from one crisis to the next. The prison in Gitarama was still a disaster, he said. Packed with humans rotting to death. Last month eighty had died. If he could persuade the army to let his medical team in to visit more than once a week, he was sure he could reduce the number of deaths.

Curic paused – then, wearily, he told Andic that there had been attempts on his life. On one occasion he'd been shot at. And recently, two men had entered the friary late one night and dragged him out into the compound, forcing him on to his knees. As they readied to shoot, Curic had demanded that he not be killed like a dog. The men hesitated and allowed Curic up on to his feet. Somehow, he managed to wrestle his way past the men and run into the garden. He climbed an avocado tree and watched as the men below spent an hour looking for him before they gave up. Curic laughed about how foolish he had felt at the time, hiding up a tree. Did Curic know who was behind the attempt, Andic asked. The priest shrugged – he didn't know specifically but he and his boss, André Sibomana, a Rwandan priest and journalist, were aware that there were people who would prefer them not to be around. Curic knew the country too well, he knew there were bad guys out there.

For a moment Andic pauses, stirring his coffee again. Then he says, 'The Catholic Church was not popular with the new government, there had been priests and even sisters implicated in the genocide. It meant you had to be careful what you said and who heard you say it.' Nevertheless, such a brazen attempt to assassinate Curic suggested the priest had become embroiled in a dispute with people who had little to fear from any investigation. Curic, his fellow priest believed, was in grave danger.

'I said to him, "Vjeko, you have been there a long time. You need a holiday. For your health. Get out – for three months, a year, but enough time to get some distance." He said, "You are right, Tomo, but I cannot leave."'

The waitress comes and busies herself with our empty cups. Andic seems poised to speak but he waits until she has left. He presses his outstretched fingers together, like a child making a church – here's the church and here's the steeple – and speaks quietly. 'This is something that I have not told anyone before,' he says. 'Everything I have just told you is true. He said all those things. But he said them later. When we were at the restaurant. Before that – the first thing after he arrived – he told me he wanted to give me his confession. He said that he had come to Nairobi so he could give his confession to someone he trusted. So. There.' Andic releases his hands and shrugs, palms upwards.

'I was his best friend. And I think he needed to tell me that he was going to die. After that, we went to the sacristy of the convent church and I heard his confession and then we went out to eat and we talked about all the things I have told you about.'

In the car park outside the hotel we shake hands. Andic is heading back to Zagreb – parish duties.

'Did you try to persuade him to leave again?' I ask.

'Yes,' Andic says. 'One more time in the restaurant. "Go," I tell him. "Leave." And he says, "No, that looks rational but I cannot." For Vjeko I think it was beyond rationality. He learned the local language by sitting in shacks drinking banana beer and he decided to stay to help others. It was connectivity. It was a question of emotion. You don't go when you feel that.'

In a wide green valley, fringed by grey austere mountains, perched over the Bosna river, lies the small town of Zepce. Here, in what they call middle Bosnia, Vejkoslav Curic was born, the second of six children, to Petar and Ana Curic – Bosnian Croats who lived a mile outside town in a little hamlet called Osova. Petar worked in the steel factory that still sits, like a vast, crushed reptile, next to the Bosna, ten miles away. Life was hard but not uncomfortable for the Curic family. They owned some land – thirty hectares of field, wood and stream. At harvest time, the five boys would help their father after school.

Curic was a confident boy. On his first day at primary school, he introduced himself to the teacher, saying, 'If you need anything, just let me know.' And he was very bright with a natural ear for languages. But his teacher was a Communist, so Curic suffered because he was a Catholic. He was the only boy to recite a song, in German, that the teacher had asked the class to learn. But he only received an average mark. Another teacher physically hurt Curic, but Petar was advised by the school not to pursue it further; the Curic family were well-known Catholics. Their complaint would go nowhere. Ana Curic is in her late seventies now. In their sitting room there is a poster-sized photograph of Curic on the wall, and in front of me, plates of meat and cheese. There is a bottle of rakija, too, and we drink toasts. Petar is not supposed to be drinking because of his health, but he takes secret sips and delivers huge winks in my direction, which Ana ignores. Even in Zepce, you had to be careful if you were a Catholic, she says. You never told people about your faith and those in the local Communist Party who were still believers would drive to Travnik to attend Mass. They wouldn't be known there.

Ana's face has the colour and texture of an overripe apple and when she tells me that, aged ten, Curic had decided he would go to Africa after hearing a missionary speak at their local church, tears spring to her eyes, which she is content to let fall. 'Nothing would stop him,' she says. 'He was very determined.' After Vjeko had taken his first Mass, before he went to Africa, Petar sold some family land and gave him the proceeds. He promptly went out and spent all the money on new cars for his brothers and sisters. And he bought his father a new tractor. I'd been told that when he left for his life in Africa, Curic took only one small brown suitcase. Ana nods. 'He didn't need anything,' she says.

A mile from their house is their local church. On the walls are photographs of Curic. Some were from Africa: children in bright blue tunics sitting on wooden benches listening to him; Curic digging with Rwandans in the fields. And some from his home town too: his first Mass; as a student wearing flared jeans and a pair of ludicrous Serpico sunglasses; a picture of him as an eleven-year-old, in white shirt and grey shorts, dark-skinned, with a dollop of hair over his forehead, at the back of a group of schoolchildren, smiling. And a picture of Curic's funeral. Andic and Curic's successor at Kivumu, Ivica Peric, are carrying the coffin, helped by two

Rwandans. Andic is trying to keep the white cloth on the coffin. He is bearded and muscular. Peric – clean-shaven – is at the back, eyeing the coffin's progress under the care of the Rwandans at the front. Sunlight from the window has bleached the photograph so it looks like a painting by Giotto. The two men look like Apostles.

High up on a hill, overlooking the small town of Kiseljak, I sit and drink with Father Vinko, a squat, powerful-looking man in his early fifties. Vinko looks older than his years; his skin is puffy and angry-looking and his eyes seem hooded – a lifetime of looking out at people through a curtain of cigarette smoke. He knew Curic well. Together they spent a week in Paris, as tourists, way back in the early eighties when, he tells me, Yugoslav priests in Paris weren't a sight you saw that often. When Curic went to work in Rwanda he wanted it to be special. Vinko says, 'He wanted to get close to the people, not just at Mass or building them houses or schools. He wanted to sleep in the same place as Africans, eat their food.' Vinko shakes his head. 'But when he did that, he got sick and realized he couldn't live like that. He couldn't help them if he lived like them. So he went to Kigali for a few weeks and learned to build houses.'

Vinko is a bull of a man and his words are blunt and uncompromising. 'Vjeko was stubborn,' he says, 'really stubborn.' He was Curic's local parish priest when Curic gave his first Mass. Every new priest chooses a 'godfather', and when Curic told Vinko of his choice, Vinko disapproved. They argued for some time – three, four hours – and still Curic wouldn't listen to the older and more experienced priest. 'He would not back down, even when he didn't know anything,' the priest says. Later, when he had left for Africa, Vinko would get calls and letters from Curic – pleading with him to come to Africa too. 'He used to say, "Africa needs priests more than Bosnia."'

It fell to Vinko to drive one early morning in 1998 and tell Curic's parents what had happened to their son. It was freezing cold and snowing. A typical January day, when you can do little except pray and wait for the weather to break. He found them already at the door. 'What has happened to our son?' they asked him. Vinko never understood how they knew something was wrong. Later that morning, they walked up the small track to the church and said a Mass for him.

'People were very upset,' says Vinko to me now, stubbing out another cigarette. 'When he came back home everyone was always excited because he had such good stories to tell. He was inspiring to listen to.'

Father Vinko's face is pock-marked, and creased like brown baking paper by his heavy smoking. He places the ends of his short, stocky fingers on the table – a concert pianist readying himself for his first chord. Then he looks at me from under his heavily lidded eyes. I think to myself, if I were in trouble, I would come and tell this man. He'd help me.

He says, 'You know, in the end, I think Vjeko was disappointed in Africa. I think he thought he could change things and he couldn't. That's my personal conclusion.'

Vinko reaches for another cigarette. He's not finished: 'I remember him telling me that the people who loved him would be the same ones who killed him.'

PART III

2012–13

'So we beat on, boats against the current,
borne back ceaselessly into the past.'

F. Scott Fitzgerald, *The Great Gatsby*

CHAPTER ELEVEN

Kabgayi

We drive for an hour before the road becomes impossible – not so much a road at all, just deep ruts that grind the undercarriage of Jean-Pierre's 4x4 which rolls and pitches – its suspension groaning. Aphrodis grimaces as his head hammers into the side window. 'Enough, Jean-Pierre,' I say, 'come on, let's walk.' And we abandon the Toyota next to a group of small huts and start to climb up the spine of a long ridge that eventually disappears into the broad green flanks of the high hills that mark our horizon. The countryside looks as though it was drawn by a child: small fields of maize and cassava that drop delinquently down, on either side, to a deep valley, festooned with extravagant patches of banana trees and the occasional small brown hut. 'The cassava will be gone soon,' Aphrodis tells me. 'The banana too.' I nod because I have heard about this plan. On the advice of agronomists, the government in Kigali has stipulated that farmers throughout Rwanda must grow only crops specified by the Ministry of Agriculture, to maximize yields and reduce the risk of soil erosion. Recalcitrant farmers caught growing unauthorized crops face being fined or having their plots confiscated. The economic logic of monoculture is indisputable – as is Rwanda's sustained economic growth over the last decade. To many here, and in the West, it is justification for the government's tough stance on inefficiencies that characterized the backwards mentality of the old Rwanda. But the planned removal of private banana plantations from some areas has upset many. The banana is a traditional crop that has, for generations, been used as a symbol of community between Rwandans, mainly through the sharing of banana beer in a communal container, a pastime that is frowned upon by government ascetics in Kigali, who view it as a dirty, unhygienic habit and a hangover from Habyarimana's day.

We trudge upwards for half an hour. Aphrodis leads the way. Two decades before, as a teenager, he had walked down this track to begin life, as a postulant, at the friary at Kivumu. He survived the genocide by being driven to the border in June 1994 by Curic (and the infuriated Rwandan army officer), but he had subsequently left the priesthood. Like many Tutsis during the Habyarimana regime, Aphrodis joined a seminary to get an education, rather than from any deep-seated conviction in the Catholic faith.

Ahead, up a dusty track, is a collection of mud huts. Some children play in the dirt. A hundred yards before them, on its own, sits a single house. Aphrodis knocks and we enter a small room with a back door that leads into an internal yard. I can see the hindquarters of a cow through the door; its tail flicks flies from the crusted turds around its rear end. In the middle of the room is a small table covered with a shabby cloth, with a small vase of fresh flowers on it. 'My mother is head of a Catholic group, Regia Maria,' Aphrodis says. 'They meet once a week and pray.'

We sit on a low bench with our backs to the wall and, shortly afterwards, Drocella Nyirabukunzi walks through the back door. She wears a dark patterned dress and, in the cool of the windowless room and possibly because of her advancing years, has sensibly wrapped herself in an *igikwembe* – the colours faded from age. Aphrodis explains that I am keen to hear about her home – since it was one of the first to be built by Vjeko Curic after the genocide. Drocella smiles. Her eyes are fiercely bright and she has small, delicate features, and hands that grip her knees and look like exposed tree roots. 'The house was a gift from God,' she says. When she returned to the village at the end of the genocide, the home in which she had lived with her husband and nine of her children had been badly damaged.

In April of that year, several days after the President's assassination, the militia had attacked the house together with some of the people in the village. Each night men came and banged on their door, shouting, 'There must be Tutsis in there, we can smell them.' Finally, all but one of her children fled, but she had stayed with her husband and one son for several more days before it became too much. Her husband refused to leave. 'I have to follow my children,' she told her husband. 'I have to protect our house,' her husband replied.

She walked at night and hid in banana groves during the day. When she met a unit of RPF soldiers she was transported to a refugee camp. Later, she learned that the eight children who had left before her had been killed in crossfire between government and RPF forces. When she finally returned home, she discovered that her one remaining son and husband were still alive. He had been a popular man in the village – a teacher, who often gave cows to his neighbours. When the leader of the militia learned that it was his former teacher who was behind the barred door of the house they were attacking he told his accomplices to stop. Even so, her husband was never the same again. Three years later, he was killed on the road. Witnesses said that he was weaving erratically when an oncoming lorry hit his bicycle.

Drocella's house was part of Curic's reconstruction programme for the diocese. The house had been rebuilt in brick with wooden lintels over the doors, concrete foundations dug deep, a tiled roof and windows in most of the rooms. Drocella leans forward and points through the door to the collection of houses up the track.

'Things are better now. I can farm and I can sleep peacefully. No one talks about politics any more. We are all the same.'

'She means talking about different ethnic groups,' Jean-Pierre explains, referring to the most profound of President Kagame's edicts that he has introduced in an attempt to leave the country's past firmly behind. People are no longer Hutu or Tutsi or Twa but simply Rwandans. Any public utterance about ethnicity is deemed to encourage division in the country and the culprit could face a lengthy prison term. Drocella hears me use the words *Tutsi* and *Hutu* and looks awkward. I change the subject and ask her about the flowers. They were given to her by former *génocidaires*, she says, who come to her house to pray and discuss their problems. Does she feel safe with the men in her house, I ask. 'Oh yes, they leave everything in prison,' she says.

Jean-Pierre and Aphrodis shake their heads and try not to laugh. 'Look where she is,' Jean-Pierre says. 'Up a hill with nowhere to go. She doesn't have a choice but to hope and pray.'

Later, after Drocella has shown me around her small home, we emerge outside. Above us, up the track, a woman pounds cassava in a wooden bowl; her two children sit next to her staring down at us. Two men drift past the cassava woman's house, watching me as I snap away with my camera. The hills behind stretch up to a low ridge, perhaps a few hundred feet higher up than where we stand. We are a long way from anywhere, I think. Stuck up on a hill, like some Welsh sheep farmer. It's a brutal hour-long journey by jeep to the main road, a two-hour walk for Drocella, through three settlements, mostly Hutu, which watch her as she makes her way down muddy paths, across small streams.

Paul Kagame is now well into his second seven-year term as leader. His party, the RPF, won a thumping majority in the parliamentary elections. He, apparently, persuaded 90 per cent of his countrymen to vote for him as President. He has indicated that he will not stand for a third term, though many here cannot imagine how he will be happy retiring to whack tennis balls on his private court in Kigali, or stare at his cows on his farm up country. He rescued the nation from moral, economic and social degradation; the country has more schools, more roads, a universal health-care system. Even plastic bags are banned. But much of the country remains desperately poor; how can he possibly leave Rwanda in the hands of others when there is still so much to do? Kagame looms over his country, a solipsistic presence through which all thought and ideas must pass. It seems unthinkable that another Rwandan could make such a demand of his people – to eliminate ethnicity from their lives; a command for Rwandans to forsake their past that was conceived in a pastel-painted presidential office long before it received its predictable ratification in the country's legislature. Rwanda has no opposition parties that might have objected to the idea – they are all in exile. Even without any real political opponents, it is still audacious to tell Rwandans to reversion oral histories that have been passed down from generation to generation. Eighty years ago, the Belgians gave Rwandans identity cards that told them who they were. But people already knew who they were without a small piece of pink paper. Now there is a new diktat from the leadership – this time for Rwandans to reboot themselves. But up here in the hills above Kivumu, Drocella knows that the people she walks past – who sit on the stoops of their huts pounding cassava just as they have done for hundreds of years – are Hutu and she knows that they know she is Drocella Nyirabukunzi, a Tutsi, the mother of a family destroyed by their hand or, at the very least, with their knowledge or connivance. I wonder if Mr Kagame would ask his wife, Jeanette, to make the same walk to market each week.

Drocella sits down carefully on her stool. The sharp features that I saw inside have been diminished by the hard sunlight. The shadows inside that hid her age have gone. Now she looks like a woman who has lost eight children and a husband. I ask Aphrodis how often he makes it up here to visit his mother. He shakes his head. 'It's difficult,' he says. 'I have a family to look after.' I take her hand and thank her for showing me her house. She nods and starts to speak. Jean-Pierre listens.

'She says she is a stone. Her children have all gone. "I'm like a tree," she says. "I can be pushed by the wind."'

Susanne Brezina first met Vjeko Curic at a dinner on 10 July 1994 at a Catholic mission in Gikongoro, in the south-west of Rwanda. As the Austrian representative of a Catholic aid agency and laden with considerable financial resources, she had been focusing her efforts on feeding the huge number of internally displaced people who were still caught up in the last remnants of the fighting between the RPF and recalcitrant government forces. The Europeans around the table wore shiny shoes and pressed shirts, and picked at their food, and decided that it was not safe to cross the front line between the two armies. When Curic arrived – he was late – he wore old jeans and had just driven his small convoy of food aid from government-held territory to the rebels' side. He sat next to Brezina and told her of his plans for his parish in Kivumu. 'Come,' he said, 'we need your help.' The next day they accompanied a Rwandan bishop, Augustin Misago, to Kibeho church. Twenty thousand people had died there in April – shot by soldiers, hacked and burnt to death by local villagers and *interahamwe*. There were bloodstains on the walls, child's handprints where they had tried to escape the inferno. Misago walked through the ruins in his pristine white cassock and talked to Curic about trying to find money to rebuild the church.

'I didn't like the Bishop,' Brezina tells me. 'I didn't like all this talk of finding money. Thousands of people had just been killed there.'

Curic sensed Brezina's irritation. 'He's a Hutu,' he told her. 'Be careful whom you trust – there are many sides to this.'

Brezina thought, well, that's useful to know; I like this guy – with his jeans and T-shirt. 'So I went to Kivumu.'

Thousands of Hutus were stuck in camps inside Rwanda and on the Zairean border, and Curic wanted to encourage people to return home. Reconciliation, he told Brezina, would come through forgiveness. The building programme was the first step on that path. Over the next few months, largely funded by Brezina's charity, Curic rebuilt hundreds of homes, using both Tutsi and Hutu labour. 'Curic knew everybody,' Brezina continues. 'As we drove through the villages around Kivumu, Curic would say, "See this guy with the wooden shutters on his bike – he's a Hutu and a carpenter, and he'll make them for half the price of the ones in Kigali. That guy there – his cousin owned a plumbing business, but he was killed in May so now he has taken it over."' Brezina was flabbergasted. How the hell did Curic know all these people? It couldn't be possible. But the shutters got made and he was right about the new owner of the plumbing business. 'The genocide was a glitch,' Curic used to say. 'I knew these people before the genocide and I know them now and they will not always hate each other.' Hutus and Tutsis needed to re-engage with each other, to talk about what had happened and why. 'If they deny their past,' he told Brezina, 'they will repeat their mistakes.' The priest didn't mind who heard his views – even the new government, who felt his message was simplistic and overly hasty, given the depth of the crime and the extent of the trauma that Rwandans had recently endured.

'Rwanda was frozen. It was like people were locked in a trauma. So Vjeko could operate as if it was still the genocide. He had leverage because he had stayed,' says Brezina.

Besides, Curic was a magnet that attracted money from Western NGOs and charities. Rwanda's government – struggling with a looted financial system and a shattered infrastructure – was in no position to complain. The Bosnian could sweep his arm across the wide deserted valleys and plan for a resurrected Rwanda where Hutu and Tutsi would farm and work together again. He brooked no argument. 'We were on a mission to help this country,' says Brezina, 'and anything that got in our way was stupid and irrelevant. We felt indestructible – anything was possible.' She found the Bosnian inspiring. Even his sermons were lively and provocative. 'You should never have more than one of anything,' he shouted to his parishioners as he marched down the aisles. 'So what shall I do with these jeans I have on under my cassock?' he asked the children. 'I have another pair in my room. Maybe I should give these ones away?' Then he pretended to take his jeans off. The women shrieked with embarrassment and laughter and sunk their heads into their laps. An *umuzungu* without any trousers.

At night, when Susanne Brezina stayed at Kivumu, she sat with the priest and listened to the sound of gunshots echoing around the valleys. Rwanda was still a deeply violent and unstable country. The defeated Hutu army, along with the militias, sat on the Zairean border, threatening to retake the country for the million or so Hutus who had remained with them in vast refugee camps. The country was plagued with incursions from Hutu militias murdering Tutsis who had taken their homes, or exacting revenge on Hutus who had decided not to flee. Many rural areas became too dangerous for surviving Tutsis. The tentacles of the former extremists, who sat in a ferment in their Zairean refugee camps, stretched deep into the Rwandan countryside. Militia were regularly sent back and Tutsi families – stuck out alone on their hills – were often vulnerable to attack. Many retreated to the relative security of Gitarama or Kigali. Much of the western half of the country fell into lawlessness, with gangs of militia roving the villages before being driven out by units of RPF soldiers engaged in a counter-insurgency campaign designed to clear the country of the extremists once and for all. The RPF was often brutal in its treatment of individuals or whole communities it suspected of harbouring *génocidaires*. Evidence grew that many ordinary Rwandans had been killed by the army, who suspected them either of being implicated in the genocide, or of sympathizing with and sheltering the Hutu militias that were launching attacks from Zaire. A UN report put a figure on the number of people killed after the genocide by the RPF: thirty thousand. Despite the allegations, few RPF soldiers were ever arrested or tried for any revenge killings. One former senior Rwandan official described to me how, in 1995, he had witnessed Kagame – then Deputy President – flying into a rage at a report that pointed to RPF crimes; he had thrown it straight into the bin.

At Kigali airport one day, as she was waiting to fly back to Austria, Brezina was approached by a fellow passenger, the UN human rights investigator Homayoun Alizadeh. He showed her pictures of a massacre that had been recently discovered in the north-west of the country. Women and children allegedly murdered by the RPF. A burnt-out village. An RPF officer approached them and demanded Alizadeh hand over his briefcase. The investigator refused. The soldier grew angry, accused them of smuggling, and forced both Brezina and Alizadeh to be strip-searched. But the UN man still refused to hand over his briefcase. Intimidated by the UN man's citing of the UN Charter, the officer finally gave up and they were both allowed on their flight.

'In 1994 you couldn't think things over – you just had to decide quickly,' Brezina tells me. 'You knew who the killers and the victims were. But a year later, it was more complicated. Everything was so mixed up. The genocide was black and white, but afterwards you were not sure whose side you were on.'

Sebastijan Markovic returned to Rwanda in August 1994 – as soon as he could, as soon as he felt it was safe. He spent two weeks at Kivumu with his old friend. Curic seemed unchanged. After supper, on that first night, he showed Markovic to his room – not the one Markovic had usually stayed in, but one further along the corridor. When Markovic asked why he had been moved, the Franciscan took him by the arm and led him to the room that Curic himself had always occupied. When he opened the door and swung the torch around the walls, Markovic was horrified to discover bloodstains. 'The RPF herded people into this room,' Curic told him, 'and murdered them, so I am staying in your old room until I have cleaned mine up.' He took Markovic outside and led him to a eucalyptus tree. In the glare of the torch's beam, he pointed to the nails driven into the wood. 'They strung up Hutus on this tree,' Curic said. He pointed to the orchard a few yards away. He wanted to show Markovic the bodies that were buried there.

Now Markovic pauses and takes his glasses off. We are in his friary in Kigali, but I have had to wait until his fellow priests have left the dining room before we can talk in confidence. 'Did you go to the orchard?' I ask him. Markovic shakes his head. 'I couldn't,' he says, 'I had seen enough, I had heard enough. And I was frightened – the risks of knowing these things, let alone seeing them and talking about them, were huge. They still are. This is RPF country. They don't tolerate that.'

I had heard the whispers. In early June 1994, as the RPF closed in on Gitarama, many Hutus – certainly soldiers, probably militia and possibly ordinary people as well – had fled to the friary at Kivumu. Curic was away – in the south of the country – running aid to the large number of internally displaced people who were still caught up in the fighting. The Hutus at his friary had been quickly surrounded by the RPF and had surrendered. That much was commonly known and talked about, but it is alleged that they were murdered by the RPF at the friary. No soldier from the RPF was ever arrested for that crime. When Curic returned to his parish he discovered what had taken place. Markovic smiles at my next question. 'But what could he do but carry on? Besides, he had seen so many massacres it was normal. He could even joke about them.' 'Are the bodies in the orchard still there?' I ask. Markovic tells me that they had been removed some time later, but Curic was left to clean up his room. It was a warning, thinks Markovic. In the eyes of the new regime the Catholic Church had been irrevocably contaminated. Even though many priests died in the genocide or tried to stop the killings, several priests and nuns had, shockingly, either actively encouraged the killers or even participated themselves. Curic may have stayed and saved the lives of many Tutsis, but he was white and representative of a discredited West that had fled the country at the precise moment that Rwandans had most needed their protection. The Bosnian was welcome to stay at Kivumu but, like Westerners who had rushed in after the genocide, he was there under sufferance. 'Did Curic see it like that?' Markovic smiles and shakes his head. No, his friend was always certain that he was needed, sure he could work around any obstructions a government erected. He remembers Curic telling him how RPF soldiers had barged into his office with a young boy who had been accused of helping *génocidaires* escape. They needed to use the phone to organize for the boy to be transported to a police station. As the boy sat on the chair, Curic slipped him five thousand francs. It would be survival money for him in prison. It was a highly risky move. If he had been caught, Curic could have been arrested and even imprisoned, but he had laughed as he had told Markovic how he had managed to push the money into the boy's pocket without the soldiers seeing.

In this volatile atmosphere, Curic had few friends. Markovic had left for Kigali to begin work rebuilding the École Technique Officielle. The one man Curic liked and trusted was his boss – André Sibomana, who had been asked to run the Kabgayi diocese following the murder of Bishop Nsengiyumva in early June 1994 by RPF soldiers. Sibomana was a charismatic but controversial priest who had, for many years, edited the national Catholic newspaper, *Kinyamateka*. He had grown up in rural poverty, but after theological college he had been picked out from his peers and sent to Europe, where he studied law and journalism. On his return he quickly took control of the oldest newspaper in Rwanda and became a prominent critic of the Habyarimana regime. At the start of the genocide his name had been on a death list but somehow he had survived, hiding out in his home parish. In the new Rwanda, Sibomana had applied an equally censorious view – regularly citing the RPF for failing to protect the community or, worse, murdering parts of it. Criticizing the predominantly Tutsi regime was always risky; to do so as a Hutu was seen, by many, as foolhardy.

At a time when an unprecedented number of charitable donations were pouring into the country and, in particular, into Kabgayi, which was the largest Catholic diocese, Sibomana needed a man whom he could trust to handle the competing demands for the hundreds of thousands of dollars that were arriving. Curic was an obvious choice: neither Hutu nor Tutsi and with a deep understanding of Rwanda. Curic readily accepted the post to run the Économat Général of the Kabgayi diocese.

In a popular café, I meet with a prominent member of an international aid agency. I have promised to reveal neither their name nor their organization's, to protect its neutrality. 'Gerard' knew Curic well in the years that followed the genocide. He liked the Bosnian and they would regularly meet up and share notes over a drink. The aid official came to rely on the priest, whose knowledge of Kinyarwanda helped him decipher the obscure responses he often received from his Rwandan employees. There was much to do in Gitarama, where Gerard was based, distributing food and medical supplies to a population that was still largely unable to fend for itself. He would be furious when he discovered that his employees had failed to do as he had asked but had, instead, formed a committee – a leader elected, speeches made – to discuss his latest directive. Curic explained that he had to play a more subtle game – getting angry was pointless.

Rwanda had an oral culture. Curic guided Gerard: 'Don't get cross; engage in the debate, let your disappointment be expressed in the fluency of your language; what you want to happen has to be expressed as a narrative, not an emotional outpouring. Rwandans always keep their emotions in check. They stop listening if you get emotional.'

Gerard saw that Curic relished his role at the Économat Général. He and Sibomana were a powerful duopoly. Curic arbitrated on all requests from the hundreds of parishes that were slowly mushrooming back into life. Schools, health clinics, support for orphans, agricultural subsidies, new housing projects – all competed for the priest's time and money. The building of thousands of new homes offered lucrative contracts to local builders who were competing for the tenders. But there was jealousy – Gerard could see that. An *umuzungu* priest with so much power divided people. An *umuzungu* priest whose closest ally was a Hutu, and a prominent critic of the new government at that, deepened the sense of resentment. Curic seemed unbothered – he had built up enough credit with the Tutsis during the genocide, he said, to feel comfortable fraternizing with Hutus now.

Gerard began to doubt that Curic's ties with the new regime were as solid as he thought. Gerard worked closely with the RPF. They were disciplined, private, circumspect with the information they released to Westerners. Not a bunch of bandits on the take, like the last lot of kleptocrats, but a military government, he realized. These men and women had been forged together by thirty years of exile, not moping around their camps in the Ugandan bush but developing a tightly controlled, disciplinarian view of the world. Now they had retaken the country and, unlike the former ministers of the so-called government in exile who were sitting like bloated lumps in their villas across the border in Zaire, they had no intention of leaving Rwanda ever again. The RPF were happy to cooperate with the West in the reconstruction of the country but Gerard – reorganizing hospitals across the country and feeding the internally displaced – was strictly controlled in how he worked. He also thought he was being watched by what he had learned was an extensive intelligence network that had been put in place within days of the end of the genocide.

Mentioning this to Curic was little help, since it only encouraged the priest to embark on a bout of politicking that began to grate. The Bosnian loved to disseminate the latest piece of news from Kigali and often launched into long perorations on its meaning. Gerard had just spent two years working in Bosnia during the civil war and dinner with Curic at the friary reminded him of the ideologically hardcore Catholics that he had come across running aid convoys into Vitez and Kiseljak. Despite all his years in Africa, Curic was still unmistakably a Bosnian Croat: the talk, the leather jacket, the Chivas Regal. More than a whiff of macho swagger. Then there was the other side to him – the determination that left Gerard breathless with admiration. On one occasion he witnessed Curic bully his way past a recalcitrant RPF officer: 'Get out of my way,' he had told him, 'remember I know what you have done, I know where the bodies are buried.' And there was Curic's phone call to his clerical superiors in Europe – defending the Balotine nuns' decision to perform abortions for women who had been raped by the *interahamwe*. Fuck the Vatican, let's deal with realities.

*

In 1996, in an effort to end the incursions into Rwanda and stymie support for the former extremist government, the RPF mounted a military invasion of Zaire's eastern Kivu provinces, which run contiguous with Rwanda's western border, where huge refugee camps had been in existence since July 1994. The camps were attacked and largely demolished. Thousands of Hutu refugees died in the violence, while many others were forcibly repatriated to Rwanda. Others retreated further into the Zairean forests. Over the course of the following years, tens of thousands of Hutu exiles began the long walk back to their homes in Rwanda. Those alleged to have been involved in the genocide would not elude justice. By 1996 more than eighty thousand Rwandans, including many returnees, had been incarcerated – apprehended on the evidence of survivors and eyewitnesses. Or sometimes on little evidence at all. A simple denunciation could be enough to prompt an arrest.

It was not a normal prison population. The usual retinue of thieves, drug dealers, fraudsters and gangsters was swamped by ordinary men and women – teachers, doctors, carpenters, local government officials, taxi drivers, farmers, tax clerks – who had either killed or encouraged others to kill in the spring of 1994. Jails that had been built to house a few hundred inmates were now home to several thousand, and conditions inside had deteriorated fast.

The Gitarama prison was one of the worst. Situated on the main road into town, it is made up of a series of low, red-brick buildings surrounded by scrubby fields on which goats gnaw at yellowed wisps of grass and groups of boys kick scuffed and tattered footballs. In 1995, after months of intense lobbying and cajoling, Curic and André Sibomana finally received permission to accompany the Red Cross into the jail. Inside the gate, in the first interior courtyard, hundreds of men stood, as if they were a welcoming committee. In fact, Curic had walked into the living quarters of the *komeza*, a Kinyarwandan word that means 'continue', but in the context of the prison, it was the description for thousands of men with neither a cell nor even any kind of space in which to sit or lie down. The men spent their days and nights weaving their way between one another and slept, if sleep were possible, where they stood.

They were at the bottom of a hierarchical system of class and power that permeated throughout the prison. Just above the *komeza* were the hundreds of prisoners crammed into one of several large rooms. In the small chapel, for instance, three hundred men sat or lay on two planks that were jammed together – a home eighteen inches wide, dubbed *un château* – and supported above the floor by two blocks, one at each end. Underneath, between the blocks, three men lay perpendicular to the bed. The gap between floor and plank was just deep enough for a man to lie face up. The heat was intense. Whether you had *un château* or a space underneath depended on your status. At the top of the social pile were military men, doctors, lawyers who were given more space – perhaps a cell with only thirty or forty *châteaux*. But where people ended up depended on the decision of the *capita général* – the boss of each building – and how he ranked you.

Just as in society, Rwandans inside the country's jails were judged, put on a list and prescribed a place. Some were forced to sleep shoved up against the open latrines. But only at night. During the day they were driven out by the queue of men trying to relieve themselves. The queue was often so long – several hours' wait – that some abstained from food in order to avoid the toilet altogether. There were few showers; men stripped and washed in the open with what little water they could find. The water collected in grubby pools under the slowly wasting bodies of those who lay, exhausted, in the dirt. Sibomana had watched rivulets run through the feet of the men and discovered that even within the *komeza* another social hierarchy existed. Those he saw lying on the ground were usually dead and in the process of rotting away. Just above them crouched the sick and wounded who were waiting to die. They had days or perhaps weeks to live. And those standing, shifting from one foot to the other, were the prisoners who were still relatively healthy. But this was deceptive. Many of the men had stood for so long in the garbage, the shit, the rotting carcasses, that their limbs were severely diseased. Feet became swollen and then eventually began to fall apart. Some had lost a complete limb or needed to have it amputated. Sibomana saw one man standing on the raw stumps of his shins. When a man finally succumbed and slumped to the ground, it was an opportunity – the possibility of a few extra inches of space – for his neighbours.

The spring rains turned Gitarama's prisoners into grey sludge. The summer heat burnt the men into listless, dehydrated husks. They were hollowed-out shells – half starving, filthy and sick – with little hope of justice. The courts were unable to cope. The government admitted that it would take two hundred years to process the accused. Men and women who walked through the gates of Rwanda's prisons did so knowing that it was almost certainly a death sentence. In Gitarama, between September 1994 and May

1995, seven thousand were incarcerated in a prison that was built to house less than a quarter of that number. In just eight months, nearly a thousand had died. One hundred a week were rotting to death. At the end of the visit Sibomana reported watching a UN spokesman reassure the assembled crowd that help was at hand. One of the prisoners reached down and ripped his own toe off and threw it in the officer's face.

Curic was incensed by conditions in the prison. Brezina remembers the priest berating the RPF officers who ran it. 'How can you possibly think that this country will be reconciled if you remove human dignity from these men?' he roared. When Curic lost his temper with the soldiers she became frightened. She was nervous of the RPF. They were different to the ramshackle, loose-tongued, easily bribed army that had governed before. They were not above corruption, of course: in Kigali, where she lived, she was once stopped in her car by soldiers and asked where she was going. To a restaurant, she told them. They ordered her out and got into the jeep and drove away. Brezina shrugs – lifting an *umuzungu*'s car in those feral days seemed a reasonable redistribution of resources. What worried her more was the fear the army instilled in Rwandans and their confidence that they could act with impunity. Shopping at a bakery one day she was standing with others in a queue when an RPF soldier walked in, barged to the front and grabbed several loaves of bread from the counter. He left, without paying, slowly walking past his fellow Rwandans, wagging his finger at those who dared to look at him.

'You are playing with fire,' she told Curic.

'So what?'

'You're no good dead.'

'It's a good way to die.'

Curic led the chorus of critics who voiced their frustration at the RPF's refusal to allow food and medical aid into the jails. Foreign journalists lapped the story up. Prison conditions became an embarrassing and thorny issue for the new government. Sebastijan Markovic worried that his friend seemed to be on a mission to antagonize Kigali. Even when he was finally given permission to bring a weekly medical team into Gitarama prison to work alongside the Red Cross and the death rate among the inmates began to drop dramatically, Curic was still dissatisfied. He wanted to build shelters for the *komeza* – to protect them from the elements. The RPF resisted. 'Why do you want to build these things for the killers,' prison guards asked Curic, 'when we don't have any shelter either? You should build them for us.' 'I can't build things for you,' Curic replied. 'Ask your government.'

Gerald detected a creeping impatience and shrillness to Curic's demands, a mixture of bravado that Brezina ascribes to his experience of the genocide and irritation that the obvious course of action – meaning, his course of action – was not immediately adopted. 'It's a waste of time,' Curic complained to a fellow priest, 'all this talking and talking and nothing gets done.' In the decade before the genocide, he had spent years scraping bits of money together, cajoling Rwandans into helping him build up his friary, brick by brick. Now, swamped with cash, Curic had the power to change things, a wider brief and, he knew, there was a far more pressing need. He won the argument at Gitarama prison: walls were extended, new roofs erected, toilets built.

Where Sibomana was more diplomatic – employing orphans to fashion hundreds of pairs of rubber sandals out of old bicycle tyres for the barefoot prisoners – Curic was overtly ambitious. Showers were planned for the inmates. The RPF guards were outraged. 'You are building showers for our enemies!' they screamed. 'They are not your enemies,' Curic the Franciscan replied, 'they are your brothers and you need to forgive and learn to live together again.'

One night I dine with the friars at Kivumu. The talk is of Curic but the effusiveness I expected is muted. For many of those who had responded to Curic's call to enter the priest-hood, the Bosnian was not the same man after the genocide. After Curic rescued Florent and drove him to the border in June '94, the young Rwandan priest stayed in Burundi – fearful of a repeat of the violence he had barely escaped from with his life. When he was close to completing his training, he returned to Kivumu to see Curic. 'Come back and help me,' Curic had said. 'I am all alone.' This was in 1996, says Florent, and Curic was not the same *padiri*. The weight he had put on. The talk of the diocese and the politics. He hardly had time to take Mass in Kivumu. He had stopped walking through the parish – he drove everywhere and he employed two novices to check on the people. Florent didn't think Curic was a Franciscan any more. He was a bureau-crat.

'He told me a story of how he had recently been having dinner with a military chief and got a call that one of his parishioners was in labour and he had had to leave the dinner. I thought, well, Vjeko, before you would not have been having dinner with the military in the first place.'

*

280

After supper I sit outside and watch the dusk fall. New pylons stretch across the valley floor and lights nearby begin to flicker into life – a corridor is illuminated, perhaps sixty yards wide, either side of the pylons. The rest of the valley remains in darkness – just as it had been when Curic first arrived – the night air thick with the smell of people who sit in houses I can't see, stirring in their sleep. I had been told that when he was a young priest, Curic instinctively favoured the Tutsis in his parish. In the backsliding world of Habyarimana's Rwanda, he had been left alone to navigate between the different currents of corruption to help those he saw were being oppressed. The new regime had quickly shown itself to be quite different. Discipline was rigidly enforced by a well-organized army, a national plan for recovery was pursued with a tough, adamantine edge that dazzled foreign governments, still sick with guilt and quick to applaud Rwanda's new sense of purposefulness and direction. Curic's public clashes with the government over prison conditions were loud and dissonant, encouraging gossipers in the Church and the business community to question his powerful position in the diocese. His friendship with André Sibomana and his public displays of sympathy for the Hutu returnees rankled with the RPF. Curic's knowingness – his linguistic confidence – bordered on presumption, coming as it did from an *umuzungu*. He came to be viewed by the more secular Tutsi returnees as a throwback to the dark days when politicians and clerics – pampered by wealth and privilege – feasted together, oblivious and unmindful of their country stagnating around them. Earlier that evening a priest had told me that Curic had shown him a letter he had received from Kigali. It was unsigned and had been delivered by hand. The letterhead said it was from the office of the Prime Minister, at that time a man called Pierre-Célestin Rwigema. The note was brief – advising Curic to leave the country. His life was in danger. 'I will not leave,' Curic had told the priest. 'The people who are dying on the border' – by which he meant the Hutus stuck in refugee camps or returning to Rwanda – 'are human beings too.'

CHAPTER TWELVE

Kibuye

Nkubito is dead. The leader of the gang that murdered Jean-Pierre's father on the road to Kibuye in April 1994 succumbed in prison, shortly after he wrote the letter to Jean-Pierre, who learned of his death through *gacaca* – the justice system that the government introduced to release the pressure on Rwanda's logjammed courts and bring about reconciliation between the ethnic groups. The forced repatriation of Hutu refugees from Zaire meant there were, by 1998, 130,000 Rwandans sitting in prison with little expectation of a trial. *Gacaca* would, after several years, significantly ease the strain on the prison system. Tens of thousands of Rwandan prisoners took part in the traditional courts and many were subsequently released back to their villages and towns. Across Rwanda, Hutu *génocidaires* sat opposite the relatives of the Tutsis, and sometimes Hutus, that they had murdered, and confessed all.

The system had its critics. Some killers offered explanations with their confessions which suggested to many victims that responsibility did not lie – in whole or in part – with them: 'I was forced to kill'; 'if I didn't I would have been killed myself'; 'the government told me it was my duty'; 'God had abandoned us'. False confessions, too – anything to escape the prisons.

Jean-Pierre refused to attend the *gacaca* that was held in Kibuye. He saw the sense of the system but it felt, for him, as though he were being asked to forgive the killers of his father. Nkubito didn't kill me, Jean-Pierre thought, he killed my father, so why is he asking me for forgiveness when he should have asked my father to forgive him? News from the *gacaca*, however, filtered back to Kigali. Nkubito was no more. But a man called Gaspard had admitted to being part of Nkubito's gang, though he denied killing Muganga Joe. Nkubito had acted alone, he said. It was all too convenient, Jean-Pierre concluded. Nkubito's gang could pin the crime on a dead man. Gaspard had already served nine years in prison and was set free shortly afterwards.

The court did release Jean-Pierre from one burden. For several years he had made the four-hour journey to Kibuye, in search of his father's last resting place. He knew roughly where his father had been killed and would spend hours, on his hands and knees, looking for evidence. It had been a fruitless search. Gaspard's testimony, however, had offered more precise details of where Joe lay. In 2009, after a long day of digging with friends and villagers, Jean-Pierre had found a small pile of bones, the remnants of a shirt and a pair of glasses that he recognized as having belonged to his father. He had taken the remains of Muganga Joe to Kigali for burial – fifteen years after he had been murdered. That same year, on a return visit to Kibuye, Jean-Pierre had confronted Gaspard. It had been an unsatisfactory meeting.

'The village is Hutu,' Jean-Pierre tells me. He has dropped his voice, wary of using such terms so openly. Nearby, in the hotel garden in which we sit, a businessman is on his mobile phone. Jean-Pierre waits until the man has begun talking. He says he thought the villagers would turn on him and kill him too. It felt dangerous there – he felt vulnerable, surrounded by people he didn't know, in a village tucked away in the hills, far from Kibuye and any protection the presence of police might provide. Gaspard, when he finally found him, was evasive. Jean-Pierre couldn't think straight, listening to the man. He was so angry he couldn't understand him. Nothing seemed to make sense.

'You could say to those killers, here, make a body, make a finger – and they will spend their lives trying to make even that little finger. But in a few minutes they manage to kill a whole body, a whole person. How do you understand that?'

The man on the mobile phone finishes his conversation, picks up his papers from the table and leaves, nodding to us as he passes. I say, 'Let's go back to Gaspard's village and find him. Let's try again.' And we agree to go.

On the way we stop at Rutongo, where Jean-Pierre's family lived in the years before the genocide. At the top of the hill sits the hospital where Joe worked. The main corridor is wide and green and open at both ends so the breeze blows through the wards either side of the passageway. Jean-Pierre points to his father's old office which occupied a corner of the building close to the reception. The reception area is open and there are several people staring at a dusty television screen that is bracketed to a concrete pillar. President Kagame is speaking and then the picture cuts to a scene of dancers performing in front of the presidential party. We are nearing the anniversary of Liberation Day – 4 July – when the RPF finally defeated the extremist government. Some question why it took the RPF three months to throw out the Hutu forces given that the RPF was a far better-trained and motivated army. Conspiracy theorists say Kagame was in no hurry to evict the extremists. Each day of conflict produced another massacre – arming Kagame with yet another stick to beat the West with until, finally, he was victorious. But Rwanda is stuffed with conspiracy theories and this one, I think, is mendacious gossip. Kagame was a highly accomplished commander who led a small invasion force of bush soldiers in a war against a government army that was dug in and militarily supplied by a global power – France. But it is interesting that such unsubstantiated whispers won't entirely disappear.

We walk down a steep hill. On one side of the track, every fifty yards or so, there are brick houses, painted white, but now covered with mud and smoke stains. Across the pitted track there is a rusted chain-link fence. Beyond, through the trees, I can see the copper mine – started by the Belgians forty years ago – which has cut a huge red welt through the mountainside. The government built the houses for middle-class Rwandans who worked in the mines or the hospital. Jean-Pierre stops.

'We used to call this place Paris because the houses were all the same and very beautiful.'

At a house halfway down the hill Jean-Pierre walks into a small square courtyard. Several children are crowded around an open fire, which is being fed by an older boy, whittling branches off a large tree trunk that has been dragged in. The children are shy and retreat to a series of dark rooms on one side of the courtyard, peering out at us. 'I shared the middle room with Mukassa Joseph,' Jean-Pierre says, nodding to where some of the children have fled, 'but I wasn't here very much because I was always at school in Zaire.' He seems embarrassed. 'It wasn't like this,' he says, pointing vaguely around. 'We had electricity. Water. Everything.'

A teenage girl is washing plastic plates in an old dented pail filled with soupy brown water, setting them down on the cracked cement paving. Periodically she pours the dirty water out and refills the pail from an old, battered twenty-litre jerrycan. A man on a stool sits and smokes and ignores us. Rubbish is everywhere. The place is filthy – a pigsty really. The walls are charred and broken down, the rooms are gloomy recesses stuffed full of rubbish and old mattresses. Jean-Pierre talks to a woman who is wearing an old patterned chemise, which flaps open to reveal a baby pressed to her breasts. She is the owner of the house and works as a security guard at the mine. Then Jean-Pierre begins a longer conversation – and he sounds tetchy. 'What are you talking about?' I ask. 'I want to know why her children are not at school,' he replies. 'They should be at school but she says that they have to help here at home. It's wrong.'

Jean-Pierre is obsessed with schools and we often talk about his children and their next step on the education ladder. The RPF – the party Jean-Pierre voted for – has invested heavily in education, but it is still compulsory only until the age of twelve and many schools are short of teachers and overcrowded. In Kivumu, the priests had bemoaned the lack of proper schooling. Six thousand children in their parish alone – educated either in the morning or afternoon because of the lack of teachers. Hutu children, they told me – the Tutsis were in the towns and sent their children to private schools. Too many were leaving school and heading straight back to their homes without being able to read or write or get a job. It was repeating the cycle of destitution and anger. 'And then what?' one priest asked. The Rwandans around the table had fallen silent. Talk like this was dangerous. Ivica Peric spoke up: 'Before, the government could control the country because it was only one ethnic group – the smaller one – that was dissatisfied. But now it's the other way round; the larger group face that situation.'

Higher education remains a distant prospect for most Rwandans and Rwanda's small middle class is often doubtful that the new universities that are opening up are good enough for their children. Jean-Pierre has sent Sandra to university in France on a scholarship and is scraping the money together to do the same for Vanessa. Serge is still at school but the plan is to try and find a way to get him to a college in the United States.

Jean-Pierre is cross with the woman's answer and walks off, to the far end of the courtyard, where he points to a small hut perched just above the house in a patch of maize. 'That's where Zeno the Batwa pygmy lived; we used to pay him five francs and he would dance for us.' The woman has followed us and smiles, recognizing Zeno's name. 'He died many years ago,' she says. 'He had a son called George but he never came back from Congo after ninety-four and I think it hurt him.'

'Are these people Hutu? Did they go to Cong—'

Jean-Pierre shakes his head and cuts me off. This new Rwanda – where talk that might indicate ethnicity is a banned subject – is frustrating. A few days ago, a Westerner sat in a restaurant with me and, under his breath, talked about *Hondas* and *Toyotas*. It took me a minute to realize what he was on about. In polite circles, and if they feel pushed to be specific about Hutus or Tutsis, Rwandans will talk about 'another section of the population'. The past is being rewritten. Instead of personal history there lies an empty, untethered space, a yawning awkwardness between people. A week before, out in the countryside, Ivica Peric and I had walked through villages where this kind of listless poverty was common – a rural underclass that remained tied to a small patch of land, living in two-room huts, lacking running water or electricity. There are two Rwandas now, largely divided along ethnic lines, Peric told me. Tutsis who lived on the hills before '94 had been killed and many of those who had survived had subsequently headed for the capital and more prosperous towns where the trickle of wealth still follows ethnic lines. Out in the hills, the vast majority of Rwandans – the vast majority of the country – are poor and Hutu. Given how close we are here in Rutongo to the capital – a mere ten miles away – and to feel such a powerful sense of abandonment, it seems implausible to imagine that I am looking at a Tutsi family down on its luck. These people are Hutu, I am sure of it – part of Rwanda's underpaid, poverty-stricken janitorial staff – possibly survivors from the refugee camps in Congo who returned a decade or more ago but have yet to escape the poverty that still afflicts much of Rwanda. 'When you are poor,' Peric had said, 'you need to know who you are.' But the government wants people to live in existential indifference to their past and to ask questions is not only forbidden but risks getting this family into trouble.

Part of my frustration, I know, stems from a meeting the day before at the presidential compound. It had not gone well. I had rung a friend who worked for President Kagame and asked if I could meet with His Excellency once more. I explained that it had been over seven years since we last talked. Much had changed in the country. Alfred said he would do what he could. The next afternoon Jean-Pierre dropped me off at the presidential gates and I was escorted down an impeccably swept path into a wide, open garden with a polished white-stone patio. Alfred met me under an awning and introduced me to Yolande, a youngish woman with a faint American accent, who was the President's Director of Communications. We chit-chatted. Behind us a gardener with a long net fished out a leaf from a blue swimming pool. Nearby, a group of young-looking white men and women, in suits, sipped Cokes around a table. Every so often they howled with laughter. I said, 'Gosh – they seem comfortable here.' Yolande smiled. 'They are from Tony Blair's Governance Initiative.' She took out her notebook.

'Anyway, to business, David. Why do you want to see His Excellency?'

I told her that I was interested in memory and what role the past plays in our lives, what role it played in a country's future.

Yolande listened attentively but began to shake her head slowly. 'The President has talked enough about the past,' she said. 'He wants to talk about the future, where Rwanda is going, not where it has come from.'

'That seems fair enough,' I said. 'I guess I am interested to know if people are able to do the same as their leader.'

'Why wouldn't they?'

'Because most of us are just trying to work out how to live now.'

'You don't think about what you will do next?'

'Well, yes,' I said, 'I probably do but not entirely successfully. And when I do, I know where I've come from. That seems important – to hang on to what I am. People like to know where they come from, don't they? It's hard to forget. Especially if you are poor.'

'Oh God, David, no. I really don't buy this argument that people think about their roots more if they are poor. *Please.*'

'You don't think when people are struggling in their lives they need to feel anchored by who they are? Or where they come from?'

'No – that is such an outdated idea! *Really.*'

Yolande paused and then placed her palms flat on the surface of the polished table and explained that the President believed Rwandans could define themselves by what they wanted to achieve, not by some ethnic label attached to them by colonialists and exploited by extremist politicians.

'It wasn't colonialists,' I countered.

'Yes, it was,' she said.

'OK, the Belgians gave you identity papers but you have always been Hutu and Tutsi. You've always existed like that.' I paused. 'It's who you are,' I added.

'Is it? So, you say that's who we are?'

'No, you do.'

Yolande looked at me, took a sip of water and sat further back in her chair. I turned to Alfred. He had taught Communications at a British university for many years before returning to Rwanda. 'Alfred, come on,' I said. 'Don't you think it's good to talk about identity rather than suppress it?'

Alfred smiled thinly.

Yolande leaned forward and closed her notebook. 'It's time to move on from those days, David. We're past all that.'

There was another burst of laughter from the nearby table. Yolande explained that one of the team was returning to Britain and this was their goodbye drinks. We continued to chit-chat for a few more minutes and then the meeting was over. Yolande walked with me past Tony Blair's acolytes towards the gates. She was conciliatory. His Excellency was very busy. Perhaps he could meet me when he was next visiting Britain. She stopped, remaining in the shade of a large tree, and shook my hand. I walked on, alone, into the bright afternoon sun. I could see Jean-Pierre's jeep in the car park. The sun burnt. I muttered as I walked – angry with myself for my presumption. An *umuzungu* telling a Rwandan who they are. *Jesus Christ.*

'You were quick,' Jean-Pierre said. 'How was His Excellency?'

'Busy.'

We drove out of the compound. Three soldiers wheeled the metal gates open. They seemed young, in their early twenties. Small boys back in 1994. I thought about Yolande and wondered how old she was and why I felt angry with her as well as with myself. 'We're past all that,' she had said, her voice rising above the din of the table next to us. Are we, I thought, as we pulled out on to the road. Are you sure, Yolande? With your privileged, college-educated voice, your perfect transatlantic manners – surely a product of the Tutsi diaspora rather than a survivor. Where were *you*, Yolande?

*

The journey to Kibuye is long and slow. The road gradually steepens as we climb into the mountains, Jean-Pierre's jeep groaning at the gradient. Later in the year he plans to buy a new car. Business is picking up. 'Kagame has been good for our country,' he says, 'we are safe now.' And with security, the inference is clear, comes growth – economic, social, spiritual. After Sandra and Vanessa, their son, Serge, quickly followed. But more than ten years later, Jean-Pierre and Odette surprised each other when she became pregnant. Cindy's arrival seems to have rejuvenated Jean-Pierre. 'The older kids call us Abraham and Sarah because we are so old to have another child,' he laughs. At a roadside stall we stop and eat slabs of goat's cheese. Later we park the car next to a pile of rubble that used to be Nyange church. In March 1994 the road in the village was being repaired – to give ministers in Habyarimana's government a more comfortable ride to their lakeside retreats. A Caterpillar truck was left by the side of the road and on 16 April 1994 it was used to push in the small brick church where two thousand Tutsis had sheltered from the *interahamwe* outside. Once the church walls had been smashed in, the militias and locals launched their attack using clubs and machetes.

The keeper of the memorial is an old man. He seems tentative as we approach. Did we want a tour? No, thanks – we haven't much time. He retreats to his small hut by the main gate. The area where the church stood is not large. Most of the building has been cleared to make way for graves – a few slabs of white cement – but the site is still fringed by debris from the genocide and ringed by a metal fence and a low, red-brick wall. Skeletal metal window frames jut out from the rubble. A printed purple banner – perhaps two feet wide and twenty feet long – is draped across the entrance. It has started to drizzle, so the material has sagged and bulged, making the writing impossible to read. But I have seen many of them – all over Rwanda, commemorating, as they do, the genocide and marking each site as a memorial to a massacre that took place there.

Commemoration of the genocide against the Tutsi.
Let us learn from history by building a better future.

'How are Rwandans supposed to stop thinking about Hutu and Tutsi when there are these banners everywhere?' I ask.

We have retreated to the car – the drizzle has become heavier. Jean-Pierre cleans his glasses and ignores my question. We sit in silence watching drops of rain race down the windscreen. Perhaps it is because of the rain or the swirling mist that has curled around our car for the last hour, reducing us to a frustrating crawl. Or maybe Jean-Pierre regrets agreeing to my idea of looking for Gaspard again. But I think I have just misjudged my friend's mood. I have been to sites like this with Jean-Pierre before. This time is no different. As we had mooched about he had grown quieter, slowly drifting away; his shoulders had dropped. I should know by now when to ask a question and when to shut up.

'You can't close these sites down,' he says flatly. 'They are part of what happened.'

He starts the car and wrenches the wheel round as we turn on to the main road.

'Don't these places just remind everybody of the past – hold everyone back?' I ask.

The keeper has emerged out of his hut and, lashed by the rain, brings his hand up in a shaky salute. Jean-Pierre wipes the condensation from the windscreen.

'Everything reminds me of the past. I go to Kibuye, I drive past men and I think, did you kill my mum and my brothers? Did *you*? And *you*? I go to a wedding and I have to make the speech as the head of the family and I know it should be my dad speaking. The killers killed one million people. This is not a joke. This is not an idea.'

We drive on in silence. At the summit some children try to flag us down, shouting – *hey, hey, hey* – waving intricate wooden toys at the car. Jean-Pierre ignores their yelps. He pushes his glasses up onto his forehead and with his thumb and forefinger squeezes his eyes so the tears collect in each corner and ride up onto his large fingers. We pick up a little more speed as we begin our descent. I switch on the car stereo and push in the tape. A Zairean voice croons, *Why are you leaving me, don't leave me. Tell me what you want.* The mist peels away. Bright sunshine reveals a wide, deep, bottle-green valley, the familiar, feudal patchwork of huts splattered across it.

'Did I ever tell you about the time when I brought a girl called Rose back home?' Jean-Pierre asks.

He turns the music down and tells me that Rose worked in the Ministry of Infrastructure. He brought her home and introduced her to his parents. When she and his mother were next door, Papa Joe had said, 'Hey, Jean-Pierre – she is a nice girl, for sure, but she is not very beautiful,' and Jean-Pierre said, 'Shut up, Dad, you can't say that,' but Jean-Pierre couldn't help laughing. And his dad started laughing too. 'OK, I'll shut up,' he said, 'but that's my opinion.'

'That's outrageous,' I say and we start to laugh.

'I know. Can you imagine that? What kind of dad can say that to his son?' He shakes his head, laughing deeply at the memory. 'They didn't know my dad said that to me. The killers. They knew nothing about that.'

A bend on the road. A grey parenthesis. Kibuye, a few miles further on. Behind, the village of Rubengera and the land that Joe and Jolie had bought and on which they were building their house. From her new kitchen Jolie would see a finger of blue from the lake, and Joe would put on his white coat and sneak away to the hospital a few times a week – just to keep his hand in. As the road straightens there is a path that leads to a collection of small houses. Jean-Pierre leaves the road, heading up the path for a few yards. Below us the ground drops away to a small creek, a series of small, carefully tended plots and a man digging. I can hear his hoe hit damp clods, a rhythmic *shtup*. Jean-Pierre points to a hole by the side of the path. 'Joe was killed here,' he says. 'They left him on the track.' A single bindweed flower hangs over the hole, which is partly covered with grass and small bushes. Jean-Pierre heard that some time after the killers left, the *préfet*, who had ordered the killing, told them to return and bury the doctor in the ditch. I say, 'Well, that would fit, because sometime in April the government had ordered militias to bury the dead rather than leave them where they had been killed.' 'Yes,' says Jean-Pierre, 'it was a health problem.'

I can hear the gurgle of the creek. A car sweeps past, the drawl of its tyres on the bend, a slow inhalation of air. Jean-Pierre tells me that a long time ago he had met Nkubito. Jean-

Pierre was a student at the time – taking a bus back to visit his grandmother in Kibuye. 'I know your father,' Nkubito had said. 'He is a friend of mine, let me pay for your bus ticket.' Jean-Pierre had thanked him but said that he would pay. They had travelled on the same bus back to Kibuye and when Jean-Pierre had arrived at his grandmother's house he had asked his father if Nkubito was a friend of his. 'Maybe,' his father had said, 'I don't know.'

The *shtup shtup shtup* has stopped and the man by the creek is leaning on his hoe, watching us. 'Sometimes,' Jean-Pierre says, 'it feels like I am pulling this heavy thing behind me. I drag it and drag it and if I stop I will die. So I go on pulling this load and there is no one to help me.'

When they dug that final time for his father, Jean-Pierre had brought his thirteen-year-old son, Serge. He used to ask lots of questions about his grandfather but this time, after they found Joe's bones, his questions dried up. It was as though that was enough for Serge, Jean-Pierre thinks. 'The young are the future – not me, or him,' he says, pointing to an old man walking towards us, almost bent double under a vast bundle of grass. The man cranes his neck and nods at us as he passes. Not long ago, Jean-Pierre says, he came across an old friend of his father. He remembered Ruziyo from when he was growing up, how he had always stopped and chatted to his father. He was old now and seemed pleased to see Muganga Joe's son and welcomed him into his house, and they sat and talked about the old days when his father was alive, and then Ruziyo shook his head and said, 'I can't understand how they could kill a man like your father. A doctor. It was wrong. I can see why they killed your mother. But your father? *No.*'

'When I heard him say this I thought, it's not over,' says Jean-Pierre.

The house that Joe had been building is still unfinished. What spare money Jean-Pierre has is going towards his children's education. But the building is sturdy, the walls and roof are up and the windows have the familiar iron railings sunk into their frames so the place is secure. There is a small brick veranda at the front and someone has carefully tended the garden. Two hectares of land surround the property, which is set a hundred yards above the main road – far enough away from the constant hum of motorbikes down below, in the village.

The house next door, where Jean-Pierre's parents were living whilst work continued on the new house, is rented out to Abdul and his family. It is falling apart – the thick plaster around its foundations has fallen away, the windows are boarded up. Abdul seems unbothered. I think he is just grateful that Jean-Pierre has not charged him rent for the past year. He makes tables and chairs, he says, but has found little work in the last six months. Taxes are too high so people don't have money to spend on furniture. The Association, which he had belonged to for many years and which functioned as a kind of work collective, has been closed down. His family survive on the crops he and his eldest son, Paul, cultivate in the grounds around the house; eating most of them, selling a few. Maize, beans, bananas; the crop of sweet potatoes is over. 'Life is the same as it always was,' he says. 'Maybe slightly better.' There are no problems with security, he can travel where he likes without having a *permis de résidence* to prove where he lives. Not that he travels much. Although he did some work for the government the year before and points to the shirt from the National Institute of Statistics he is wearing. *If You Don't Count, You Don't Count*, it reads. We are standing in a sodden field of maize and from here I can see that part of the roof of the house is collapsing and the rainwater has collected into fetid puddles that seep into the mouldy stonework at the back of the house. Abdul clutches a stalk of maize – 'The government provides free fertilizer,' he says, 'and that's a good thing.' Education too – his kids would never have got past primary school before '94.

Did he know Muganga Joe? Abdul drops his head. He remembers him. He used to see him smoking outside the house. 'This is our history,' he says, and mutters to himself. He seems upset, rocking on his feet. Jean-Pierre shrugs – maybe he knows the killers. Or was part of it.

Abdul's son, Paul, interrupts. 'It is a bad part of our history, when we were divided by the Europeans. We know it can happen, so I am worried about that and so are my friends. We talk about it a lot.'

'But we are all Rwandans now,' his father says, as if to reassure him.

'Sure, I feel Rwandan,' Paul replies.

'Yes, me too,' says Abdul. 'It doesn't matter if you are Hutu or Tutsi – it's all the same now.'

Jean-Pierre walks back towards the front of the house. Abdul's wife emerges from inside with a large baby under one arm. 'This is where my mum and brothers were killed,' Jean-Pierre says, pointing to a patch of bare grass near the door. The gang had told her to come out of the house; his brothers had followed their mother outside. They were beaten to death. Below the house, through the maize, I can see another purple banner draped across a building. Purple – Rwanda's colour of mourning – is a striking contrast to the greens and browns of the countryside.

Abdul and Paul have caught us up. Paul is keen to practise his English. He is in his third year of secondary school. What does he want to be, I ask. 'A doctor.' 'Every kid wants to be a doctor,' mutters Jean-Pierre. And it is true – it was a refrain we heard at a school we had recently visited, in a village several miles off the main road to Butare. The headmaster, Vénuste, and I had sat in a classroom full of fifteen-year-olds. 'Doctor,' they all chimed in answer to my inevitable question. Why did they want to be doctors, I asked Vénuste. He smiled – it was a good thing to be, no? But we had tussled when the headmaster explained that Hutu and Tutsi were terms only used in history lessons about the genocide. Otherwise pupils were taught they were Rwandan. What did his pupils think they were? What people felt they were was hard to know, Vénuste said. Did he think avoiding their ethnicity would help them understand what happened to their country, I asked. Vénuste explained that it was helpful to tell his pupils the specifics of what happened – how the politicians were at fault – rather than concentrate on who you were. Around the classroom the pupils continued to copy out the densely packed English sentences on the blackboard – a geography lesson. Few of the children spoke English yet here they were, obediently turning out neat cursive on river erosion in their exercise books. 'Everything will depend on our leaders,' Vénuste reassured me. 'They need to cherish us.'

We walked to the primary-school building and Vénuste told me that twenty-four staff taught fifteen hundred pupils. Parents had little choice but to send their children here. There was another school but it was not close. Vénuste pointed off to the west and there, situated three valleys away, I could just make out the aluminium roof of a building shining in the afternoon haze. I said that I had not heard a Rwandan use the word 'cherish' before. Why did he choose that word? 'Well,' Vénuste said, 'I think we are still fragile. If our leaders are like those that went before then I don't know what will happen.'

Vénuste's words echo inside me as Jean-Pierre and I make our way down the path from his parents' house to the car. Abdul and his family watch us as we leave, four fragile figures silhouetted against the afternoon sky. 'Come back and see us,' Paul had said in English. 'Work hard,' I replied. I think of President Kagame and a government that still retains the military discipline that took it from the refugee camps of Uganda back to Rwanda's state ministries. Kagame's fluttery, high-pitched speech belies his steeliness, his certainty. *You will be a doctor, you will grow only maize, you will speak English, you will be a Rwandan.* He has placed himself, like a roadblock, between old enmities. Like the leaders before him, he can boss his countrymen, still mostly poor and subservient, to do as he commands since they are as needful for him to be right – to keep them safe – as he is for them to obey him.

Jean-Pierre puzzles over the map and I think about the roadblocks in 1994 that smelt of death long after the militias had fled. And then, slowly, we begin to make our way to the village where Gaspard lives.

CHAPTER THIRTEEN

Kivumu

When Gerard, the aid worker, drove up the stony path to Kivumu, at the end of another long and difficult day, desperate for a cold beer and some conversation, he would often find Vjeko Curic sitting in the living room of the friary with his head in his hands, in tears. 'He was depressed, no doubt,' says Gerard.

This was in early 1997. Curic had continued to receive funding for his construction projects, which he believed were the route to ethnic reconciliation, but Rwanda had lurched back into violence. The former extremist government had redoubled its military incursions from the refugee camps in what was now the Democratic Republic of the Congo. The border became a militarized zone as the RPF fought to drive units of militia and former soldiers of the extremist government back out of the country. Westerners had been killed. In February a Canadian priest – known for his equanimity towards both Tutsis and Hutus – had been murdered in the north of the country. The perpetrator was, according to witnesses, a former member of the Tutsi rebel army but he was reportedly released soon after. Two weeks earlier, three Spanish aid workers were killed in their home late one night and there was confusion over who was responsible. Some allege that the killers were soldiers from the former Hutu government army; others are less sure and point to the fact that the RPF had a heavy presence in the area, having undertaken to protect Western aid workers and human rights investigators. The deaths had prompted most aid agencies to pack their bags and leave Rwanda, demanding greater security before they returned. Curic was on his own again, and unlike in '94 when the enemy stood at a roadblock, it was impossible to know who to trust and who would sooner do him in. The letter from the Prime Minister's office had unnerved him. A friend brought him a bullet-proof vest from Europe which he gratefully accepted. 'Look,' he said to Oswald, as he showed it off, 'I am safe now.' But the smile seemed hollow. Sebastijan Markovic, his old Salesian friend, despaired of the situation. Curic confided that he felt threatened from all sides. André Sibomana, Curic's boss, asked Markovic to persuade their friend to leave, but it was impossible, Markovic says, to do so.

'If he'd left he would be saying to everyone, "I am afraid."'

Gerard had stayed – one of the few Westerners to remain in Gitarama. It was a depressing world in which to work. The *interahamwe* had recently begun turning up, casting a pall of fear over the town. Most mornings Gerard arrived at his office to discover a body had been dumped there – probably the victim of a bloody, retributive murder. His staff, mainly Tutsi, were already in the office, having stepped over the body. 'Has anyone contacted the morgue to have the body picked up?' Gerard would ask. No one spoke.

The culture of silence that permeated Rwanda before the genocide had not disappeared; if anything, the paranoia in the town had made it worse. Silence was a defence against the accusatory, conspiratorial world in which Rwandans lived. To speak up, let alone volunteer to move what was most likely a dead Hutu from the steps of the office, risked being branded an extremist sympathizer. Rumours of who had returned to Gitarama forced people to stay at home in a self-imposed curfew. The market slowed, half his staff never showed up. Most nights Gerard was too exhausted to make the fifty-minute drive to Kigali and a decent meal, and he'd return instead to the small, decrepit motel he roomed at on the outskirts of Gitarama. He'd sit and watch shitty black-market videos – *Mr Bean* and *Die Hard* – that his staff found for him. Or he'd head over to Kivumu and see Curic.

The priest, Gerard tells me, would rub his face with his hands and quickly cheer up. Oswald would cook something spicy, and as they ate Curic talked about the old, pre-colonial Rwanda, when the Tutsi monarchs ruled the south and the Hutu dynasties controlled much of the north. Curic had become fascinated with *ubwiru* – the secret language of the Tutsi royal courts. Families that were part of this world used it to convey coded messages between themselves. Children were initiated into this oral tradition learning, by heart, poems that took hours to recite. The stories and poetry were constantly updated and passed on covertly from generation to generation. To the untrained ear the verses seemed to make no sense, but Curic had spent years studying *ubwiru* and relished his knowledge and understanding of a secret world. Even though the RPF had positioned some Hutus in nominally powerful positions in the first post-genocide government, Curic, better than most, grasped that power emanated from a Tutsi elite, which he felt he was privy to. Gerard knew that mining the different political seams would appeal to the Bosnian, but wondered whether the priest overestimated how much sway his nuanced and privileged understanding of the Tutsis' masonic world actually had. 'Get out of here – take some time off,' Gerard advised him. But he wouldn't. 'I won't be faced down by them,' he told the aid worker. Gerard pauses, weighing his words. 'Look, I liked Curic, and he was a really good guy,' he tells me. 'But Bosnians are macho. They like the game and they want to be in the game – it's how they survive.'

In 1970, when Curic left home for his Franciscan boarding school in Visoko, along with the subjects usually taught, the thirteen-year-old was also schooled in the history of the Franciscans in Bosnia. They called themselves 'Uncles' – an appropriately avuncular title, perhaps, given their love of wine and a good sing-song. The name, in fact, originated in the fifteenth century when the Franciscans were the only Catholic order that dared stay in Bosnia after the invasion of the Turks. They became the protective shield around the small band of Catholics, carefully negotiating a deal with Sultan Mehmet that would allow them to remain and fulfil their pastoral duties. Five centuries later, in Tito's Communist Yugoslavia, the Franciscans, once again, found accommodation with the regime in power. In Visoko, much of the monastery building was divided between a military orphanage and the headquarters of a local rail company, but once again, the Franciscans' political acumen allowed them to map a route through a newly proclaimed atheist country.

The school continued and pupils like Curic were quietly trained for the priesthood every year.

The Gimnazija looms over Visoko. The town used to be a mix of Serbs, Croats and Muslims. But since the end of the Bosnian war, the Serbs have left and only a fraction of the town remains Catholic. Father Ivan Nujic pulls out the old school ledgers and runs his finger down the pages until he finds Curic's name. His marks are neatly annotated – fours and maximum fives mostly. 'You needed to get that,' says Ivan. 'You can repeat a year once but after that we can't keep forgiving you. You have to want to study – if you don't then, *phssssht*, you go. Twenty-five enter when they are thirteen, but only ten of them will complete the four years here.'

Faded black and white photographs hang from the walls of the corridors. Young men, hair neatly parted in fifties styles, jackets buttoned, stare intently at the camera. Choosing the priesthood in the Tito era, however loose an arrangement the dictator had with the Soviet Union, was still a risk. Ivan says, 'The Communists hated us. Wearing a cross could cause you trouble. There were spies everywhere. Even here at the school, some of the students were paid to spy on us. So we had to be a family – even the teachers were like big brothers, protecting the pupils from the state.'

Ivan points to the picture of a young man. 'That's my brother,' he says. 'But he left – he ran.'

'Is he a priest?' I ask.

'No, he's a lawyer in Switzerland.'

'Do you see him?'

Ivan flicks his hand dismissively. 'Sometimes.'

Outside, looking through the window, I see that some of the walls are still pockmarked with bullet holes from the war. The dormitories are tidy, bedside reading neatly stacked, floors polished, a few clothes hanging in shared wardrobes.

Father Josip now runs the school. He remembers Curic returning to talk to the boys in the late eighties, telling them of life in Africa, encouraging them to become missionaries. Josip was tempted himself. He became president of the Missionary Society; they sent stamps to the Central Office in Sarajevo – a hundred stamps and they could build a house in Africa. But Bosnia was a missionary country too, he says. The Catholics were outnumbered by Orthodox Serbs and Muslims. And they were persecuted by the Communists. 'If you were a popular priest the Communists would "invite" you for an interview. "Why are you a priest?" they would ask. "You are young and good-looking, come and join the Party."' Father Josip uses the word '*lupa*'. Ivan had as well.

'What does it mean?' I ask.

'It means being watched. Like under a microscope.'

'Was Africa an escape for Curic?' I ask.

Josip says, 'When Curic was at school here, his father worked in Germany. He would stay there for two or three months at a time. The money was so much better. One time, he managed to get a week's leave, but when he got home to Zepce he was detained by the police and held in a cell until it was time to return to Germany. There was no freedom here. Yugoslavia was a prison. We were watched, if you had your own ideas you were seen as dangerous. It was a burden.'

On 31 January 1998, Oswald left Kivumu friary for his weekly shop in Gitarama. His ancient bike shook as it sped down the dirt path towards the main road. The brakes were old so he used the soles of his shoes to rein in his speed; they scraped and stuttered across the ground, jarring his knees, and before the last sharp bend, where the path dropped steeply and joined the asphalt road, Oswald slid his long right leg across the metal frame and leapt on to the verge running alongside as if the bike were an unruly bullock. It was an undignified dismount, but the Kivumu turning joined the main road on a dangerous bend that saw minibuses wrap themselves around the corner with no thought to the people who walked on the narrow strip between the tall eucalyptus trees that lined the road and the carriageway itself. Béatrice Ncogoza, having survived the genocide, had been killed two years earlier – hit by a *mutatu* – as she made her way into town. Five children were left for her husband Pierre-Célestin to look after; Olivier, now ten, was still mute after the attack at the school in Kivumu, when Father Vjeko had stopped the killers and driven the family to Kabgayi hospital.

Oswald was still living as a refugee in Congo when Béatrice was thrown by the force of the minibus's impact into the stone water culvert that ran down the side of the road, dry most of the year and littered with parched eucalyptus leaves, gurgling in the wet season, when the rain fell off the steep hills through which the road had been cut, decades before. Oswald had left Kivumu on 8 June 1994. For three days before that, the friary had been occupied by government troops, forced to retreat after soldiers from the RPF dropped down noiselessly on to the main road from the surrounding hills and began a final, lethal assault on the last vestiges of resistance in Gitarama. Kabgayi had fallen to the rebels a few days earlier, although there were pockets of *interahamwe* – anonymous in their workaday clothes and difficult for the RPF to identify – which had kept the thousands of refugees from straying too far from the camp. Curic was in the south of the country, running aid from Burundi into camps near Gikongoro. Kivumu was slowly being encircled. Oswald could not rely on Curic to protect him once the Tutsi forces overran the friary – which they surely would. The government soldiers sat listlessly around the compound, beaten, hangdog tired. 'Be strong,' the priest had told Oswald the last time he saw him, 'and we will win.' Oswald was a Hutu and he decided that surviving was more important than winning. He left before dawn and would not see Kivumu again for two years.

On that day in January 1998 Oswald returned from his shopping trip at around twelve. Curic had gone to visit one of the local construction sites where new houses were being built. Oswald prepared lunch. At two that afternoon, Curic returned. He was accompanied by two Rwandans. Oswald recognized one – a soldier who had visited the friary before. The other man Oswald had never seen before. Curic told Oswald to go and buy some Fanta and cigarettes for the unidentified man and, once again, Oswald set off on his bicycle. By the time he returned, the three men were preparing to leave. Curic explained that he was driving into Kigali and would be giving the two men a lift. As Oswald opened the jeep door for them, Curic whispered, 'Be careful: these men are telling lies against you.' Those were the last words Curic ever spoke to his cook and confidant. Later, some of his friends puzzled over this remark and concluded he was being flippant – perhaps the whisky was talking. Others viewed it more darkly but they kept their counsel.

Curic drove the two men into Kigali and dropped them off at the city limits. At the Kiyovu roundabout – where the commercial district meets one of the main arterial roads out of town – traffic was heavy. The morning gloom had long burnt off and the city broiled. Curic wore jeans, a collarless shirt and a pair of sneakers – his crucifix swung from a piece of leather around his neck – a uniform that had become unmistakable to his parishioners.

He drove on alone, to the diocese's General Bursary, where accounts about what happened next start to differ. Some say that Curic stopped at a bar nearby and for several minutes joined a few people who were drinking there before jumping back into his jeep along with another man – probably a soldier. Others dispute this. Curic never left his car, they say, but spoke to people on the terrace through his window, before a man who Curic may or may not have invited into the car climbed in.

It was only as his white jeep drove off and the tyres made a sudden screeching noise that people took notice. Some children, who had been chasing grasshoppers around a lamp post, said that they heard some shouting from inside a white jeep, which then lurched across the road. There was an almighty fight going on inside. In the blur as it passed there was no chance to identify the man next to Curic. All people were sure of was that as well as driving, the *umuzungu* was lashing out, with his one free hand, at someone. The jeep bounced off a lamp post and then skidded across the road. It was then, eyewitnesses said, that they heard the gunshots. There were a lot of them – at least six, though some argued there were as many as ten. Anyway, there were loud cracks – incredibly loud, one woman said – that shocked passers-by, prompting them to run for the ditch by the side of the road.

The jeep crashed into a low wall. The assailant ran from

the car. Apparently he was limping. Some nearby security guards called out to the man, who said, 'An *umuzungu* fired at me, I finished him off.' The guards were surprised. The idea of a white man shooting at a Rwandan was hard to compute. They brought the limping man to their superintendent, who told the guards to leave: he would handle things from here and call the police. Shortly afterwards, the man escaped and was never seen again.

When bystanders approached the jeep they found Curic slumped across the passenger seat. The windscreen was smashed – either by the impact of the car hitting the wall or by a bullet from the gun. One of the bullets had torn into the driver's door, and another had exploded into the seat. They pulled the priest from the wreck and laid him down on the hot, sticky tarmac. Despite the crush of onlookers, several people immediately identified him; he was the *padiri* from Kivumu. People shuffled closer to the prone body, curious at this peculiar sight – a white man, lying on a busy street, covered in blood – but unsure what to do. Someone talked about getting a doctor. But it didn't matter, because by the time he had been heaved out of the jeep and placed on the road he was already dead.

The afternoon has faded into twilight. I can hear the metal doors from the compound opening and the sound of footsteps, but in the thick grey light the concrete outbuildings have softened and folded into the falling dusk. As if in remembrance of the two hours Oswald and I have sat together talking – about all manner of things – and in keeping with the day's end, our voices, too, have grown quiet. I am glad to have taken up the offer made by Ivica Peric to make a return trip out from Kigali. Kivumu feels like a refuge and it is no hardship to decide that it is too late to hack back into the city. Besides, Oswald is a great cook.

Oswald tactfully pauses as I scribble his words down. He is a shy man usually, but this afternoon he seems to have relished the chance to talk about Curic, and I have struggled to keep up with his recollections. Oswald heard of Curic's murder when soldiers came to his house, he whispers. They came at four in the morning, and he was interrogated for two hours before being taken to a police cell where he would be questioned again and remain incarcerated for thirty hours more. Oswald's big-boned face seems to wrestle with his emotions. He smiles ruefully and then drops his head down to massage his neck, eluding my gaze. They took a long time to see he was not a killer, he says. I try to imagine the experience of being a Rwandan Hutu, in the paranoid and violent days of 1998, under suspicion for the murder of your white boss. When he looks back up he tells me that it was no surprise that Curic had been killed. For some months the priest had been frightened.

Shadows shuffle past – young priests on their way to the small chapel next door. I hear the hum of the electric strip light and the scratch of the match to light the single candle. Father Ivica strides past to join them. Evening prayers. Oswald looks back towards the kitchen and I see that he needs to start preparing supper. I apologize but he smiles again and as he gets to his feet his huge frame seems to loom even larger in the darkness that has enveloped us. In 1996, when Curic heard that Oswald had arrived back at the friary, having emerged alive from one of the refugee camps in Goma, he ran, apparently, to the kitchen to greet him, and then dragged the big man into the dining room. 'Oswald is back!' Curic announced, pouring glasses of rakija for the priests who stood awkwardly by their chairs. 'Now things will be better.'

We walk through the compound towards the kitchen. I tell Oswald that I was surprised when he said that Curic was frightened. Everybody else tells me that he never feared anything.

'He *was* brave,' says Oswald, 'but it was frightening for him because he could see how things would end up. He had a favourite saying, which he had learned a long time ago. "*Agasozi kagusabye amaraso ntukayarenza.*"'

I look out past the cowshed. The valley is dark. There could be no valley at all. There is no light and, other than the muffled chants from the priests at prayer, there is no sound. Oswald tells me what the saying means: 'When the hills ask for your blood you can never refuse.'

CHAPTER FOURTEEN

Kibuye

On our way to Gaspard's village, we drive away from Lake Kivu – a shiny sea. A church sits up on a promontory. The church is made with thick brown slabs of rock, like a Presbyterian kirk, and juts out over a deep valley. 'St Jean,' Jean-Pierre says. 'My mum's aunties and uncles were all killed there.' The road steepens and we grind through the gears and then stop at a small junction, halfway up the side of a hill. There is a single-lane track off to the left that cuts around the hillside, curving into the distance. Below us, tiers of farmland stretch down to the floor of the valley, but above us the land is less cultivated. 'This is it,' says Jean-Pierre, and the jeep begins to push slowly through the bush, which seems to be falling on to us from the hillside. When we find a few huts by the side of the track Jean-Pierre stops and asks for Gaspard. He is dumbfounded by their answer. 'What are they saying?' I ask. Jean-Pierre says, 'Gaspard is back in jail.'

People have gathered around the car. Jean-Pierre fires questions at them. 'When did he go back to prison?' A year ago – maybe longer. A few suggestions but no one can be precise. 'Which prison?' Gitarama. Or Butare. People can't remember. 'What had he done?' The crowd look sullen now. A Rwandan they don't know is asking questions, with an *umuzungu* taking notes. It's not normal. 'Where is his house?' They begin talking to themselves. Jean-Pierre drives on. 'I don't trust them,' he says under his breath. The track bends around the hill and up into a new valley – a curl of red mud squeezed on to a vast green canvas. We stop a woman. She points up the hill. 'Gaspard's house is up there,' she says. We can't see where 'there' is because the hill is steep and covered in bush. 'His wife is still at the house,' the woman says, walking away from us, a baby pinned by an old shawl to the small of her back.

There is hardly even a path to follow so we begin to climb through the bush. Some children join us. They say they know the house we are looking for and the eldest becomes our guide. We walk for twenty minutes. Jean-Pierre puffs behind me, cursing when his shoes slip on the mud. 'We didn't come here when I saw Gaspard before,' he says. 'Maybe he didn't want you to know where he lived,' I say. We find ourselves walking on to the plots of small houses – dull, damp squats, half hidden in dark banana groves, surrounded by thick euphorbia hedges. Clothes hang from pieces of string. Women are sitting outside on stools. It feels as though they have not moved for hundreds of years. 'The house is close now,' says our guide; his toes spread and grip as he climbs. Behind me trail five younger children. The bush begins to thin and triangles of sunlight break through the trees and shine through banana leaves, making them seem like vast green quills. I can see fragments of the valley below and out to the west Lake Kivu is like a desert. Above, in a clearing, is

Gaspard's house. It is L-shaped – red wooden boards shutter the windows, the door is red too. No one answers our knock. The door is locked. We sit and wait.

After ten minutes a boy walks around the bend of the hill towards the house, carrying a yellow water container on his shoulder. It is Gaspard's son, we are told. Jean-Pierre explains that he is looking for Gaspard. 'He is in prison,' the boy says. There is a sheen of sweat on his face. He has wide high cheekbones and a perfectly symmetrical face. He is older than I first thought – perhaps eighteen – and is dressed in a tidy blue shirt and khaki trousers. 'Did you have far to carry your water?' I ask. The boy shakes his head – a few miles but he had come from school which is a little further. Jean-Pierre asks him where his father is. The boy drops his head. 'Prison,' he repeats. Does he know why his father is in prison? 'No,' says the boy and Jean-Pierre frowns. The children have settled down in the grass near where we stand, a few yards from the house. They chew on stalks and listen attentively. The boy's eyes are watchful. His answers are short. Where is his mother? 'At the market.' Does he have any brothers or sisters? 'Yes, but they have left.' 'Do you think about your father?' I ask. 'I try not to,' he says, 'because it makes me feel crazy.' 'So you don't miss him?' He shrugs. Gaspard has been in prison for eleven of the eighteen years his son has been alive. We talk about school. He wants to be a doctor. One small boy in our entourage has had enough and wanders into the banana grove and starts beating a stalk with his stick. I think to myself, this would be a good place to have a camp if you were eight years old, high up, the perfect place to defend. Like Jack had in *Lord of the Flies* before Piggy barged in.

'What is your name?' Jean-Pierre asks.

The boy pauses. 'Gaspard.'

Jean-Pierre exhales. 'Gaspard,' he says, shaking his head. 'You are called Gaspard too?' He is growing impatient. 'I want to tell him that his father was in Nkubito's gang when my father was killed.'

I am feeling uneasy. This is difficult. 'Be careful,' I say.

'I'm not angry with *him*,' Jean-Pierre says. 'But I think he needs to understand.' He turns to the boy and begins questioning him again – pausing to let me keep up. 'How long is he in prison for?'

'Thirty years.'

'Did he go to court?'

'Yes,' says the boy, 'and to *gacaca*.'

'So what do you think he did to just walk off this hill and give testimony and get thirty years?'

'I don't know.'

'What does thirty years tell you?'

The boy is quiet. Jean-Pierre is angry and says to me, 'He is treating us like we are stupid. Thirty years means the court knows he killed a lot of people.' Jean-Pierre looks at the boy and tries again. '*Thirty years.* Come on – what do you think that means?' The boy says he doesn't know. 'You don't know?' Jean-Pierre turns to the children. 'What did his father do?'

Our guide speaks up. 'He killed people.'

Gaspard's son looks carefully at the guide-cum-informer, and says, 'It was a political time. People did things.'

'But you have to know,' Jean-Pierre says. 'You have to be able to say, "My father killed." If you don't—'

Jean-Pierre slaps his thigh and we sit – this small group – and, for a while, nothing is said. The boy stands quietly opposite Jean-Pierre, who has bowed his head, troubled, rubbing the back of his neck. The children watch Jean-Pierre and the boy and wait. Below, further down the hill, I can hear the echo of a metal pot being struck – *ko-pok ko-pok ko-pok*. A hoot of laughter. The world seems to have returned to this place. Women pick their beans and scrape the dirt off their children's clothes, and kids run screaming down the hill to school each morning. Men farm and hack back the bush. They'll sometimes gather to drink and curse the rain or lack of it. Up here, though, I feel far away. Weighed down, as if in suspension. Jean-Pierre lets out a long, weary sigh and looks back up at the boy.

'It's OK to love your father. I loved my father too.'

He heaves himself up and begins to walk down the path away from Gaspard's house and we follow, a silent trail in obedient single file, oldest to youngest, leaving the teenager still standing next to the water container, watching us as we disappear from view.

In late-afternoon sun we drive back to Kigali. There are small conical hills that drop away below the mountain road down to a bend in the river, each one lower than the last, like steps for a giant coming off his mountain lair for his evening draught of water in the valley floor.

'A future killer,' says Jean-Pierre finally, after a long silence.

'You can't say that, Jean-Pierre. You don't know.'

He shakes his head. 'If they don't face the truth, how do we move on?'

'It was very difficult for him. Us standing there like that. He was ashamed.'

'Of course. But, David, he did not kill. He was not there.

He can stand apart. He is smart – he knows. He can separate himself from his father and not betray him. He only has to say he knows. Then he is free because then he can make a choice.'

Shame had crushed the boy into silence earlier that afternoon. I doubt that I would act any differently if it had been me. Yet, however uncomfortable I feel about our meeting, Jean-Pierre offers a way out for Gaspard's son – from the shame and the resentment that surely followed our departure. Stuck three-quarters of the way up a hill, still heaving jerrycans of water to a fatherless home, that absence raw and implicit and unspoken, Gaspard's son is bound by the crimes of his father. To submit meekly to a government-peddled trope, which I find hard to imagine he entirely believes, offers him no release. 'But we are still fragile,' Rwandan friends tell me – and they, after all, should know – so perhaps that justifies the tacit agreement of many Rwandans to the oppressive silence imposed from above, which smothers this country.

I had met an old RPF stalwart called Tito Rutaremara, now a senator in the Parliament, and he had told me how the justice system, *gacaca*, had made people understand why the killing had happened. The killers had testified so now we knew. Extremists had encouraged people to kill, and it was true that some had wanted to join in, but most had not and were pushed into killing. People knew now why it had happened and so the country could move on. 'Can you just draw a line under it like that?' I asked. Time passing does not necessarily alleviate the wounds people feel. I told him about Tutsi friends who still mistrust Hutus. I told him I had Hutu friends who complained, under their breaths, that thousands had died at the hands of the RPF after the genocide, yet there was no *gacaca* for the families of those victims. Tito nodded – it was true that Rwanda was not liberated from its past but the government had laid down the foundations for a new country and was now in what he called Phase Three – rebuilding. When each Rwandan ate three meals a day, had health care, earned a living wage and sent their children to school for nine years, then they would be liberated, he told me.

'You mean,' I asked, 'when you have nothing you are more rooted in your past and you cannot move on?'

Tito nodded. 'That can be true,' he said carefully.

I told him I had always thought that was the case, but had recently felt that it was too simplistic. The past – the hurt of it or the shame of it – needs space to be explored and acknowledged. Then people can be released from it. Tito nodded again and told me a story – a girl he knew had spoken of how members of her family had killed, and once she had talked about it she had felt a release.

'Exactly,' I say, 'it's about people opening up – especially young people who want to understand – and your government will not let them do that.'

Tito paused. 'Well, you have to show how these things were organized by the state. That can provide the same release for young people.'

'That's not the same,' I said.

We pass Nyange, with its ruined church, again. Just near the rubble of the church is a school, perched at the edge of the village, overlooking the valley. Three years after the genocide, a roving band of *interahamwe* barged into the school one night and told the children who boarded there to split themselves into Hutus and Tutsis. The students refused, telling the intruders that they were Rwandans. So the men killed them. Later, as news of the murders spread, the government praised the students for ignoring their ethnicity and thinking of themselves as Rwandan. But no one really knows what those dead children thought. Perhaps they did feel Rwandan, or perhaps they had obediently said what they had been taught to say – and, deep down, still thought of themselves as Tutsi and Hutu. Or maybe they thought simply that they were schoolmates and should stick together. I think of them, terrified, shoved up against the wall, blearily wiping the sleep from their eyes, the hour too dark and the school far enough away from the rest of the village for them to know, surely, that help was never likely to arrive. They had been forced to make a choice as to who they were and no one had done that for them. In those difficult few moments before death, in a room silenced by the consequences of their decision, I wonder if that choice had felt like freedom.

The sun has dropped fast. Jean-Pierre guns the engine as we tip over the summit and begin our descent. Long shadows loom across the valleys ahead of us. Small flues of light catch the edges of escarpments. Houses suddenly burn brightly and then disappear as the valleys slip into shadow.

LAST WORD

One hot midsummer's day I return to Osova and spend the afternoon with Ana Curic. Some years have passed since I was last here. Petar, her husband, lies in the kitchen on a fold-up bed. He is frail, with hardly the strength to speak, but his eyes light up when I walk in and he motions to Ana to retrieve the rakija from the room next door. We drink a toast. Ana recently had an operation on her leg. The painkillers she took after she returned home were useless, she says. So she began to pray and within a day her leg gave her no trouble at all. Branimir, my translator, shakes his head. 'Old woman talk,' he says. Ana returns from next door with the rakija and a box of family photographs and sorts through them as we talk.

The pictures have misted over at the edges and are brown with age. A family stand next to a car. A couple hold a baby, smiling, a pacifier in the baby's mouth. Snow – small dark figures silhouetted against white. A man holds a suitcase – Petar heading to Germany; three boys in dark jackets and ties, a priest standing behind them. Small fragments of life. Then, dashes of colour emerge from the pile. Africa.

Green everywhere. Children on wooden benches, their faces turned up, bathed in light, bright blue school tunics and dark, handsome shaven heads. Another of hoeing – the hoes raised in unison. Women stare solemnly into the camera. Then Curic – leading a line of Rwandans up a hill, each of them balancing a water container on their head, the valley falling away behind them. Curic with a baby, Curic bent over, head hovering above a bucket, in flip-flops and shirtless, laughing. A Mass – Curic holding the chasuble. Ana tells me that they didn't know about the genocide until the following year. There was just no news at all. It was Ivica, Curic's successor, who told them that he was alive – that there had been any trouble at all. 'It was a relief not to have known,' she says. As it was they were struggling with a war on their own doorstep. Vjeko had told them a little about it when he visited in 1996. 'How was it to see him again?' I ask. Ana laughs and throws her arms up and shakes her head at the memory. 'It was wonderful!' she says. He walked up the road and there he was. She wrapped her arms around him and said, 'I am going to kidnap you and never let you leave.' Ana shows me a picture of Curic when he arrived. She is planting a kiss on his cheek and he has one arm around her. The other holds her wrist in front of him, as if stopping her from getting too close. She explains that Curic had opened his suitcase and placed pictures – dozens and dozens of them – on the kitchen table. 'Look at them,' he said. All the pictures were of small children. 'They are orphans,' he told her. 'Their parents were killed in the genocide or afterwards. I have to go to Germany and Canada and raise money for these children.' Ana had looked at the pictures. 'It was terrible,' she says, 'their faces, they looked so desperate.' She stops and begins to cry. Petar rests his hand on Ana's arm, slowly patting it.

'I told him he was my son,' Ana says through her tears. 'That I needed him here, at least for a little while. But I knew I had lost him. He was with us – in the room – but in his head, he was far away.'

Curic left for meetings with potential funders in Germany two days later. It had been his first trip back home for five years and it would be his last. Ana and I walk down to the end of the garden, and in a woodshed, with tarpaulin draped carefully over it, is the tractor that Curic had bought his parents with the money his father had given him before he left for Africa. There is rust on the bodywork and the tyres have lost their air and have sunk, exhausted, into the grass. Ana tells me they are selling it. Petar is not strong enough to drive it any more. But the engine is still good and she knows a family in the village that will want it.

The village of Beramo lies fifteen miles south of Kigali. There is a shop and a school and a patch of grass, like a village green, fringed with small, single-storey houses. Near the church is a field of maize. Below the maize the land drops away gently over several miles to the Nyabarongo river snaking eastwards along the valley floor. Jean-Pierre stands in the field, with a smile that I have rarely seen before – broad and playful – and explains that the house he will build on this field, which he now owns, will be set back from the road and have a wide veranda looking across the valley.

Friends are building next door – the husband works with Odette at EWSA and they are close to finishing a large, square, concrete house with metal gates and a high wall that is already topped with broken glass to deter intruders. Jean-Pierre says, 'I don't want one of these high walls. I want to look out. A low fence will do.' Building will start next year – as long as he has saved enough money to pay for Vanessa's college fees. She goes to Nairobi in the autumn. She has told her father that she plans to change her name. She doesn't want to be called Sagahutu any more. 'I'm OK about it,' Jean-Pierre tells me. 'It's her life.' He shrugs. Serge, too, will leave for college soon. Then it will just be Jean-Pierre and Odette, looking after their little one, Cindy.

We walk back up to the road. Jean-Pierre points to the church. 'There,' he says, 'a church for Odette – so she will be happy.' 'But it's a Catholic church, Jean-Pierre, Odette's an evangelical Protestant.' He laughs. 'That's OK, she will like it. It's all the same, right?'

A group of men who, earlier, had watched us arrive approach Jean-Pierre. They seem cautious, a little shy. They mutter questions at the new landowner. When will he start to build? Will he have people coming from Kigali? Or will there be any building jobs for them? They look poor and a little desperate, fidgeting as they listen to Jean-Pierre, who stands by his jeep, hands on hips and tells them that he is sure there will be work for them. They back away, thanking him. 'Can you imagine,' Jean-Pierre says, looking at the men walking slowly back to their houses. 'Ten years ago I would not have built here, I would not have felt safe. But now it's fine.'

'Are you sure?' I ask. 'These people – well, who knows what they were doing in ninety-four.'

'You can never be sure, can you?' says Jean-Pierre.

We bask in the slanted afternoon light, slouched against

the jeep, and look out at the wide horizon. The sun is warm and we talk about nothing. Then we fall silent and I think, 'I am fine. Really.' And I close my eyes and what I see is this: there is an old red-earth road, which runs past a church. There are trees on the right, and small mud-brick houses line both sides. The road is dusty and worn from the traffic of people that have walked down from the hills where it begins to the church just a few yards away. Before it was a road it was a track, and before then, it was a goat trail. One day – and probably quite soon – gangs of men will come with large machines and tarmac the road.

But some time after that, the earth will fold in on these hills once more and the road will disappear. The people will fold into the earth and the hills will hold their bones. Under the earth is their blood. And below the earth, soaked with their blood, is a hole. It is dark and a man is scrabbling up the sides of the hole towards what he thinks might be a small crack of light. The man stops, sucking in a faint spill of air that he feels on his skin. As he rests a picture appears in his mind. It is early morning and a small child lies on her bed. She is awake and looks at him as he stands by the door, looking back across the room at her. Through the gauze of the mosquito net that surrounds her bed he can see her slowly blink, watching him. He greets her, and even though he barely breathed her name it echoes around the room. The room falls quiet again but outside he can hear the buzz of a small motorbike. The child watches him. The man in the hole opens his eyes and begins to work his way slowly towards the light.

I wake with a jolt. Jean-Pierre has started the jeep. 'Come on,' he says, 'we are late. Odette will be angry.' I climb in.

Jean-Pierre points at the maize field where one day he will build his house. 'In the evening,' he says, 'the village goes completely quiet, and if you stand with your back to the road, you can watch the shadows fall right across the valley and you cannot hear a sound.'

FURTHER READING

Africa Rights, *Death, Despair and Defiance*, Africa Rights, 1995.

Alison Des Forges, *Leave None to Tell the Story: Genocide in Rwanda*, Human Rights Watch, 1999.

Philip Gourevitch, *We Wish to Inform You that Tomorrow We Will Be Killed with All Our Families,* Farrar, Straus and Giroux, 1998.

Jean Hatzfeld, *A Time for Machetes: the Rwandan Genocide – the Killers Speak*, Serpent's Tail, 2005.

Jean Hatzfeld, *Into the Quick of Life: the Rwandan Genocide – the Survivors Speak*, Serpent's Tail, 2005.

Adrian House, *Francis of Assisi*, Pimlico, 2000.

Timothy Longman, *Christianity and Genocide in Rwanda*, Cambridge University Press, 2010.

Linda Melvern, *A People Betrayed: The Role of the West in Rwanda's Genocide*, Zed Books, 2000.

Catharine Newbury, *The Cohesion of Oppression – Clientship and Ethnicity in Rwanda, 1860–1960*, Columbia University Press, 1988.

Gerard Prunier, *The Rwanda Crisis: History of a Genocide*, Columbia University Press, 1995.

Carol Rittner, John K. Roth, Wendy Whitworth, *Genocide in Rwanda – Complicity of the Churches?*, Aegis, 2004.

André Sibomana, *Hope for Rwanda: Conversations with Laure Guilbert and Hervé Deguine*, Pluto Press, 1999.

Patrick de St Exupéry, *L'inavouable*, Editions des Arenes, 2004.

Scott Strauss, *The Order of Genocide: Race, Power and War in Rwanda*, Cornell University Press, 2006.

Scott Strauss and Lars Waldorf (eds), *Remaking Rwanda*, University of Wisconsin Press, 2011.

Carina Tertsakian, *Le Château – the Lives of Prisoners in Rwanda*, Arves Books, 2008.

United Nations Blue Books Vol. 10, *The United Nations and Rwanda 1993–1996*.

Author's note

The title of the book was inspired by the Rwandan saying, '*Agasozi kagusabye amaraso ntukayarenza*'. Literally translated, it means 'When the hill asks for your blood', but Vjeko Curic, who loved the saying and was perhaps inspired by the hills that surrounded Kivumu, was prone to pluralize it. With apologies to Rwandan linguists, I have done the same.

ACKNOWLEDGEMENTS

In Rwanda, I am indebted to Jean-Pierre Sagahutu and his wife, Odette, for their patience, support and generosity. Sebastijan Markovic offered invaluable memories and the Salesian friary in Kimihurura, Kigali was a welcome refuge. In Kivumu, my thanks to Ivica Peric and his Franciscan friars for their time and hospitality. I am grateful to Oswald Ngendahimana and Aphrodis Nsengumuremyi for their memories. Vénuste Nsengimana, Tito Rutaremara, Hervé Deguine, Yolande Makolo, Isaac Ndatabaye, Jolie Murenzi, Pierre-Célestin Ncogoza, Assumpta Mugiraneza, Alfred Ndahiro and Aimable Gatete all generously offered their recollections and insights.

There are, however, a number of people whom, owing to the political atmosphere in Rwanda, I am unable to publicly acknowledge. They know who they are and I thank them for the risk they took, and the trust they showed, in providing me with information about both past and present Rwanda.

In Bosnia, thanks to Ana and the late Petar Curic for their recollections and to Tomislav Peric and his family for their hospitality. Danijel Nikolic, Branimir Mlakic and Matija Kurevija were long-suffering guides, translators and companions. Ivan Nujic, Tomo Andic and Pero Vrebac were vital sources of information.

Camille Mpumuje and Charlotte Cooper-Richardson provided expert Kinyarwanda and French translations and Lucy McCann and the staff of Oxford University's Bodleian Library of Commonwealth and African Studies at Rhodes House were an always helpful source of information.

I owe a deep debt of gratitude to Helen Vesperini for her friendship, expertise and wise counsel over a number of years and for her careful reading of later drafts. I could not have written the passages on Rwanda's prisons without the help of Carina Tertsakian's remarkable book, *Le Château*, and I am also grateful to her for her much-valued advice with the manuscript. My thanks, too, to Susanne Brezina, who patiently answered my many questions. Parts or whole drafts of the book were read at various times by Allan Little, Sibille de Cartier d'Yves, Lauren Ezell and Lucy Hannah. Thanks to all for their comments and advice.

Camilla Hornby, formerly of Curtis Brown, patiently offered me wisdom and encouragement throughout the early stages of the book and my literary agent, Karolina Sutton, also at Curtis Brown, has been equally steadfast. At Transworld, my thanks to Rochelle Venables, to Kate Green and the publicity team and to Elisabeth Marriman, Suzanne Bridson and Kate Samano for their beady-eyed and skilful copyediting. And my sincere thanks go to my editor, Jane Lawson, for her superb editorial judgement as well as for her creativity and understanding. Lastly, to my family – Jules, Thea and Roly: whether near or far, as this book has progressed, I am deeply grateful for your support and love.

David Belton worked as a producer at BBC *Newsnight* in the 1990s where, amongst many foreign assignments, he covered the civil war in Bosnia and the genocide in Rwanda. In 2002, he co-wrote the story and produced the award-winning feature film *Shooting Dogs*, based on real events that had taken place during the Rwandan genocide. He has since produced and directed many critically acclaimed and award-winning documentaries for British and American television. He lives in Oxford with his family.